Deliver Us From Mother

Stella McCormick

McCORMICK HOUSE PRESS

First Printing, 2026

For the little girl who thought this was normal.

Trigger Warning

This book contains depictions of emotional, physical, and psychological abuse, religious manipulation, and coercive control within a family setting. It also explores themes of trauma, isolation, self-harm, suicide, drugs, sexual assault, and the lasting effects of narcissistic parenting. Profanity is used at various points throughout the book.

Some passages may be distressing or triggering for readers who have experienced similar forms of abuse or trauma. Please take care while reading and engage only at a pace that feels safe for you.

If you find yourself in need of support, consider reaching out to trusted friends, a counselor, or a helpline such as the **National Domestic Violence Hotline (1-800-799-7233)** or **988 Suicide & Crisis Lifeline (in the U.S.)**.

You are not alone.

Author's Note

This book is a work of nonfiction based on my personal experiences and memories. Some names, identifying details, and certain events may have been changed to protect the privacy of individuals and to respect confidentiality. While every effort has been made to portray events truthfully as I remember them, memory is subjective and can often be affected by trauma, and others may recall these events differently.

Contents

Introduction

To the outside world, we were a loving family. Mom, Dad, five kids, and a few animals living the American Dream while devoting our lives to Christ. Inside, we lived within a closed system, so carefully crafted by my mother that even reality bent to her will. It took me years to understand that what my mother created was not just an abusive home – it was a cult. Not a sprawling compound on a rural property, not a charismatic preacher gathering followers in a church basement, but a single-family cult contained inside the walls of our home and the mind of one woman.

Since stepping away and looking back on my upbringing, I have discovered seven key characteristics that define a single-family cult. While these characteristics can also be applied to larger, more organized cults, I am unpacking each one and explaining how they apply to single-family cults, specifically the cult my mother created. If the following few pages start becoming eerily familiar to you, please start asking questions and thinking critically so you can understand your upbringing for exactly what it was – a cult.

***

1. The Charismatic or Authoritarian Leader

One parent or family member often rules with an "iron fist," demanding unquestioning loyalty. This leader is typically narcissistic, refuses to admit fault, and blames all problems on others.

Every cult has a leader who must be believed. My mother didn't need a pulpit; her presence alone was enough. She could draw people into her orbit with her smile and her words. She could manipulate anyone's mind, and they would do her bidding. She could fill a room with her certainty, bend reality with her anger, and convince anyone that her cruelty was divine instruction. She had an answer for everything and a Biblical justification for every move she made. The line between what was her word and what was God's Word was often blurred.

She didn't call herself a prophet, but she acted like one, wholeheartedly believing she knew more than anyone else on earth about Christianity, holiness, parenting, homeschooling, and literally everything else. We learned very quickly that disobeying her was disobeying God. To us, she seemed to know things ordinary people didn't; she seemed superior to any other adult in our lives. Her charisma was a quiet kind of lightning: unpredictable and dangerous. We followed her like terrified and loyal disciples. We mistook control for love because love was what she said it was. In her eyes, we weren't children learning how to live, we were followers learning how to obey.

***

2. Coercive Control

The leader uses a pattern of abusive behaviors to dominate family members and limit their independence. This can include verbal threats, humiliation, financial abuse, stalking, and monitoring of the family's actions and communications.

Control in our house wasn't just about rules; it was about ownership. My mother monitored everything – not just what we could and couldn't do, but also what we could and couldn't think. She controlled our thoughts, emotions, and expressions. What we wore, what we said, what we believed – none of it belonged to us. It was like every feeling passed through her filter before it reached the world. She decided when we could smile, when we could eat, when we were forgiven, and when we were loved.

She could switch from warmth to fury in an instant, and we learned to predict her storms like amateur meteorologists. Over time, the goal was not to be good; the goal was to be invisible. I learned very quickly that there was safety in smallness. Don't cry too loud, don't question, don't show fear unless she wants to see it. She isolated us emotionally and spiritually, so even our private thoughts felt unsafe. The fear wasn't just of punishment but of her disappointment, which seemed to carry the weight of eternal judgment. When she smiled, the air was lighter. When she frowned, the walls tightened. Although even in her smile, we could sense impending danger. We were taught to submit, always carrying the fear of losing her love.

***

3. The Family Narrative

A fabricated set of family lore or stories justifies the leader's behavior and the family's practices. This narrative can present the family as more moral or special than it is and can be used to gaslight members into doubting their own perceptions.

Every cult has a story – a mythology that explains why it must exist and why its leader and their behavior are justified. My mother's story was that we were too godly for any earthly church, we understood the world's temptations and sinful nature far more than anyone else, and the world wholly misunderstood our way of life. She saw herself as the victim of ungrateful children and a mother intent on saving her family from worldly corruption. She was good because she said she was, and the world was bad because she said it was.

Inside the perceived reality of her story, she could do nothing wrong. Her cruelty was discipline, her violence was accountability, her control was protection. She was an ever-patient, ever-suffering martyr, sacrificing everything for the ungrateful children she was burdened with. We, desperate to earn her love, accepted our roles as the disobedient flock in need of redemption. This was the story we were told, and when you hear the same story enough times, you begin to believe it and adopt it as fact.

***

4. Forced Conformity and Loss of Individuality

The leader dictates family members' roles, beliefs, and behaviors. This suppresses personal growth and critical thinking, forcing members to adopt the group's narrative to be accepted.

We were not allowed to have preferences, opinions, or identities that differed from her will. She chose our clothes, dictated our tone of voice, and corrected our posture. If we laughed too loudly, she said we were disrespectful. If we cried, we were weak. Our religious beliefs were chosen for us. Even our body language had to conform to the image she wanted the world to see. We weren't allowed to be individuals; we were built to be perfect little godly children, always acting as a living tribute to her impeccable parenting.

The more we became who she wanted us to be, the more love we could earn. But the more we resisted conformity, the more we were punished. Eventually, I couldn't tell where her voice ended and mine began, but that was her plan: to erase us so completely that her voice spoke through our mouths.

***

5. Intense Secrecy

The family is often isolated from the outside world, with the leader promoting an "us vs. them" mentality. Family members are forbidden from speaking about problems to outsiders, with the family's public image prioritized above the well-being of its members.

Our home was like Vegas: "What happens here stays here" was our motto. It wasn't a warning; it was a law. To the outside world, she played the role of a devoted mother, smiling at neighbors, singing at church, and quoting verses about God's love and forgiveness. We were taught to smile in public as well, but to stay silent. Silence in public was loyalty to her.

We learned that the truth was dangerous; if we told, we were liars, but if we stayed quiet, we were safe. She always told us, "No one would understand our family," or "Nobody will believe you if you tell them what goes on at home." Secrecy became sacred, and silence became survival. We couldn't have known then, but our quiet was her camouflage.

***

6. Manipulation Through Guilt and Fear

The leader conditions family members to feel that any problems are their fault. Questions or attempts to challenge the family's rules are met with punishment, shame, or gaslighting.

My mother never needed locks or chains to keep us obedient – she had guilt and fear. She could turn any act of independence into a sin, and any boundary into selfishness. She could make us feel responsible for her happiness, her loneliness, and her anger. If she screamed, it was because we made her. If she hit, it was because "we forced her hand." If we wanted to leave, she reminded us of everything she'd sacrificed for us and everything she'd done for us. If we cried or complained, she asked how we could be so ungrateful. Guilt was the chain that kept us tethered long after we left the house.

Fear was her second language; she spoke it fluently – in the lift of her eyebrow, the sharpness of her breath, the soft tone she used before all hell was about to break loose. She used fear as a weapon: fear of God, fear of punishment, fear of losing her love or approval, fear of being cast out of the family. We feared her disappointment more than we feared God. We carried her voice in our heads like a second conscience: always whispering, always condemning. Somehow, she made us responsible for her suffering.

***

7. Limited Contact with the Outside World

Family cults often discourage contact with outside friends and relatives, portraying the world outside the family as dangerous or corrupt. If new people join the family through marriage, they are often required to adopt the family's beliefs and may be cut off from their own relatives.

The outside world was my mother's greatest enemy. She told us people out there were dangerous and deceptive, that they would corrupt us and poison us with lies, and they would present us with worldly temptations and lure us into sin. She said nobody out there would ever love us the way she did. For our own protection, she kept us away from neighbors, family, and anyone else who might question her authority or lead us down a path of sin. Even when we appeared to participate in normal life – church, Vacation Bible School, summer camp – she stood guard, keeping a watchful eye over every interaction.

The isolation didn't end when I left home. It followed me and lived inside me. For years, I distrusted kindness, mistook love for manipulation, and waited for freedom to turn into punishment. Leaving her house is not enough to break the isolation; you have to leave her version of reality altogether. You must recognize that true freedom does not come simply with the absence of walls, but with the deconstruction of the walls she built inside you.

***

These seven characteristics, when combined, create a world in which control, secrecy, sameness, guilt, fear, and isolation are disguised as "love." These traits built the walls of my childhood and shaped every version of myself I've ever had to kill or reclaim. We were not a family. We were a collection of confused children trapped inside one woman's carefully crafted reality. For a long time, I thought survival meant silence. I now know survival means telling the truth.

This book is not an act of revenge, but rather an act of remembrance. It is my testimony, not to her power, but to its undoing. In order to tell the truth about my mother and to show the world the truth about my childhood, I have to finally reveal the inner workings of the cult she called "family." I write these words to dismantle her reality, brick by brick, until nothing remains but what was always meant to be mine: my voice.

NOTE:

Children raised in family cults are often groomed to be dependent and submissive, losing their sense of self in the process. Prolonged exposure to coercive control and manipulation can result in long-term mental health issues, including anxiety, depression, PTSD, and low self-esteem. Leaving a family cult can be an extremely difficult process, emotionally mirroring the recovery of those who leave larger cults. Members may have limited life skills and be isolated from a healthy support system.

If any part of this story feels familiar, whether you're currently in a controlling family or religious environment, have recently left one, or are still healing from its effects, you are not alone. The following organizations may be able to provide support, education, crisis services, and recovery resources.

***

National Domestic Violence Hotline
Phone: 1-800-799-SAFE (7233)
Text: Text START to 88788
Website: TheHotline.org

***

Suicide & Crisis Lifeline
988 – call or text
Website: 988Lifeline.org

***

Crisis Text Line
Text HOME to 741741

***

Intervention101
Phone: 215-467-4939
Website: Intervention101.com

***

reFOCUS
Website: refocus.org

***

International Cultic Studies Association
Website: InternationalCulticStudies.org

***

Recovering From Religion
Phone: 844-368-2848 (84-I-Doubt-It)
Chat on their website: RecoveringFromReligion.org

***

Adult Children of Alcoholics and Dysfunctional Families
Phone: 310-534-1815
Website: AdultChildren.org

***

Daughters of Narcissistic Mothers
Website: DaughtersOfNarcissisticMothers.com

Key Characteristic #1

CHARISMATIC OR AUTHORITARIAN LEADER

Through my childlike eyes, she was everything. She was superior to all, inferior to none. She was all-knowing, all-powerful, perfect, and without sin – words that are typically used to describe a deity. She was always correct, and while Dad could do things wrong or make mistakes, she never could. I thought all moms were like this; I thought all girls grew up to be perfect, wise moms, never making dumb mistakes or getting themselves into trouble. I had something to look forward to, and someday I figured I would be like her and stop being so naughty and disobedient. Someday, I would be a mom, and I would know everything, and I wouldn't sin anymore. I could be everything she was… *if only I could just be like her now,* I thought, *then I wouldn't get in trouble so much.*

She had a powerful hold over people – us kids, Dad, other kids, other grown-ups – people did her bidding without her having to do much convincing. It was like people just believed every word that came out of her mouth simply because she was the one who'd said it. That went for us, too; we did as she said, no matter what. Partly because that's what we were supposed to do – obey our parents – but also because if we were successful, we might get a chance at earning her acceptance. I was always eager to please her, always eager to earn her love, always eager for her attention.

I did get a good bit of her attention, but it was usually not in a good way. It was typically because I'd been naughty or disobedient, and she had to discipline me or have Dad discipline me. I didn't like that attention; I wanted the other kind. The kind she sometimes gave the younger kids when they'd been good. Sometimes, she would sit on the couch and read them books, and sometimes she'd even let them sit on her lap. I wasn't allowed to sit on her lap by then – I was too big, she said, and she wasn't going to treat me like a baby. I didn't want to be treated like a baby; I wanted to be treated like a big girl, but being a big girl seemed impossible. I had more responsibilities, and I could never quite complete everything on time or to her satisfaction. But I kept trying because surely one day I'd be successful, and she'd be so proud of me.

I always knew to wait and see what kind of mood she was in before I could tell if it would be a good day or a bad day. Sometimes it started as a good day but ended up being a bad one. It was like her mood dictated the weather inside the house, and every movement, word, and glance had to be carefully measured. If she was calm, the air felt gentle and light; we could breathe easily, speak a little louder, maybe even laugh, and the sunlight could make its way through the windows.

But when anger or disappointment crept in, the whole house tightened. Voices dropped to whispers, footsteps softened on the carpet, doors shut quietly, and even the younger kids seemed to sense the shift in pressure. The whole house braced for impact. We learned to read her face like a forecast, searching for any sign of a storm before it broke, and it was too late to take cover. A sigh could mean rain; a slammed drawer meant thunder. It didn't take long to understand that peace wasn't something we were given – it was something we earned by staying small, quiet, and compliant until the skies cleared again.

We all knew our place within the family hierarchy: hers was at the top, unquestioned and absolute. Dad stood beside her in public, the smiling figurehead of a family that looked obedient and devout from the outside. But behind closed doors, his authority vanished. In those early years, he sometimes tried to give us little tastes of freedom. I remember him taking us to get $1 kids' hot chocolates from a drive-thru coffee shop called Moxie Java using the allowance she gave him. He always reminded us not to tell her, or the secret outings may have to end. Those moments felt like tiny rebellions, proof that somewhere beneath his silence, he saw us and he cared.

But over time, even those small gestures disappeared. He seemed to learn that resistance, no matter how gentle, only fueled her fury. Eventually, he stopped trying altogether and simply became an extension of her. He nodded when she spoke, echoed her opinions, and avoided her wrath as best he could, just like the rest of us. The message was clear: loyalty to her meant peace at home, and any act of rebellion was treason. There was no partnership in their marriage, only her command and his compliance.

1

In The Beginning, There Was Mother

1997 – 2004 | AGES 0-6

***

2001, age 4

Last night I was sitting at the table for dinner. I didn't feel good; my head hurt, and my tummy felt funny. There were mushrooms on my plate, and I didn't want them. They smelled bad and made my tummy feel worse. Mommy got mad and yelled at me to eat them. I said I didn't want to, but she said I had to. She pushed the mushrooms into my mouth, held my jaw closed, and told me to chew. I tried, but I felt so sick, and then I threw up on my plate. I thought she'd let me stop eating, but she didn't. She yelled at me to scrape the throw-up over to the other side of my plate and finish eating my mushrooms. I was crying, but she told me to stop, or I'd be in more trouble. I stayed in my chair and tried to eat, even though everything tasted yucky, and I was scared. I wanted to go to bed, but I couldn't until I finished. I just kept wishing it would be over. Daddy was sitting at the table too, but he didn't help me. He just ate his mushrooms like he was supposed to.

***

My earliest memories are of life in a small home in Caldwell, Idaho. It was a pretty small house, and when my younger siblings kept coming, Dad split the two-car garage down the middle, turning one side into another bedroom. My parents had five children in about six years, three girls then two boys; I am number two, so I don't remember a time when I didn't have several siblings around. We lived in that house till the summer I turned seven. Of course, this was years before my parents began forgetting my birthday, so I do have memories of cakes and presents sprinkled throughout my younger years. That house saw some of the best times I can recall, though those times seem to be drifting further behind the other, less enjoyable memories.

Back then, we still had a TV (the kind that today's kids would probably call "vintage" or "old-fashioned"), and we were allowed to watch PBS Kids, but only select shows. I remember Between the Lions, Reading Rainbow, Dragon Tales, Caillou, Teletubbies, and Sagwa. CyberChase was banned, so we had to turn the TV off as soon as it came on.

Once my brothers were born, we also watched Clifford, Thomas the Tank Engine, and Bob the Builder. I have a few vague memories of some other shows like The Comfy Couch, and my older sister remembers a few more like Zoom. We were only allowed to watch one episode of a show per child per day; Mom had a chart on the fridge, and we chose which show we wanted each day for the rest of the week. My first choice was always Sagwa.

When we weren't in trouble, we could all watch even if the show was selected by someone else. If we were bad, not only would we lose the show we chose, but we wouldn't be allowed to watch the other shows either. Sometimes, Mom would ground me in my room during my show, but she would still let the other kids watch it, even though it was the one I'd picked. If I was really quiet, I could still hear the show through the wall or the door, but Mom figured that out. She'd put the radio right outside my bedroom door and tune it so it was just the static between stations. She'd turn it up so I couldn't hear the TV.

Movies growing up consisted of Veggie Tales and 3-2-1 Penguins, mostly. I remember watching a few random movies that we rented from the church library, but most of my memories are of either VeggieTales or the Wee Sing Hymnal movies. Even with Veggie Tales, however, some were banned. Mom said some didn't have a strong enough Biblical connection, so we weren't allowed to watch them. She didn't like "King George and the Ducky" because it was the story of King David sending another man to battle so he could steal Bathsheba, the man's wife. I guess she got over that, because we ended up watching it a lot.

Mom didn't like "Sumo of the Opera," "Lord of the Beans," "Minnesota Cuke and the Search for Samson's Hairbrush," "Dr. Jiggle and Mr. Sly," the Sherlock Holmes spoof, any of the LarryBoy ones, the Wizard of Oz spoof, and a LOT of others, actually. We never watched any of those. She only allowed us to watch the ones that were directly based on a Bible story. She said VeggieTales went "downhill" after about 2005, so we really only watched the older ones. On repeat. All the time.

I remember changing diapers because Mom was too busy. I remember putting the bathroom stool by the crib to get the baby out because I was too short to reach over the side. I remember doing laundry, washing dishes, cleaning the table, cleaning the bathroom, and cleaning our room and the boys' room... I remember a lot of cleaning. So much cleaning, yet our house was always so cluttered. There was stuff everywhere; I don't know what the stuff was, necessarily; it was just stuff, and it was everywhere. Some of it was laundry – clean and dirty – in laundry baskets all over the house. I remember getting into a lot of trouble for laundry. Not picking up dirty laundry. Not putting away clean laundry. Not transferring loads – I had to use the bathroom stool for that, too. Again, too short.

I remember being babysat each time a new sibling was born; we would have a sleepover at someone's house and come home the next day to a new baby. I remember enjoying the few days right after getting a new baby brother; Mom was usually sitting in the living room or resting in her room, she didn't get mad at me as much, and I thought it was cool that people from church kept bringing us cool new foods for dinner. We always ate the same things – couscous, rice, potatoes, tuna – so I remember the variety of dinner options was exciting. I liked that Mom was too tired or sore to hit us. I liked that Dad was the primary parent for a little while. He wasn't as tough on us as Mom was. But it didn't last long; eventually, she'd get back up, and life would go back to normal.

***

2002, age 5

Daddy scared me really bad tonight. He came into my room to say goodnight to us girls, but when he turned to walk out the door, he hit his head on the CD rack that's hanging on the wall. He yelled really loud and punched the wall really hard with his fist and made a really big hole. We were really scared, and I think my sister was crying. Later that night, he came back in and told us he would never ever hit one of us, but I'm really scared of making him mad now.

* * *

Most of my memories from those years consist of being scared of my parents in general; there was constant yelling between Mom and Dad, between them and us, between everyone, really. It was such a loud house, yelling and screaming, things being thrown, dishes being broken, doors being slammed, holes being punched in walls... just loud. Always.

I remember hiding in the pantry a lot. Mom and Dad would be screaming, I would be scared, so I hid in the pantry. I didn't like getting hit by a flailing hand if I got too close during their fight; that would be my own fault, and I'd get in trouble for it later. I also hated getting in the way of something being thrown across the room. Usually, my sister and I would get the younger kids together in one of the bedrooms, close the door, and play with them until the yelling stopped or one of them came to get us. I remember always feeling like I was in trouble. I was always in trouble anyway, so that feeling makes sense, I guess. I remember thinking I could never do anything right, even though I was trying my hardest.

I knew exactly where the first-aid kit was because it was being used almost every day. I learned early how to put Band-Aids on, how to choose which shape and size best fit the injury, how to pour hydrogen peroxide over deeper or dirtier wounds, and how to pull slivers with tweezers gently so the slivers didn't break. I was set on becoming an EMT when I grew up. I knew it stood for Emergency Medical Technician, that they rode in ambulances, and that they treated injuries. I figured I could do it since my sister and I always took care of all our own injuries, plus our younger siblings', and I also liked ambulances. I got an EMT or paramedic toy set, complete with a coat, stethoscope, and all the first-aid supplies I'd ever need for my 4th or 5th birthday. I remember Mom telling me I would hate being an EMT because I would have to see a lot of blood, but I already saw a lot of blood at home, so I didn't see the difference.

One night, we were sitting at the dinner table, and my younger sister was sitting in a highchair, kicking her feet against the table. She kicked too hard, and the entire chair fell back; her head hit the kitchen floor with what I remember to be a really loud thud. She didn't cry for a few seconds, and Dad started freaking out. Mom was yelling, and my older sister and I had to take the boys to their bedroom.

I remember sneaking out of the bedroom and peeking around the hallway wall to see what was happening. My younger sister was finally screaming and crying, but Mom and Dad's screaming was even louder than hers. Dad was yelling at Mom to call 911, and Mom was screaming at Dad that she didn't need to. Everything was so chaotic, and I remember being more scared than I'd ever been before. I think Dad ended up calling 911 because the EMTs arrived at the house a little while later. They had all their bags and tools out, huddled around my sister on the living room floor. My older sister and I were watching from the hallway, keeping the bedroom door closed so the boys didn't come out.

I don't know what happened, but eventually the EMTs left, and my younger sister was sitting in the living room. We went back into the bedroom with the boys to wait for Mom or Dad to come to get us. It seemed like forever, but eventually Mom called us to say that we could come out. Dad was on the couch, holding my younger sister, and I think he was holding an ice pack to the back of her head while she ate some crackers. Mom said dinner was over, even though we had barely started eating when it all happened, and she told us to start doing our chores. The boys got to eat, but they were basically babies, and they almost always got to finish eating. My older sister and I went to bed that night, and Dad was still holding my younger sister on the couch. Mom and Dad weren't speaking to each other, and Mom seemed extra mad.

I remember Mom coming in – not to say goodnight, she never did that – but to tell us never to call 911, ever. She said if we call 911 and the police or EMTs come, their job is to take us away and give us to another family. I asked why they didn't take us that night, and she said because we obeyed for once and hid in the bedroom. I wanted to ask why they didn't take my younger sister, but I was too scared; Mom was already mad, and I didn't want to make it worse. Dad came in later that night to put my younger sister to bed, and he saw that we were both still awake.

Looking back, I assume we were probably pretty shaken by the whole thing, and I'm sure we looked scared. Dad told us everything was okay, that our sister would be fine in the morning, and that we should always call 911 if there's an emergency or if we think someone is hurt or in danger. He seemed pretty mad, too, so I don't remember either of us asking any questions. I was so confused about the purpose of 911 and the role of EMTs after that. I abandoned my life goal of becoming an EMT because I didn't want to be someone who went into people's houses, took their little kids, and gave them to different families.

***

2002, age 5

We didn't get dinner again tonight. That's been happening a lot. Mommy says it's because we're bad or we didn't listen or obey during the day, but most of the time, I don't even know what I did wrong. She says, "You don't deserve to eat tonight," and we just have to go to bed hungry.

She and Daddy always eat, though, probably because they weren't bad all day like I was. Sometimes she'll give us a piece of bread and a cup of water, and she says that's plenty. My stomach growls so loudly when I lie in bed, but I can't say anything, or I might get us all in more trouble. I just pull the blanket over my head and pretend I'm not hungry, or try to dream about yummy food, so when I wake up, it feels like I ate dinner.

***

Mom always told us she legally only had to feed us once a day, so as long as we ate once, we were fine and she wasn't breaking any laws. She said our bodies also didn't necessarily need more than one meal a day, and if we whined or complained about it, we were being greedy. She reminded us almost daily that there are children in Africa who don't get to eat at all, so we should be thankful for the food we do get and not beg for more. She also reminded us about children in Africa who were starving whenever there was food left on a plate; we had to finish every last bite on our plate before leaving the table because we were lucky to even get any food compared to the starving African children.

I remember going to bed without dinner a LOT. Mom said it was because we had been naughty that day and didn't deserve to eat. We still had to do our evening chores; then we'd go to bed. If we cried that we were hungry or begged for food, she said we would lose the privilege of breakfast the next day, too. I learned just to be quiet, do my chores, and go to bed without arguing. It was better just to do as she said and not risk losing another meal.

Sometimes we had "bread and water" for dinner: a slice of plain bread and a glass of water, so that wasn't so bad. I remember taking my time to eat it, thinking I would feel fuller if I took longer. That didn't last long, though, because Mom started setting a time limit for dinner, and if we didn't finish our bread and water, she took them away. After that, I ate it pretty quickly so I wouldn't lose it.

We had WIC and food stamps during those years, and I remember going grocery shopping with Mom and having to match each food stamp or WIC check to each item. Back then, they didn't give out debit or EBT cards; they were physical pieces of paper, each one showing which items the check or voucher covered and the quantity. Mom would hand my older sister and me each the next paper in the stack. We would run down the aisle, get the correct food item, and run back to put it in the cart. Sometimes, I'd have to go back and get something else because I did it wrong – if she gave me a check for "one apple or grape juice" and I brought back apple juice, she'd inevitably want grape juice, so I'd have to redo that check.

I remember getting yelled at in the store if I didn't get the correct brand for something, too. One time, I brought back two boxes of Mac n' cheese, and I got yelled at for bringing back a "name-brand" box; she yelled at me that if I wanted to have the most expensive brand, I could pay for it myself. I grew up always checking prices and knew to choose the cheapest option, which was usually the store brand. I only made each mistake once, the correct items and brands being seared into my brain, but I bet if you asked her, she'd probably say I never learned anything.

I remember we each got to paint our own tiny jar once. Then Mom sent us outside to collect as many tiny rocks as we could find. When we brought them inside, she said that at the end of each day, we would get either a rock or a penny. A rock meant we were naughty that day, and a penny meant we were good. At the end of the week, if we had more pennies than rocks, we would get a treat.

I remember thinking it wasn't fair because the boys always got all the pennies, since they were the youngest and couldn't get in trouble as much as the girls. I don't remember ever having more pennies than rocks, and I don't remember ever getting a treat. Mom told me I was just a naturally bad kid, and I couldn't help but be naughty all the time. After a while, I remember thinking that if I was just bound to get all rocks anyway, there was no point in even trying to be good. I gave up trying to get pennies; it was never going to happen anyway, so why bother?

I don't remember Mom ever "tucking us in" at bedtime or coming to say goodnight. Dad did almost every night – he'd give us a hug and say, "I love you, goodnight". But Mom never did that. At least not that I remember. I actually don't remember her ever hugging me. I think if she did, it would've been weird. She didn't really like to touch us unless it was part of discipline.

I remember asking Dad why Mom wasn't coming in to say goodnight, and he said Mom was upset that we were naughty all day. He said that maybe if we obeyed tomorrow and listened to Mom, then she would say goodnight to us the next night. I remember trying to be as good as possible the next day, always obeying, listening to her, doing what she said as quickly as I could, but she still put a rock in my jar and didn't come to say goodnight. I stopped trying to get her to say goodnight after a while; I knew it wasn't going to happen, no matter how good I was that day.

We still did Christmas during those years; I remember a few years when Mom would put up a fake tree and decorate it. We weren't allowed to help because she said we would do it wrong or break something. She usually did it at night while we were asleep. I remember thinking it would be fun to help her wrap the lights, hang the ornaments, and put the angel on the top. She didn't put the presents under the tree till the night before Christmas.

I always knew it was her because she told us every year that Santa wasn't real. The other kids at church believed Santa brought their presents, and Mom said we weren't allowed to tell them he wasn't real, or we'd get in trouble. One time, I told a kid at church that the tooth fairy wasn't real and that their parents put the money under their pillow. They started crying, and I got in big trouble.

For birthdays, we would pick a cake from one of the Wilton catalogs, and Mom would make it for us. Sometimes I had to pick several cakes until I found one she approved of. We weren't allowed to have a birthday party and invite friends over unless it was our 6th or 16th birthday. I remember being shocked when I found out other families didn't do "6 and 16" and just had parties every year, regardless of what age they were turning. I thought "6 and 16" was just a regular birthday party rule for everyone.

I remember one time the light bulb in the ceiling fan in the girls' room went out. Mom replaced the light bulb during the day, and that night, while we were getting into bed, the glass cover fell to the ground and shattered. Mom and Dad started screaming at all of us girls and demanded to know who touched it and loosened it because it clearly wouldn't have fallen by itself. None of us had touched it, so we all denied it. They took us to the living room, lined us up, and sat on the couch while they waited. They said they would wait until one of us confessed.

We did that a lot – line up till someone confessed to something, but usually none of us had done it, so we just waited till someone caved and took the blame so we could get it over with. I spoke up and said that Mom had replaced the light bulb earlier that day and that the glass cover might not have been tightened all the way. Mom said she never touched it or replaced the bulb, so I got in trouble for calling her a liar. After that, I just took the blame for causing the glass cover to crash and break – I figured I was already in trouble for calling Mom a liar, so I may as well just get in trouble for all of it. The sooner one of us just said we did it, the sooner we could all go back to bed.

Usually, during these lineups, while we waited for someone to confess to something, Dad read us Bible verses about children obeying their parents, lying being a sin, telling the truth, etc. They would just keep reading Bible verses and telling us how disappointed God was with us until one of us confessed. They would sometimes change their tone – from screaming at us to talking softly – and make us believe it would be better for us if we just confessed. Sometimes they told us they just wanted to know who did it and that we wouldn't even get in trouble. Then one of us would cave and confess and figure out they were lying because we'd just be in even more trouble.

Other times, if nobody confessed, we'd all get spanked. We'd have to line up and watch one person get spanked, then the next, then the next. We'd get through one round of each of us getting spanked, then Dad would ask again if anyone wanted to confess. If nobody did – because, again, usually none of us had actually done the thing – he would start another round of spankings. We would do that until someone caved; then they'd get in even more trouble. I remember feeling like there was never a good way to navigate those lineups. If I were truthful and said I didn't do it, I would get in trouble. If I lied and said I did do it, I got in trouble. We could never win.

Right before Dad spanked us, he'd always look at us and say, "I'm doing this because I love you." And then he'd spank us; we'd get back in line, and he'd say the same to the next person. Over and over. Because he loved us.

"I love you, but I don't like you." That was another one. They both said that, but mostly Dad. Mom didn't like to use the words "I love you" very often, or if she did, I didn't hear. If we did something bad, Dad would tell us he loved us, but he didn't love our behavior. He loved us, but he didn't like us. He loved us, but he didn't love how we were treating Mom. "I love you, but..."

I don't remember hearing "I love you" on its own; it was always followed by something. "But," a favor, a punishment, a hit... always something. Never just, "I love you."

***

2003, age 6

Mommy flicks us on the lips and cheeks a lot when she's mad. Sometimes it hurts so bad my eyes water, but I'm not allowed to cry because Mommy says crying is for babies. Sometimes the spots turn red and swell up, and sometimes there's some blood, but then Mommy says I have to wash the blood off my face, or I'll get in trouble for being dirty; only babies can't wash their own faces, and I'm not a baby. Sometimes, if I still have marks on my face when we go to church, people ask me about them, and I just say I fell. Sometimes I say the cats scratched me or I fell off my bike. Mommy says to say those things, and I have to because if I don't, I'll get in so much trouble when we get home.

***

I always knew Mom was in charge. I knew to listen to Mom first, Dad second. I knew that if Dad told me I could do something, I would have to make sure Mom approved, too. Dad didn't make decisions; Mom did. Dad was also wrong a lot, and Mom made sure everyone knew when he was. She was always right, and I remember wondering why Dad was always messing up.

I thought grown-ups were supposed to be smart and know how to do things, but Dad always seemed to make mistakes, and Mom had to correct him a lot. Dad got in trouble a lot, but Mom never did. I thought all families were like that. I thought all dads just messed up, and the moms had to correct them. I thought moms just knew more than dads.

When I was five, I learned in church that if you don't say the prayer and have Jesus in your heart, you have to go to Hell, where you'll burn forever after you die. We also did communion that day, and all the grown-ups and my older sister got to have crackers and grape juice in church. I wanted some too, but Mom said I couldn't have any until I had Jesus in my heart.

I didn't know if Jesus was in my heart or not – I didn't know how to tell. I knew one thing, though: I absolutely did not want to burn in Hell forever when all my family and friends were going to Heaven. I also didn't want to feel left out during communion when I had to pass the plates without taking any snacks.

I remember asking Mom how to get Jesus in my heart so I could avoid going to Hell and have communion. She told me to repeat the prayer after her, and I did. Then she said I had Jesus in my heart. I didn't feel any different, but I figured if Mom said Jesus was in my heart, she must be right because Jesus was in hers, so I guess she would know.

One Sunday at church, Dad and the pastor baptized me in the little pool on the stage. I had to wear black so it wouldn't be see-through in the pool, and I wouldn't be immodest. I also had to bring a change of clothes to church since I'd get all wet and would have to change before getting in the van to go home. All the grown-ups were crying, kept hugging me, and said they were so proud of me; I was just happy I wasn't going to Hell and that I could share communion with my older sister.

Mom seemed so happy the day I got baptized. She let me sit by her during the service, smiled at me a lot, and told all the other grown-ups that I had asked Jesus to be in my heart and that I was getting baptized that day. She smiled so big when all the other grown-ups congratulated me. I felt so happy that I had done something to make her proud of me. I didn't think I'd ever done anything that good before; it was such a good feeling to know she was proud of me and seemed to finally like me.

We stayed late after church, and the pastor gave me a gift bag with a Bible, some bookmarks, and candy. Mom was smiling so big; she was so happy. But when we went home, she took the bag and told me to put my wet baptism clothes in the washer before they started to smell. I started a load of laundry in the washer, then found her in the kitchen.

I expected her to be nice to me and smile at me like she'd been doing all morning at church. Instead, she snapped at me to change out of my Sunday clothes and to start helping my sister set the table for lunch. I figured she was just distracted by trying to get lunch ready and put the kids down for their naps. I waited till the afternoon to talk to her again; I asked her if I did a good job at church, and she yelled at me for trying to make everything about me.

She said I was so selfish and self-centered and that I was just eating up all the attention. I didn't know what that meant, but I was pretty sure it meant she wasn't proud of me anymore. I asked Dad if I could get baptized again the next Sunday so Mom would be happy and proud of me, but he said I could only do it once.

I don't remember a time when I didn't know what "sin" was. I knew kids were born with sin already, but that God hated sin and didn't want us to sin. I thought it was weird that God made us Himself, put sin in us, but didn't want us to sin. I asked Mom why God wouldn't just make us without putting sin in us, and she got mad at me for questioning the Bible. I learned pretty quickly that I'm not supposed to ask questions about the Bible or God. She did say God used to make people without sin, such as Adam and Eve, but Satan made Eve sin, so now everyone has sin. I just knew I already had sin, and I couldn't get rid of it no matter how hard I tried.

Even after Mom said I had Jesus in my heart after the prayer and the baptism, I still got in trouble every day, so I wasn't sure it worked. I prayed every night for months for Jesus to stay in my heart so I wouldn't be naughty and get in trouble all the time, but every single day, I'd just get in trouble for something new. I didn't think Jesus wanted to be in my heart since I was always so bad.

When they told us we were moving the summer I was about to turn seven, Mom gave each of us girls a plastic bin with a lid. All my stuff had to fit into that bin – blankets, stuffed animals, toys, and clothes. She said anything that didn't fit would be thrown away. Thankfully, I didn't have that much stuff, so I didn't have to throw anything away. After that, I made sure I never collected very much stuff so that each time we moved, I could keep what was mine.

I also didn't bother collecting much since Mom just threw a lot of our stuff away anyway. Sometimes, when she felt like cleaning or was mad, she'd come into our room with a black garbage bag, just put stuff in it, and put it in the trash can outside. I told Dad once, and he said Mom probably just put the bag in the garage, and we would get our stuff back if we were good. I don't think she did that, though, because I never saw that stuff again each time she did that.

One time, she threw all my Sunday shoes away, and I had to wear tennis shoes with my Sunday clothes to church. I was so embarrassed because the shoes didn't match any of my dresses; they weren't fancy like the stuff we were supposed to wear to church, and other kids made fun of me for wearing regular tennis shoes with Sunday clothes. She said that when I got money for my birthday or Christmas, I could buy myself a new pair of Sunday shoes.

Looking back, I can see now that the foundation of control had already been laid long before I ever realized I was trapped. At the time, it just felt like family, like faith, like earning love by obeying a lot of rules. I didn't know the difference between devotion and indoctrination; I was too young and too deep inside to see where one ended and the other began. Every belief was spoon-fed truth, and every boundary was disguised as protection. The walls didn't go up overnight; they were built brick by brick, with fear, guilt, and obligation as the mortar. By the time I was old enough to question anything, it was already too late. My thoughts weren't my own. I wasn't chained, but I might as well have been. Innocence had met indoctrination, and indoctrination had won.

Key Characteristic #2

COERCIVE CONTROL

Her power was maintained through anger – the loud crack of a hand across a face, the sharp sting of a finger flicking a lip. Her anger filled every inch of every space. Disappointment made her strike, not retreat. Her rage was physical and tangible, like a slammed door or a thrown object. Punishment came often and taught us to measure our words, or movements, and even our breathing.

Surveillance was constant; she noticed everything. How long we lingered in another room, how long it took us to complete a task or chore, the look on our faces when she spoke, whether our public smiles seemed convincing enough. She controlled not only what we did, but also what we said. There was no privacy inside our home, but it was for our own safety and protection. Fear became the air we breathed, and submission was the only language she understood.

Food, clothes, chores, affection, punishment... everything was currency in her system of control. Meals weren't about nourishment; they were about obedience. We had to earn a meal, and it was something that could be easily taken away. She decided who deserved seconds, who deserved to go to bed hungry, and who deserved to sit at the table with an empty plate and watch the others eat. Chores were abundant and mandatory, a never-ending test of loyalty disguised as responsibility. Affection came with strings attached; we could earn it through compliance, but it could be revoked at the first sign of defiance. Any positive attention we received came with a requirement to do something for her in return. Everything we touched, ate, said, or felt was filtered through her obsession with dominance. Love was conditional, rationed, and used to remind us of who was in charge.

Her control wasn't only in the slaps, the chores, or the constant surveillance; it also seeped into how we thought and how we felt. Obedience became the means by which we could earn affection. Following her rules might garner us attention, a smile, and maybe even some fleeting motherly warmth. If we stepped out of line, guilt wrapped around us like chains. Disobedience wasn't just met with punishment; it was sinful and made us unworthy of love. We didn't recognize it as manipulation but simply as the fact that rules are sacred and that breaking them incurs devastating consequences. Over time, it became second nature for us to measure our worth by compliance and our failures by rebellion. Every act, thought, and feeling had to measure up to her standard, and the line between obedience and love seemed to disappear entirely.

I quickly learned that my thoughts were not safe when I allowed them out of my head. I remember telling my dad that I had been "mean to Mommy in my mind." That evening, I didn't get dinner. The lesson was clear: the tiniest act of defiance, even just a thought, could have serious consequences. We weren't just punished for actions but also for intent, imagination, and feelings that might someday spill out. There was no sanctuary or solace inside my own head; fear followed me there and taught me to police my mind as much as I did my actions. Obedience had to be total, extending even to the invisible corners of my mind.

Among us children, there was always subtle competition and occasional betrayal, but mostly just quiet understanding. We learned early on that our only safety was in each other. Dad wasn't going to help us, so we had to help ourselves. The older ones stepped in where they could, deflecting her anger, taking the blame, and distracting her long enough for the younger ones to hide or go unnoticed. It wasn't affection that bound us together, but necessity. We operated like a small, secret unit, communicating through glances and silence, always alert, always ready. Yet for all our unity, we were largely strangers in all the ways that mattered. Survival left no room for softness. We didn't talk about fear or sadness with each other, and we didn't comfort each other after each storm had passed. We just carried on, side by side, together but distant, each of us scarred in similar ways, but alone inside our pain. We played together during the day but kept our thoughts to ourselves at night.

In hindsight, normal boundaries and common luxuries did not exist in our home. Comfort was rationed and not freely given; it was provided to us according to her mood, whims, and satisfaction with our behavior. We were not given hugs or praise, so a simple kind word or smile held enormous meaning to us, as it was rarely given as a reward for compliance. She controlled when we could feel safe, and if we needed reassurance, we were out of luck. Being scared during a thunderstorm meant you were asking to be treated like a baby. Everything that should've been natural, such as physical touch, affection, and the simple certainty of care, was mediated by her authority. Our needs became the tools she used to reinforce her power.

There were moments when it all made sense to me – or at least, I thought it did. I followed the rules; I did what I was told, and for a fleeting moment, the house felt safe. I didn't see it as control; in my mind, these were just the rules we had to follow to keep ourselves out of trouble and stay protected. She was protecting us by making us follow the rules. I knew I needed to obey because it was logical and necessary.

Over time, obedience felt like an instinct, not a choice. I didn't think before I complied, and I didn't weigh the cost or question the fairness of whatever order she gave me. Fear had been drilled so deeply into me that following the rules was a reflex and a way to survive the day and avoid her storm. Even when her orders seemed confusing, I usually felt that defiance was too dangerous to risk. My body learned the rhythm of submission before my mind even understood it. Compliance became a silent contract I didn't even know I signed, and the distinction between my own will and her control was gone.

2

No Rod Spared

2004 – 2005 | AGES 7-8

***

2004, age 7

Mommy slaps us a lot, I'm mostly used to it now, I think. I used to cry when she slapped me across the face because it stung, and my eyes would water, and if she hit my ear, then my ear would ring a little bit, but I've learned not to cry much anymore because it just makes her madder. I don't flinch or back away anymore, either; if I do that or pull back or try to cover my face, she says it's crazy that I'd think she would hit me, and then I get in more trouble. Now I just stand as still as I can when she gets close to me, even though my whole body wants to move away. It's better if I'm still; she'll slap me and then just move on to someone else, and I'll be okay for a while. I can wait till I'm in bed tonight to cry.

***

We moved to Nampa, Idaho, in the summer of 2004. That was the first summer we went to the camp. I don't know where she heard of it, but Mom found Shiloh Bible Camp in the Idaho mountains and took my older sister and me, plus one friend each, to summer camp for a week. I couldn't wait to come home. I brought a friend from church, but she found another group of girls on the first day of camp and didn't really speak to me the rest of the week.

All the other girls in my cabin were older and bigger than me; it was a camp for 3rd-5th-grade girls, and I had barely turned seven, and I was fairly small, and I'm pretty sure I was set to start 2nd grade in the fall, so I'm not sure why Mom brought me. All the other girls were in 5th grade, probably 10 or 11, and they played pranks on me and teased me a lot. I lost some baby teeth, and the grown-up teeth hadn't come in yet, so they called me a baby.

They told me they wanted to take a picture with me and had me sit on a tree stump, but as soon as I sat down and smiled for the picture, they all started laughing. The stump was covered in sap, and the entire seat of my shorts was sticky. They were laughing at me and throwing dirt at me so it would stick to the sap. They said I had a dirty diaper, just like a baby.

Whenever we went to the river for swimming time in the afternoons, the girls made fun of me for having a one-piece swimsuit instead of a two-piece. I tried to explain that I wasn't allowed to wear a two-piece because it would show my stomach and be immodest, but they just laughed at me anyway.

There was a guy leading groups of kids on canoe trips, and I decided to go. We were at the deepest part of the river, and the girls in my canoe started rocking it till it tipped, and everyone fell out. I wasn't strong enough to pull myself back up the side of the canoe to get back in, and the girls started paddling and left me behind. The instructor had to come back for me and pull me up into his canoe. I was bleeding pretty badly from scrapes on my knees, elbows, and feet from trying to climb back into the canoe.

Mom was at the camp with us as a cabin leader, and I found her and told her about the girls, the tree stump, the canoe, etc. She got mad and said that I was trying to get attention. She said I needed to grow up and stop being such a baby because everyone else is having a great time and I'm the only one with a problem. I don't remember much else about that week at camp; I just remember counting down the days till I could go home and hoping I never had to come back.

Later that year, Mom and Dad decided we were going to start doing more with the camp; we went to fall retreats and winter camps, and we spent the entire next summer there. We had a teenager babysit us kids during most of the weeks of camp, but then we had to attend the week of camp that was our grade. Some of the older girls who had bullied me the year before were some of the girls who were sent to help babysit us. They always left me behind, only liked my younger siblings because they were cute and small, and whenever Mom came back to our RV, they told her I'd been naughty all day. Then I'd get in trouble with Mom and not get to play with the other leaders' kids after dinner with my sisters.

I hated being at the camp that summer; I was still smaller than all the other girls in my cabin during the week I attended as a camper. Mom didn't believe me or didn't care when I said I was being teased, and I kept having asthma attacks during game times and had to go to the nurse's office to use my inhaler. Mom got mad at me for that, too, saying I was looking for attention again. I remember thinking I just needed to blend into the background and not get any attention at all; maybe then Mom would be happy with me.

Sometime in the summer of 2005, I went with the rest of the campers to the river during the afternoon swimming time. I remember being a decent swimmer as a kid because we always got put in swimming lessons during the school year, so I swam across the river to the far bank and sat on the rocks with some of the girls from my cabin. One of the girls pushed me off, and the others started laughing, but I was treading water and figured I'd just swim back to the other side and find someone else to hang out with.

All I remember next is being pushed down under the water; I tried to come back up, but there were too many feet and hands holding me down, and I couldn't surface. I started thrashing as much as I could to get the lifeguard's attention, but it seemed like I was underwater forever. One of the girls' feet kicked me in the chest, and I couldn't breathe. My vision went blurry, and I inhaled a mouthful of water.

I don't remember much that happened after that until I was being dragged up the other bank by the lifeguard. I coughed up a bunch of water, and the lifeguard said I wasn't allowed to swim anymore that day, and I had to sit by her till the bus took everyone back. I felt like I was in trouble, and nobody listened to me when I told them what happened. The other girls just sneered at me from across the river.

When we got back, the lifeguard told Mom she had to save me, and I got in trouble with Mom, too. She yelled at me for trying to get attention, trying to make everything about me, and trying to show off by swimming in deep water when I knew I couldn't swim. I tried to explain that I swam over just fine, and I was treading water, about to swim back, when they pushed me down, but she wouldn't listen. She said it was typical of me to blame other innocent people for something I did by myself. When I got back to my cabin, the girls had taken my sleeping bag and suitcase and thrown them out the front door; all my stuff was scattered everywhere in the woods, stuck to sap-covered stumps, and my sleeping bag was filthy.

From 2005 to 2007, we spent our entire summers at the camp. We lived in our house in Nampa during the school year, then moved into an RV at the camp for the summer, except Dad. Dad had to stay in Nampa and keep working, but he would come to see us on weekends. I liked it when he came because it took some of the pressure off of me. Mom got mad at me less when Dad was around. Other families also spent their summers at the camp, and some of them had kids our age, so we had a few friends there. The only friends we had back home were each other, pretty much.

***

2004, age 7

Mommy and Daddy yell so much every single day, but it's okay because my sister and I know what to do now. When we see Daddy pull in the driveway when he comes home from work, we make sure the little kids are in their room playing down the hall, and then we come back and hide in the laundry room. Our laundry room is in our bathroom, and there's a curtain hanging in front of the washer and dryer, so we go behind the curtain but leave the bathroom door open so we can hear. We listen for Daddy to walk inside, then we wait, and if there's a lot of yelling and screaming, we know we'll stay there for a while. Once we don't hear anything for a bit, we come out. Sometimes they're still mad, so we go hide again, but when everything's okay, we say hi to Daddy and then go get the other kids so they can come out and say hi. We don't want them to hear Mommy and Daddy yell because it might make them cry, and then Mommy and Daddy will just get even madder. It's better to just be quiet and hide till everything's okay.

***

We used to go to the Baptist church in Caldwell, where we had tons of friends in our Sunday School classes. Most of those friends came to my 6th birthday party when we lived in the old house. But once we moved, we didn't really have friends anymore because we didn't really have a church anymore, either. Mom didn't like any of the churches we tried.

We tried different churches every Sunday for a while, and Mom called it "church shopping," but we couldn't really find one she liked. One time, she said she didn't like a church because there was a black guy in a leadership position. I didn't understand why that was bad, but she just said we couldn't go back there. I remember her telling us black and brown people were dangerous, so I figured that might have been why.

Another time we tried a church, but the pastor's wife was wearing skinny jeans and high heels, so Mom said we weren't going back. Usually, though, we couldn't stay at a church because Mom didn't agree with the pastor's sermon or the church's theology. She said they interpreted the Bible differently, or wrongly, or that they believed things that weren't true. I remember her telling us we have to be careful because people will read the Bible and think it says one thing when, really, it says something else. She said people interpret the Bible to say whatever they want it to say. She also didn't like staying at churches that didn't let her be in charge of the Sunday School or Children's Church curriculum. She said one church taught Noah's Ark wrong, and another one was teaching about David and Bathsheba, which isn't a story that kids are supposed to learn.

Mom could never find a homeschool curriculum she liked, either. She usually preferred Amish or Mennonite brands but often ended up switching mid-year, mixing several brands, or abandoning one altogether if she found something she didn't like. There was always a Bible story told wrong, a prayer written wrong, a message told wrong, or something that just didn't align with whatever she believed. We tried Rod & Staff, Sonlight, Christian Light Education, Simply Charlotte Mason, Pathway Readers, Apologia, etc. I remember using Exploring Creation Science during high school because all the other science textbooks she found talked about "millions of years" and we believed in a young Earth.

Life of Fred math wasn't inherently a Christian curriculum, I don't think; I believe the author was Christian, though, which is why she allowed it. We did Amish and Mennonite math up until 8th grade; girls didn't really need to know any more math than that - we just needed to know fractions since we'd be baking and cooking in the kitchen for our families. Once the Amish ones were done, we moved on to Life of Fred so we'd have something to do for high school.

We attended many homeschool conventions held at churches or Christian colleges, so everyone there was expected to be Christian. Mom had grudges against certain families if they were a different denomination than us like Methodist or Lutheran, (or, God forbid, Mormon or Catholic which weren't even "real" Christians), if they went to a different type of church than we did, if they dressed in secular or worldly clothing, if they allowed their children to do secular sports or dance, if they had tattoos and piercings, if they wore makeup, or if they were just generally different than my Mom's idea of the perfect Christian homeschool family. The only perfect Christian homeschool mom, of course, was herself. Nobody homeschooled as purely as she did. Mom even had beef with families who used a different curriculum from ours; for example, anyone who used Abeka wasn't a real Christian. (Abeka is a Christian homeschool curriculum, by the way.) Church wasn't the only thing that she was too godly for.

Anyway, we got pretty used to attending a different church every Sunday, so I always knew not to make any friends or get too used to the Sunday School classes. I remember learning the same Bible story three Sundays in a row at three different churches once; I guess each church just happened to be teaching the same things that month. I also never worried about wearing the same dress week after week because we weren't going to be around any of the same people.

One time, my sister and I thought it would be funny to give our Sunday School teachers fake names since they would never see us again. We only did that a few times before Mom and Dad found out, and we, of course, got in trouble for that. We were lying; lying is a sin; sin is disobedience to God and disrespect to our parents, and we were also apparently making our parents look bad by lying.

After what I'm guessing was probably a year of church shopping, I think they got tired of always striking out. Mom just couldn't find a church that was as godly as she was. We did find a few churches where we'd stay for a few Sundays, maybe even a few months, but it never lasted very long. Since they couldn't find a church that aligned with their beliefs or that taught the "true" interpretation of the Bible, we just started doing church at home.

I remember asking if we were still supposed to dress up, and Mom said there was no point because nobody was going to see us. That was confusing to me because we'd always been told that we dress up on Sundays to go to church because it's respectful to God – you always want to look your best, and dressing up was a way to worship God. I thought if dressing up was for God, then we'd have to do it anyway, even though we were just staying home, but I guess not.

We didn't really have a routine at first; we'd wake up and come to the living room or the kitchen table. Sometimes we sang a song (that was always super awkward), and then Mom would tell Dad which Bible verses to read. They usually centered on children obeying their parents, sins such as lying and disobedience, parents' responsibility to discipline their children, and similar topics.

The timeline is fuzzy to me, but I also remember other times when one or two other families would come over for "church" on Sundays. On those Sundays, we did dress up even though we weren't leaving the house. I guess it was because other people would be seeing us. My sister and I would take the kids to another room and read a kids' Bible story, or take them outside to play.

The parents would do church inside; there was one time I had gotten in trouble for something, and I had to stay inside with the parents and not go outside to play. They made me read the Bible verses out loud and explain what I thought they meant. The other parents smiled at me, but Mom looked pissed. I don't know how I could've messed up reading Bible verses, but I was pretty good at messing up everything I ever did, so I wasn't really surprised that she was mad at me.

I don't remember other families coming for very long, so I think it probably lasted only a couple of months. We did other things like "do your own devotions" mornings; I think Mom and Dad just didn't want to do church some weeks, so they just had us do "quiet time" and read our own Bibles or children's Bible story-books. Other times, we'd watch a VeggieTales movie, and that would be "church."

***

2005, age 8

Mommy likes to punish us by putting us "on the wall". We have to stand facing the walls with our arms up above our heads, but we can't touch the wall with any part of our bodies, or we get more time added. My arms get so tired they start shaking, and sometimes my fingers go numb, but it's better if I can just stay still and finish my time instead of resting my arms to take a break because then it'll just end up being longer. Normally, we start with 30 minutes, but if we move at all or touch the wall, we get more time. Yesterday, two of us got put on the wall right after lunch, and we weren't allowed to move till Daddy got home from work that night. My arms felt like they were on fire. I try to count in my head or make up stories to make the time go by faster, but it never really works.

***

It was pretty clear to me that unless Mom and Dad were talking about God and the Bible in the context of discipline, they were uncomfortable and awkward, and made us feel uncomfortable and awkward. If they talked "Bible" during family devotions, at-home church, or any other situation that wasn't inherently meant for punishment, it was like they choked up and didn't know what to say. We never knew what to do, and it always felt super weird.

But if they were quoting verses and talking about Jesus while yelling at us, disciplining us, or anything else like that, it came out naturally. I think that's why I always felt like I was in trouble when any adult ever quoted a verse to me or asked me questions about the Bible. I mostly heard Christian stuff in the context of punishment, so that's what I associated it with.

That's why it seemed so strange and out of character to me when Mom and Dad decided to start spending more and more time at the camp. They were cabin leaders, taught chapel lessons, prayed with teenage campers at winter camps and retreats; I found all of that super awkward, and I hardly recognized those people as my parents. They never prayed with us, or at least they never did with me, so I felt so uncomfortable watching them pray with other older teenagers who weren't their own kids. I remember wondering why they used their soft "prayer" or "godly" voices with other kids, prayed with them, told them Jesus loved them, etc., when they never did that stuff with us.

They seemed to enjoy being with the campers more than with us. Mom told me all the time that other campers had a better relationship with God than I did because I didn't pray enough. I told Mom once that I heard her teaching another girl how to pray and asked why she never taught me how to pray. She snapped at me and said I know how to pray; I just want more attention. She said that those other kids she prays with and talks to don't have good homes, but I do. They haven't learned about God their whole lives, but I have. I'm lucky to have the family I have, and I should be thankful for what I have.

Another time, I saw Mom praying with some teenage girls, and I went over to join them. Mom stopped mid-prayer and told me to go away and find something else to do, that she was busy and I needed to leave her alone. I said that I just wanted to pray with them, and she said, "Well, go pray somewhere else then." I remember being confused and wondering why I wasn't allowed to pray with her and those girls; I was taught you can pray anytime and anywhere, but apparently, I missed the part about not now and not with Mom.

I told Dad that she wouldn't let me pray with them, and he said I was probably bothering her and I just needed to leave her alone and let her witness to those girls and lead them to Christ. I still wasn't sure why my being there would've hindered them from being led to Christ, but I figured I'd just pray alone from then on. I didn't want to mess up anyone else's relationship with God.

Back then, we still did Christmas to an extent. Mom and Dad were veering away from the tree, presents, decorations, and all that, and toward waking up, reading the Bible, and that's it. They said it was selfish to have presents when we were supposed to be celebrating Jesus, and also, Mom said it was a Pagan holiday and Jesus' real birthday was in September.

Anyway, around 2005, I still remember doing some semblance of Christmas. My older sister and I would have been around 8 or 9 years old. Our main bathroom doubled as a laundry room, so it was a pretty decent-sized room. The floor was nothing but dirty laundry, always. It was thrown in there, piled as high as my waist, and spread from the bathtub to the washer and dryer - probably a span of ten or twelve feet. So much laundry.

On Christmas Eve, there was a mountain of laundry that hadn't been done. Mom told my older sister and me that we wouldn't get Christmas unless all the laundry was washed, dried, folded, and put away by the time she woke up the next morning. We spent all night doing laundry – non-stop back-to-back loads until it was light outside. We transferred loads in the washer and dryer, folded and put away the laundry, and tried our best to keep each other awake.

In the morning, Mom came down the hall. We had just finished, but she said it didn't count because some of the piles of clothes were on the floor outside people's rooms and not properly put away. We had left piles outside the rooms since everyone was sleeping during the night while we were doing laundry, and we didn't want to wake anyone up. Mom said since we didn't completely finish like we were told to, we would only get half our presents.

She took several presents from under the tree and put them in her room. I remember being so tired I could barely keep my eyes open while we were opening presents and reading the Bible. Mom got mad that I was falling asleep and said I must not care about the Bible. She made me read the entire passage aloud, even though Dad had already finished reading it.

3

To Train Up A Child

2006 – 2007 | AGES 9-10

***

2006, age 9

I have nail marks on my arm again. Mommy likes to grab our arms really hard, and she always keeps her nails long and sharp, so they dig into our skin. It hurts so bad sometimes I want to cry, but it's better if I just hold still and wait it out. If I try to pull away, she just grabs tighter and squeezes extra hard. Sometimes Daddy is home when she does it, and he tells us not to resist; he never tells her to stop. Daddy says, "If you stop resisting, she'll stop". I tried that so many times, but it felt never-ending. Sometimes, if we pull, Mommy will suddenly let go really fast, and we stumble or fall backward, hitting the wall or falling to the floor. If we get hurt, she says it's our fault for moving too much, and maybe that's true because if I can just hold still for a little longer, maybe she'll let go sooner next time.

* * *

Summers were spent at the camp, and the school year was spent in Nampa at our house. We lived down the street from my grandparents – Mom's parents – so we saw them basically every day. My sisters loved spending time with Nana, but I always got bored. They did artsy stuff with flowers and paint and drawings, and I just didn't enjoy stuff like that. Usually, when we went to their house, they would play with Nana, and I would do homework with Grandpa. Mom always said I was too difficult to deal with, and I wouldn't listen to her when she tried to help me with math.

The truth was, she never tried to help me with math. I didn't understand things sometimes, and I'd ask her to explain, and she'd yell at me that I clearly didn't read the instructions. Grandpa explained things to me in ways that made sense, though. I didn't really mind doing homework at their house while everyone else played, because at least I couldn't get in trouble for anything. Mom left us alone while Grandpa helped me with math, so I couldn't really complain.

Grandpa was kind of like Dad. Dad did whatever Mom told him to do, and Grandpa did whatever Nana told him to do. Grandpa would sneak us little treats sometimes, sort of like Dad used to, until Mom or Nana found out and he had to stop. Sometimes he would get sugar cubes, line them up on the counter, put one drop of lemon or lime juice on each, and let us eat them. The sweetness of the sugar cut the sourness of the lemon juice, and we loved it.

One time, when we were staying the night at their house, my older sister and I couldn't sleep. We went to the kitchen, and Grandpa was in there making pancakes. He told us to whisper so we didn't wake up Nana. We sat at the table eating pancakes in the middle of the night, whisper-giggling with Grandpa, and then he shooed us back to bed. We never told Nana or Mom, but we always wondered why he was making pancakes in the middle of the night. That happened several more times over the years, though, so we figured maybe he had trouble sleeping, too. A smell had us walking into the kitchen during another sleepover, only to find him making salmon. He had just pulled a large baking sheet of salmon out of the oven, and we stood around the kitchen island eating it and whispering until he shooed us off to bed again.

I loved those random midnight snacks with just Grandpa and my sister; it felt like everything else didn't matter at the moment, and we could just enjoy the silence with our pancakes or salmon, go back to bed, and Mom and Nana were none the wiser. It reminded me of Dad's little adventures to get $1 hot chocolates that we could never tell Mom about. I remember feeling a little happier that someone else did care about us, even if he wasn't willing to care about us in the daylight when people were watching. I figured Grandpa was probably scared of Mom, too, just like Dad. And sure enough, those small moments faded away all too quickly. Grandpa was just another extension of Mom – again, just like Dad.

***

2006, age 9

Sometimes when he gets home from work, Mommy will tell Daddy we did something bad, and then he'll say, "Did you do that?" and we say no because we actually didn't do it, and then he'll say, "Are you calling Mommy a liar?" and we get in trouble either way after that. If we say no, we're not calling her a liar, then we get in trouble for doing the bad thing. If we say yes, she is lying, we get in trouble for calling her a liar, and then we also get in trouble for doing the bad thing. I think it makes her happy when we get in trouble because she smiles while Daddy spanks us.

***

I remember wanting to run away almost every day while we lived at this house. I could never do anything right; I was always in trouble; I had no friends other than my sister; and I just felt like Mom was going to hate me forever. I wanted to run away because I thought I'd be able to find a different family that might want me. I remember taking one of our horses out of the pen and riding him down the street to Nana's house. I thought if I told her how bad Mom was, she might believe me and take me to a different family or just let me live with her. Nana got really mad at me and told me to ride Cookie back home immediately; she got in her car and drove alongside me to make sure I went home. She told me to put Cookie away while she went inside to talk to Mom.

I got in a lot of trouble that day; Mom called me a "horse thief" and told me that back in the olden days, I would've been hanged. She said that since I took Cookie out without permission, I was assigned *all* the outside chores instead of just my portion. I had to do my sister's chores too, which included everything to do with both horses – mucking, feeding, grooming, etc, plus everything with the chickens as well.

I acted really mad about having to do all the extra chores outside every day, but I actually preferred it and was kind of glad that was the punishment she gave me. I would rather be outside with the animals than inside with Mom. I hung out with the horses and chickens for hours, making sure every inch of the pens and coops was spotless just so it would take me longer and I could delay going inside. I think, eventually, Mom figured out I enjoyed it, and she switched my punishment to all the inside chores instead, and I wasn't allowed to go outside anymore for quite a while.

One of Mom's favorite punishments during those years was washing our mouths out with soap. If we talked back to her, said something bad, called someone a name, said something mean... sometimes if we literally just said anything at all, she'd do the soap thing. She bought a specific soap that tasted really bad, which was used solely to wash our mouths out. She'd put the bar of soap in our mouths, sticking out about halfway since it was a full bar, and we had to hold it there without letting our teeth touch it. If we bit it, we got a new bar and more time.

She usually started with ten minutes for something small, but I once had to hold a bar in my mouth for sixty minutes. I had so much soapy spit in my mouth that I needed to spit it out, and I started to choke, but she made me swallow it and added more time. If we cried, we got more time; if we whined, we got more time; if we took it out for a second to give our mouth a break, we got way more time. I hated the soap thing so much.

There were many times Mom would duct tape us together when two of us had been "mean" to each other, we were fighting, we were just generally not getting along, or Mom simply decided we'd been bad. I remember having my wrist taped to my older sister's wrist many times, and we had to complete our chores, school, or other tasks while being taped together. When Mom finally decided we had been taped together long enough, she would rip off the tape, often taking hair and skin with it, as it had been attached to us for hours.

***

2007, age 10

We get spanked a LOT. Like almost every day. We have spanking math, too: one spanking is three "swats" or hits. So if Mommy says I earned ten spankings, I know I get thirty swats. Usually, she starts with 10, but we get spankings added on if we keep being bad. One time, I earned so many spankings I couldn't do the math that high, so I don't know how many swats it was, but it felt like hundreds.

I hate getting spankings because everyone else has to line up and watch, and I have to pull my pants and underwear down so Daddy can spank me, and everyone sees me naked. I try not to look when someone else is getting spanked, but if I close my eyes, Mommy yells at me; she says I have to watch so I know what will happen to me if I'm bad. I hate watching. I'd rather get spanked than watch. Sometimes someone will laugh, cry, make a face, or make a noise, and then Mommy says they have to be spanked next because they couldn't be quiet. Sometimes I get so scared or uncomfortable from trying not to cry that my legs start shaking, and it's really hard to stay still.

Lately, Mommy says I'm bound to be naughty that day anyway, so I have to get up really early with Daddy so he can give me ten spankings, which is thirty hits, before he goes to work. I guess I'm just going to get in trouble during the day anyway, so they just decided to spank me ahead of time since I'll end up deserving it regardless. But I still end up getting spanked when Daddy comes home, so I don't think it really matters if I'm good or bad. Sometimes, Mommy has us line up, and she meets him at the door with the switch right when he comes home from work, so we can get the spankings out of the way before dinner.

***

We did the spanking lineups a lot at that house, too. One person got spanked while the others lined up and watched. Mom stood on the opposite side of the room and watched us, smirking.

As soon as Dad got done spanking one person, Mom would tell him who smiled, moved, cried, looked away, closed their eyes, etc., and that person would be next. I learned to just watch the person being spanked, keep my eyes open and my mouth shut, and just be silent until it was over. Sometimes, Mom would still say I had moved even when I hadn't, just so I would be next. She did that a lot - make up that someone moved just so they'd be spanked next. Spanking lineups went on for what seemed like hours.

I got pre-spanked for a while; Mom woke me up while it was still dark outside, Dad gave me ten spankings, so thirty swats, and then he went to work. They said I was bound to be bad that day anyway, so they figured they'd just get my spankings out of the way for whatever sin I was going to commit that day. Mom told me everyone is born with sin in them, but that I was born with more sin than any of my siblings. She said I was born bad; I just couldn't help but sin all the time.

The pre-spanking went on for a few months, and then Mom started tallying the spankings we earned throughout the day on a whiteboard hanging in the dining room. That was how I learned how to do tally marks. Throughout the day, as we misbehaved and earned more spankings, she would add tally marks next to our names. Since I wasn't being pre-spanked anymore, Mom just put ten tally marks next to my name first thing in the morning, just right off the bat. I usually had the most tally marks by the end of the day, and if I complained about that, I got more.

Each tally was one spanking, and each spanking was three swats. That's also how I learned multiples of three. I knew that five tally marks were fifteen swats, twenty tallies were sixty swats, etc. Usually Mom started with ten spankings, so thirty swats, and then she'd add spankings from there as we did more bad things throughout the day. Dad would come home from work, check the whiteboard, and give each of us however many spankings we'd earned. It was rare that one of us didn't have any tally marks, but if that did happen, that person still had to stand in the lineup and watch, which usually led to them getting spanked anyway since they'd inevitably move or close their eyes or do something to make Mom say they were next.

I don't know if we did this every time, but I do remember having to count my own spankings while Dad was spanking me. He'd do three swats, and I'd say, "One," then he'd do three more, and I'd say, "Two." And on and on, etc. I'd count one spanking for every three hits until I'd reached the number of spankings I'd earned for the day. Sometimes, Dad would do "one more, just for good measure."

I remember counting to 100 once; I don't know how many spankings I earned that day, or what I did to earn them. I just remember having to count to over 100... Now that I'm thinking about it, I don't even know if that was the number of swats or the number of spankings. If it were 100 spankings, that would've been over 300 swats... I wouldn't be surprised if it was, but I just don't remember. I remember counting past 100, and that's it. I was probably eight or nine. I don't even know what I did that day to warrant that many spankings. Sometimes, I wonder if I blocked that memory out.

After our spankings, we immediately went back to whatever we were supposed to be doing. Making dinner, doing chores, getting ready for bed... whatever it was, we just went right back to it. We didn't sit and cry; we didn't talk about it with each other, and we didn't comfort each other. I wonder now if that was part of how our brains told us to survive in order to protect us; I wonder if we just ignored what had happened and got on with our day so our brains wouldn't make "spanking" seem like such a big deal. Today, it seems like something so insignificant in my childhood, yet I understand now that it was abuse. When I tell people about it, they don't understand how I can be so nonchalant; honestly, sometimes I don't understand either.

We usually got spanked with plastic spaghetti spoons or wooden spoons from the kitchen. While writing this, I Googled the spaghetti things that were our normal "switches" because I've never seen them in anyone's home but my own growing up. Initially, I had to add "early 2000s" to my search, and one thing called them "vintage." If you search "Tupperware spaghetti pasta fork strain n' serve," you'll find it. Ours were white and speckled, and we had three.

I don't remember ever using them for spaghetti; they were always used as a switch for spankings. If we were told, "Go get a switch," that's what we were supposed to grab. Mom and Dad said they were the perfect switch because of the holes - the air would glide through the holes as they swung, and they struck our butts swiftly and firmly due to the aerodynamics or whatever. I don't know. Apparently, they were the best thing to spank with as they inflicted maximum pain, and Mom recommended them to everyone she met.

Mom hung those normal "switches" on hooks by the whiteboard; when people came over to our house and saw them, Mom explained they were used for spanking, and she hung them up as a daily visual reminder for us. Nobody ever questioned that, and a few parents said it was a good idea and that they might start doing that, too.

A lot of times, when we got spanked with wooden spoons, Dad would hit us so hard that the spoon would break. We got in trouble for breaking the spoon, and then Mom would confiscate our birthday or Christmas money we had gotten from our grandparents because she said she had to use that to pay for a new wooden spoon. If we got spanked with a spoon or spatula or something else from the kitchen, we had to hand wash it after our spanking since it had touched our butt.

Dad was always the one who carried out the spankings, although Mom also inflicted physical punishment in other ways. In the belief system my parents embraced, discipline was viewed as the father's responsibility, while the mother's role was supposed to be to nurture and support. At least, that's what they preached.

My parents used several different books as instruction manuals on how to raise good, Christian children, how to discipline according to God's Word, and how to ensure their children were fully immersed in their chosen religion. They also followed many teachings associated with the Institute in Basic Life Principles (IBLP), which was the cult made famous by the Duggar family and their "19 Kids and Counting" show. Mom was obsessed with Michelle Duggar and adopted many of her mannerisms, child-rearing philosophies, and household practices.

Although I don't believe this couple was officially part of IBLP, the group endorsed a book authored by Michael and Debi Pearl called, *To Train Up A Child.* This book was their advice on how to raise children according to the Bible, but was later *allegedly* linked to three deaths of children whose parents practiced the Pearl's teachings.

The Pearls advise spanking children to break their will, withholding food, and conditioning a child's mind so they will obey without question. They liken training children to training horses and conditioning animals. They outline the size of spanking tools that should be used based on the age of the child, beginning with children under one year old. They describe how to "blanket train" babies - infants to one-year-olds - by laying the baby on a blanket with very few toys and hitting the baby with a ruler if the baby tries to leave the blanket.

They tell parents to use whatever force is necessary to get their children to surrender, even if it means sitting on them while spanking them. They emphasize that parents must defeat the child. They must "break" their children. Unquestioning obedience is the ultimate goal.

Evangelical and Fundamentalist Christians devoured this book, my parents included. I remember it sitting on a bookshelf in our home, well-worn, but I didn't know what it was until recently. Someone who heard my story mentioned the Pearl's book, so I looked it up and immediately recognized the cover. I knew it was in our home, and I knew my parents had read it. I honestly wasn't surprised.

Another obsession of my parents, and a significant leader among Evangelical Christians in the early 2000s, was James Dobson, who began Focus on the Family. He authored books, preached, and hosted several radio stations, which we listened to frequently. He was a huge proponent of Christian parents "breaking the will" of their children as well, and made his position on traditional gender roles within the family well known.

Marriage was between a man and a woman; the man was the breadwinner, and the woman was the homemaker; and children were to be taught these gender roles and taught about heterosexuality only. Women were to focus on being mothers and were not to seek work outside the home. He described marriage as a transaction where women exchange sex for protection; they were to marry a man and give him sex, and in exchange, he would protect them from other men who might be attracted to their sexual appeal.

Dobson suggested spanking should begin around 15 months old and said the spanking tool ought to be kept in a place where the child can always see it, so they are reminded of their parent's authority over them. I figure this is why our "switches" were hung on the wall in plain sight.

James Dobson authored the books *A Strong-Willed Child* and *Dare to Discipline,* both of which I remember seeing on our bookshelves at home. Mom even gave me copies at one point so I would have them for when I had my own children. In one of these books, he stated that if a child was allowed to challenge their parents, they would grow up to challenge God. Therefore, any display of "challenging" a parent must be met with swift discipline.

Dobson suggested that if a child cries after being spanked, the parent should give them a little more of what caused the tears in the first place. Between Dobson, the Pearls, and many others, the 1980s through the early 2000s were ripe with pro-corporal punishment books aimed toward Fundamentalist Christian parents. Clearly, my parents bought into this way of parenting, but, in my opinion, they used these teachings to create a foundation and then built their own version of discipline on top of it. Their version continued to evolve and worsen until they were, quite literally, torturing their children but still calling it Biblical discipline. They always said they were following the Bible, following God's commandment to raise their children in the Lord, and providing us with godly discipline and accountability. Except it was all abuse.

Throughout our childhood, almost on a daily basis, Mom told us that if we continued being naughty or bad, she would call the police and have us arrested. She told us she would drop us off at the police or fire station and not come pick us up. Sometimes, we would drive by a jail or prison, and she would point at it and say that was where we would go if we didn't behave.

One time, Mom told my older sister that if she didn't stop crying, she would take her to a hospital, and the doctors would strap her down and give her a shot that would make her go to sleep and never wake up. I remember being told several times that someone would come to take us, and we would have to live with another family and have different parents for the rest of our lives. I wanted to run away, so I got excited a lot of times when she'd say that, and I'd say I was fine with it and that she should go ahead and do it. I don't think she thought of it as a threat very much after that.

There were a lot of times when I would be crying so hard I couldn't catch my breath. Mom and Dad would always say that if I didn't stop, they would get rid of me, and they said the same thing to my older sister. One time, when she wouldn't stop crying, Dad said, "That's it, she goes," and walked away. I was sent to bed after that, and when I woke up the next morning, I thought my sister would be gone.

Mom and Dad did a lot of things to my older sister. They both did the wrist thing a lot, where they grabbed her wrists and squeezed tighter and tighter while she tried to twist and get away. Dad grabbed her neck a lot, often squeezing more and more until she nearly passed out. Eventually, she let him do it for a few seconds and then pretended to pass out so he'd stop sooner. That worked for a while.

Sometimes when he grabbed her neck, he'd slam her backward into the wall and pin her there while she writhed and twisted and tried to get away. He'd lift her up, holding her against the wall by her neck while her feet were dangling just above the floor, and then suddenly drop her and watch her fall in a pile of limbs on the ground, desperately trying to crawl away from him while she caught her breath. Mom stood by and watched, smiled, laughed... it was entertainment for her, I suppose.

He and Mom always said, "The more you fight, the more it's gonna hurt," and "The longer you fight, the longer I'll keep going." The three of us girls all had very different survival tactics or coping mechanisms when it came to that kind of physical stuff. My older sister would fight till she was red in the face, unable to breathe, collapsing on the floor by the end, having exhausted all her strength and energy.

I did the same when I was younger, but as I got older and saw what happened to her more often, I became the opposite. She fought; I froze. I became a rag doll, going limp, convincing myself that if I just stay still, don't fight, just give in, it'll be over sooner. They'll get tired or bored because I'm not fighting back, and they'll stop.

My younger sister's coping mechanism was different than ours, though. I've seen it described in psychology books as "fight, flight, freeze, fawn," the body's automatic defense responses to harmful situations. Fighting is responding to a threat by becoming confrontational, standing up to it, or trying to "fight" it. Flight is escaping from the threat, running away, or hiding. Freezing is becoming still, unable to move or act in the face of the threat. Fawning is an attempt to please the threat to avoid harm.

My older sister fought, I froze, and my younger sister fawned. She tried to come alongside Mom and be her right-hand girl, so to speak. She made up stories about things my older sister and I did, painting herself as the victim and getting us in trouble.

She told Mom we hit her, slapped her, tripped her, cut her... anything she could think of that would get us in trouble. And Mom always believed her, never second-guessed anything. As we got older, it was telling Mom we were doing drugs, drinking alcohol, getting pregnant, speeding... Again, anything she could think of that might get us in hot water with Mom and Dad and keep her in the safety zone. She pleased Mom by coming up with reasons to punish other siblings.

I hated her for it. We were never friends growing up; we never played together, and we never got along. She stabbed me in the back my entire life, and didn't stop once we reached adulthood. Constantly confiding in Mom about things I was doing, even if they were completely made up. We never even had a chance at a relationship.

Now that I understand my childhood and upbringing more clearly, now that I can see what it really was and that we were all simply trying our best to survive, I no longer harbor hate or resentment toward my younger sister. It took me years to get to this point, but now I understand it was her survival tactic, and she was only trying to save herself. We all were. We had to.

I understand that, to some, it may not justify her behavior, but it does explain it. I understand that she was just a child, abused and neglected, surviving the best way she knew how. I understand that throwing other siblings under the bus in an effort to get the target off her own back was how her brain kept her safe. I hate that she was in a situation that caused her to behave like that, but I don't hate *her*, not anymore.

I can see now how deeply controlled I was, though at the time I couldn't have named it. I can feel the weight of it now – the invisible threads that pulled at me from the moment I woke up until I went to sleep, guiding my words, my thoughts, and even my heartbeat. Every word I spoke, every thought I hid, every choice I made belonged to Mom long before it belonged to me.

I didn't know I was being controlled; I thought I was just being a good daughter. I thought her anger, her punishments, her constant watchfulness were proof she cared. But the truth I only realized much later is that love doesn't need to cage you, doesn't need to haunt you in your own mind, and doesn't thrive on fear.

The obedience I gave so freely, the sacrifices I didn't even recognize, were not love – they were survival. And in that survival, in that quiet, constant molding of who I was permitted to be, I lost pieces of myself I wouldn't find again for years. Only now, looking back, can I see the full shape of the cage she built, and the long, slow work it has taken to step out of it.

Key Characteristic #3

THE FAMILY NARRATIVE

In our home, everything was about the story we told the world. My mother didn't just believe we were Christians – she believed our family was a holy example, a shining standard of devotion that no one else could match. We weren't allowed to be ordinary, flawed, or human in the eyes of others. Every decision, every word, every action was a reflection of the family, and therefore a reflection of her.

At some point, they decided our family was called to be missionaries. That meant the children were missionaries, too; not just as individuals, but as extensions of our parents, embodiments of their faith, their righteousness, their ideals. We carried the weight of their image wherever we went, silently performing for an audience we didn't fully understand. We weren't allowed to stumble, to falter, or to show doubt, because to do so was to tarnish the family story.

The narrative wasn't just about appearing good; it was about being better than everyone else, holier, more devout, more faithful. Our family was admired, envied, and held up as a model of spiritual perfection in the community. And because of that admiration, my mother insisted on a higher standard. The ordinary rules that applied to other children didn't apply to us. Our mistakes were magnified, our successes were measured against impossible expectations, and our thoughts, even private ones, had to align with the image she was building.

We learned early that our identities were inseparable from the family narrative. There was no room for individuality, for curiosity, for doubt. We existed to reinforce the story she had written about us in her own mind: a perfect family, chosen, devoted, and exemplary. Any deviation was not just personal failure; it was a threat to the narrative, a crack in the facade, and a risk we were trained to fear.

I can see now how deeply this story shaped us. It made obedience feel like destiny, conformity feel like devotion, and self-expression feel like betrayal. Our lives were never just our own; they were chapters in a story that belonged to her, a story she controlled completely. And we carried it with us, silently, performing every day, learning to measure our worth not by who we were, but by how perfectly we represented her and the family she built.

4

Holier Than Thou

2007-2009 | AGE 10-12

***

2007, age 10

Mommy does the crying thing a lot. A lot of days when Daddy gets home from work, Mommy all of a sudden starts crying as soon as he walks in the door, and he asks what's wrong, and she says we were horrible all day, didn't listen or obey, didn't help with chores, and were just naughty all day. Even if we were good all day, and we're all just being quiet and being nice in the living room or playing outside when he walks inside, she'll just start crying out of nowhere, so he believes her when she says we were all really bad that day. Then we all have to line up to get spanked, or sometimes we have to go to bed without dinner, or sometimes we have to sit at the table and just watch them eat so we can still do our chores afterward. I hate the crying thing because a lot of the time, we didn't even do anything naughty. I don't know why she does that.

***

Mom and Dad decided to move again in 2007; I don't remember a lot of the details or the reasons for any of this, but my grandparents bought a second house near Twin Falls, Idaho. It was about two or three hours away from our neighborhood in Nampa, but Mom and Dad sent us kids to live with them at their second house while they bought a new house in Boise. Again, I'm really not sure what their reasoning was – I was only 9 or 10 at the time; I just knew my older sister and I were in charge of the younger kids at Nana's second house three hours away, and that we lived there for several months with Mom and Dad only visiting on a few weekends.

I don't remember doing any schoolwork while we were there; I only remember watching Tom Sawyer, Fiddler on the Roof, and Seven Brides for Seven Brothers on repeat, playing Candyland, and coloring in princess coloring books. We didn't go to church; we didn't do devotions; we never really left the house. All my memories from that time are extremely blurry, and I really don't know where Mom and Dad were staying. I've talked to my older sister about this, and she remembers about the same amount as I do. Basically nothing.

One thing I do remember, though, is how calm that time was; it was just us kids - Nana pretty much left us alone. We got up in the morning, hung out, and went to bed. There was no yelling, no screaming, and no fear except for when Nana said Mom and Dad were coming down to visit for the weekend. Everything was so calm. So peaceful. So quiet. And I don't remember missing my parents at all. I only realized that while writing this book - I never missed them. Not only that, I think I was actually relieved they weren't around. I think we all were.

Eventually, Mom and Dad came and got us, and we moved into our new house in Boise. For a while, my older sister had her own room, and I shared with my younger sister, but at some point, I believe in 2008, our aunt and her baby came to live with us, so all three girls shared our room again. I never had my own room growing up; I always shared with my sisters, and there were even some points when all five of us shared one room.

We didn't live in the Boise house for very long, but I've always remembered that it was the cleanest house we've ever lived in. Almost all our stuff was in storage, and we only unpacked what we absolutely needed. I remember being confused about why that was; it always seemed like we couldn't get too comfortable in that house and that we might move again at any moment. We had our clothes, dishes, school supplies, and most of our furniture, but it was literally an almost-spotless house since all the clutter and random stuff was in a storage unit.

I remember living in that house for only about a year, and during that school year, we homeschooled another girl we knew from the camp. Mom said she was failing all her public school classes, so her parents decided to pay my parents to homeschool her and catch her up. Mom said public school doesn't teach as much as homeschool, anyway. I remember thinking that was weird since I was pretty sure we were way behind compared to public-schooled kids; we hardly ever did school, we just did chores and got in trouble all day.

She was in 10th grade at the time, and I was in 5th. That was the only year growing up that we ever had a rigid school schedule, presumably because we had an outsider in our home and Mom had to keep up appearances and make it seem like we actually did school. We had an hourly schedule posted all around our house, color-coded by kid. I was always green. We were each assigned a color, I think at birth, and that was our color for the rest of time.

We followed the schedule on any day that the girl came to be homeschooled at our house, but if she wasn't coming one day for whatever reason, it was like the schedule didn't exist. We only did "official" school days when she was there, so when someone else was watching, basically.

I didn't mind not going to school when I was younger; when I wasn't doing chores or serving a punishment, I was reading books. I read all the Boxcar Children books multiple times over, Nancy Drew, Hardy Boys, Trixie Belden, and whatever else I could bring home from the library and get approved by Mom. She vetoed a lot more than she approved, but I got pretty good at finding books that were boring enough for her to approve of, but interesting enough for me to actually enjoy.

The girl only did homeschooling with us for that one school year, and then I guess she went back to public school. I actually don't even think it was the whole school year; I believe it was only the spring semester. Years later – I think I was in my 20s by then – she died by suicide, and Mom said she wished she hadn't wasted her time on someone who was just going to kill herself a few years later.

When I say we barely did school, that's pretty accurate. During the fall semester, the year we lived in the Boise house – before the girl came to homeschool with us – we cut down a giant pine tree in our front yard. Dad and another camp guy cut it and pulled it down, and it fell across our entire driveway, front yard, and the street and sidewalk. We got the public areas cleaned up pretty quickly, but then we spent the next several months working on the rest of the tree. Every day, we would wake up, get our "tree clothes" on, which consisted of clothes we didn't mind getting sap on and throwing away later, and then we'd go outside and start on the tree.

We each had a pair of clippers and gloves. We had piles for needles, twigs, small branches, larger branches, logs, etc. We dismantled the tree twig by twig, and it took MONTHS. We worked on the tree all morning, came in for lunch, went back outside in the afternoon, and Dad would use the chainsaw on bigger pieces in the evenings. In hindsight, I can't imagine that a tree removal service would've been that expensive, but Mom loved to brag to anyone she met that for "homeschool" today we did science, learned about nature, learned about trees... basically making cleaning up a giant pine tree in our yard sound like top-tier home education. We didn't do actual schoolwork for months.

***

2008, age 11

A lot of times, Mommy makes us clean our rooms so they're perfect when Daddy gets home from work, but then right when he's pulling in the driveway, she goes to our rooms and throws everything in our drawers on the floor, rips our blankets off our beds, shoves all our stuff off our dressers, and just makes a big mess. And then we don't have enough time to clean it back up before Daddy walks in the door, so he thinks we didn't listen and obey, and we didn't clean our rooms. We did clean our rooms, but he didn't get there fast enough to see them before Mommy made them messy again. We have to do extra cleaning when he sees our messy rooms, and sometimes we get less dinner or have privileges taken away. They take away privileges a lot.

***

Doing religious things as a family was always super awkward, even though religion was literally the focus of our family, it would seem. Mom and Dad went through phases where we would have morning devotionals every day as a family, evening devotionals or Bible study together, or they would read us missionary storybooks about real-life missionaries who went to other countries and either died or nearly escaped death trying to bring the Gospel to secluded African tribes or something like that.

I don't know why it was awkward; it just always made me feel weird. Mom and Dad mentioned Bible verses, God, and other religious things all the time, but it was always related to punishment, discipline, or accountability when we had done something bad. The times they decided to do family Bible study in the evenings, for example, always made me feel like we were all in trouble because the study usually turned to passages about children obeying parents, parents disciplining children, taming the tongue, or other related passages. They always ended the night with a warning to be good the next day, to remember what the Bible says, and that God wants us to obey our parents.

Sometimes we did morning devotions with Mom, and other times we did them on our own. When we did them with her, she always used her "godly" voice, like soft and whimsical, almost, when she read verses and talked about the Bible lesson. I hated that voice because that was the voice she used to speak to other people who weren't us kids. She sounded so nice and Christian when she spoke to other people, but she never sounded like that with us. That voice made me uncomfortable, but that's the one she'd use for morning devotions.

I liked when we could do morning devotions on our own, because sometimes I could choose whatever passage of the Bible I wanted to read. She usually assigned something for us to read, but sometimes we could pick. For a while, we had to either take notes or verbally report back to her what we had learned. That sucked because a lot of the New Testament sounds the same, so if one devotional report sounded too similar to the previous day's report, we got in trouble.

Dad had a "Christian" voice, too; it was softer, like Mom's, but it sounded very condescending. He sounded like he was talking "at" us rather than "to" us and always made me feel like I was in trouble. He would always find a way to tie in the bad or naughty things we'd done that day – as reported to him by Mom – with the devotional or Bible verse he was quoting to us.

I got pretty good at guessing which verse from the Bible Dad would quote at me each evening, based on what Mom said I'd done that day. I mostly got verses from the Book of James, which talks a lot about being quick to hear, slow to speak, slow to anger, taming the tongue, and not saying good and evil things with the same tongue, etc. That was usually because I had been "talking back" to Mom. I did that a lot, or at least that was usually what I got in trouble for almost every single day during those years. Dad said I had "anger issues" and part of it was because I wasn't praying and reading my Bible enough. He said if I had a closer relationship with God, I wouldn't treat Mom so badly. He also said I partly got my anger issues from him so it might be hereditary, but he said that wasn't an excuse for my behavior.

I had a lot of notebooks that I would write my verses in when I was being punished. Dad would give me a verse – again, usually something from James – and I would have to write it about 100-200 times. When I was done, he would inspect my work, I would recite the verse to him, explain to him what it meant, explain how it applied to me based on why I was in trouble, then I would go downstairs and apologize to Mom and recite the verse and meaning to her as well.

At first, Mom gave me a notebook since we had tons of school supplies. After a while, though, I was getting in trouble so much that she said I had to start paying for my own notebooks. I used money I got from my grandparents for birthdays or Christmas to buy notebooks, and I also started writing as small as I could so each notebook would last a little longer before I had to buy another.

Growing up, my sisters and I had to have all our clothing approved by Dad. We didn't usually get "new" clothes, but we got hand-me-downs from girls at church (if we were currently attending a church), and sometimes we got new stuff from thrift stores if Mom was feeling generous. For shirts, we had to raise our arms straight up, and Dad had to make sure our shirts still overlapped our waistbands when our arms were raised. Tank tops had to be at least three fingers wide, but that only lasted until we started wearing bras. After that, no tank tops.

For pants, we had to lift up our shirts and spin around so Dad could see if the tops of our pants were too tight. Our pants were usually too tight for his and Mom's liking, so we ended up wearing a lot of skirts. Shorts had to come several inches below our fingertips when our arms were straight down at our sides. Usually, that meant the shortest we could go was right above our knees. Bottoms had to come up to our belly buttons as well; anything lower than our belly buttons was immodest and meant we were trying to draw attention to ourselves.

As we grew up and hit puberty, Dad had to make sure he couldn't see our bra straps or the shape of our boobs. If he could tell we had boobs *at all,* we needed a baggier shirt. If he could tell we had a butt *at all,* we needed baggier pants. It got harder and harder to get clothes approved; we wore pretty baggy clothes all the time, and Mom handmade a lot of basic clothes with no shape. Mom also bought all our bras and underwear, and we didn't get to choose any fun colors or patterns. She went to Wal-Mart, bought what she wanted us to have, and we didn't get to have a say. Oh, and the boys never had clothing rules.

Mom and Dad made it clear to us that modesty was mandatory for girls. God wanted us to cover up, not show too much skin, not show off our figure, and not look excessively fancy. If a girl tried to be fancy, it meant she was trying to attract a boy, and that was a sin. Girls had to dress modestly so boys didn't stumble. Girls had to dress modestly to protect boys' hearts. If a girl dressed immodestly and a boy was attracted to her, he was being sinful, but it was the girl's fault for causing him to stumble. In order to be a godly woman, you had to be modest and covered up. Mom said if we wore anything that was not approved by her or Dad, we were disrespecting God and trying to be prostitutes.

* * *

2008, age 11

Mommy and Daddy forgot my birthday again this year. It was yesterday, but they just remembered today. I guess they were busy. Since we go to the Bible Camp for the summers now, and my birthday is in June, they usually don't remember unless I bring it up. If I do, I get in trouble for being selfish and wanting everything to be about me. That's happened for a few years now, so yesterday I didn't say anything to see if they would remember, and they didn't. My sister asked me at bedtime last night, "Isn't today your birthday?" and I said yes. I felt like crying, but I tried really hard not to because Mommy always says crying is for babies, and also, it's not like it was a big birthday like 16 or something; I'm just 11, so I think it's just a forgettable age, maybe.

This morning, Mommy said I got a birthday card in the mail from my grandparents. She yelled at me for not reminding her that yesterday was my birthday and said that since I clearly didn't want a celebration, we wouldn't have one. We had dinner like normal tonight, then she put some candles in a watermelon, and they sang Happy Birthday. I hate when people sing me Happy Birthday. I blew out the candles; we got to eat watermelon, and she gave me a few presents wrapped in kitchen towels. She said they would've been wrapped properly if I had given her more time, so I guess that's my fault. Hopefully, next year they'll remember on their own, but if they don't, I think I'll just let it go.

***

I remember Mom and Dad calling a family meeting at some point, so we all gathered in the living room. Whenever they called family meetings, we went to the living room and sat on the floor at their feet. Dad always sat in his recliner, and Mom sat on the couch. Usually, it was because we were all in trouble for something, they decided to do a family devotion or family Bible study (awkward, as always), or they had something important to tell us.

At this particular family meeting, they asked us how we felt about them becoming missionaries. I remember being confused because we had always been told "everyone is a missionary, and everywhere is a mission field", so I thought we already were missionaries. They said the difference is that they'd be "official" missionaries, and we would raise support from friends and family instead of working real jobs. One of us asked what it would mean for us kids, and Mom said we would live full-time at the Bible camp, and that would be our mission field.

Since they asked how we felt about it, I mistakenly thought they were asking for our opinions. I said I didn't want to live at the camp full-time, and that I'd rather we just keep our normal life where Dad works, and we do school, and we live in a normal house. I remember a few of my siblings agreeing, although I'm not sure the boys understood everything since they were the youngest.

Mom got mad at me for disagreeing with her and Dad, and she said they were just informing us that "this is what we're doing," not really asking for our opinion. She said they'd already signed up, completed all the paperwork to become missionaries, and that everything was already done. I was confused why they would tell us they wanted to know how we felt about it when they'd already done it.

After the family meeting, they sent everyone else to bed but kept my older sister and me in the living room. Mom and Dad said that, since we were the oldest, we needed to set a good example for the younger kids. Mom said I needed to pray and ask Jesus for forgiveness for not wanting to be missionaries. They said my sister and I were an extension of Mom and Dad, so we needed to act like missionaries at all times and make sure the younger kids did as well. Mom said she and Dad would be very busy moving forward, so it would be up to my sister and me to take care of the house and the kids while they did their missionary stuff and prepared to move to the camp.

They sent us to bed, and I remember whispering with my sister until late into the night about what this meant for us. I stayed up really late praying to God for forgiveness, like I was told to, and prayed that I hadn't already messed up the missionary thing for Mom and Dad. I knew I could never really do anything right, so I was probably going to mess it up at some point, but I prayed I could just be a good missionary and not make Mom and Dad look bad, just like they'd said.

We got really good at putting together newsletters; Mom would create and print them, one of us would fold them, one would stuff them into envelopes, one would seal them, one would put the labels on, and the fifth would sort them by zip code and put them in the mailing bins. There were hundreds – it seemed like thousands to me – and it took us hours. We knew we weren't going to do any school on newsletter days, and Mom said it could count as one of our classes. We normally sent out newsletters once a month, but at the very beginning, it was more often, I think, because we had to get people to send us money to get us started.

I felt weird asking hundreds of people for money; it seemed like a fake job. Everyone else works a real job to make money, and then they each give us a little bit of their money so we can have income and do missionary things. I thought that was weird, but Mom said that's how it worked. Other missionaries did it too, and we would get their newsletters in the mail asking for money for their families. I asked Mom if we were going to give them money, and she said no. She said we're the ones trying to get money, so we're not going to give our money to anyone else asking for money. I figured the grown-ups knew what they were doing; I'd stick to my folding and stuffing and sealing and labeling and sorting jobs.

I always read the newsletters Mom wrote, and it always sounded like she was writing about someone else's family, not ours. She wrote a little paragraph about each of us kids, and she sounded so proud of each of us and wrote about all our accomplishments. I'd never heard her talk about any of that stuff to us in person, so I asked her about it, and she said she needed to put that in there so people wouldn't know how naughty and bad we kids always were. She said if they knew we were brats, they wouldn't give us money.

She always put pictures in the newsletters, too, and they were usually "funny" pictures of us kids, but they were always super embarrassing to us. Sometimes she wrote about how naughty we were, but she would word it nicely and biblically, so it sounded good, like, "This month, we're learning the meaning of Ephesians 6:1, where it says for children to obey their parents" or "we've been studying the Book of James and how we need to tame our tongues and think before we speak". I remember thinking she liked to embarrass us because she did it so often.

***

2009, age 12

Mom stuck out her foot and tripped me again today. She does that a lot, and sometimes I can see her foot moving before I trip, so I can catch myself from falling, but she's really quick, and sometimes I don't expect it. Today she tripped me in the kitchen while I was unloading the dishwasher, and I fell and dropped a plate on the floor, and it shattered. We get in so much trouble if dishes break, so I knew the rest of the day was pretty much over for me at that point. She yanks our hair a lot, too, or if she wants us to go somewhere, she'll pull us by our hair to get us there. Our hair is so long now that it's usually in braids or ponytails, so it makes an easy handle for her to grab. I know it's better for me to just stay out of her way, and I always try to be nice to her and do everything she says so she'll leave me alone, but so far it hasn't worked. It seems like just my presence makes her mad.

***

We gradually moved all our stuff to the camp and rented out the Boise house for a while; I don't remember the timeline there, but I know we rented it out for what I think was a few years before selling it. By then, we were fully at the camp. When we stayed at the camp during the summers, we stayed in an RV that was permanently parked near the main building. But when we moved up there to live full-time, we moved into a double-wide built at the far end of the property.

There was a master bedroom at one end, then two bedrooms at the other end, so we had a girl's room and a boy's room. While we lived there, Mom and Dad were building a larger house across the parking lot at the other corner of the property. It was going to be our house; we were going to live there for the rest of time, and the double-wide would be for the summer missionaries – young adults who raised support and served at the camp just during the summer months.

We constantly had men from the camp coming to help with the new house, and they would eat meals at our house every day. I don't really remember doing school at all while the house was being built. When there were things we couldn't help with – concrete, trusses, etc. – we cooked three meals a day for whoever was working on the house. Otherwise, we were working on the new house too; we helped place rebar to prepare for concrete, we taped drywall, we cleaned up the worksite nonstop… we basically helped in every stage of the building process, and Mom said that counted as school. She bragged to people that we did "construction" as part of our homeschooling. She claimed everything as a "class," including masonry, carpentry, roofing, etc. But I don't remember doing actual school.

While we were living in the double-wide – I believe the winter of 2008-2009 – Dad worked at a ski resort as a lift operator. We got pretty cheap season tickets since he was an employee, so we went skiing almost every day for several months. That was the year the ski resort closed due to financial issues and foreclosure, I think in March of 2009. But from opening day in 2008 till the day it closed in 2009, we skied almost every day. We woke up and got dressed in our snow clothes, skied from 8:00 in the morning to 4:00 in the afternoon when the slopes closed, and came home to sit in front of the wood stove to thaw out. Mom told people we skied in the morning – she called it "PT" or "exercise class," of course, because everything came back to homeschool – and then we did our schoolwork in the evenings. Except I don't actually remember doing our schoolwork in the evenings since we always had to do all our chores after being gone all day.

Once the new house was done, we moved all our stuff from one house to the other during the day, again, not doing schoolwork. The old house became housing for summer missionaries that year, and we lived in the new house. We were there for a few years until the whole missionary thing fell apart.

Key Characteristic #4

FORCED CONFORMITY AND LACK OF INDIVIDUALITY

In our house, individuality was not allowed. Every piece of who we were was measured against her standards and reshaped until it fit her mold. She didn't just want obedience; she wanted perfection. She wanted each of us to be a mirror, shining back her beliefs, preferences, emotions, and showing our devout adoration for her. Anything that deviated was defiance, and anything that made us stand out was rebellion. Personal expression was dangerous territory. The clothes we wore, the music we liked, the books we enjoyed – everything was subject to her approval. A pretty shirt, a song she disliked, or a hairstyle that showcased talent and artistic flair could summon her wrath. She called it "guidance", but it was control. Our personalities became a threat to her authority, and she made sure we knew it.

Hobbies, friendships, and dreams were filtered through her first. If she didn't like it, it was forbidden. If she didn't like a friend or that friend's mother, the friendship ended. If we showed interest in something outside her worldview, she twisted it into sin or mocked us for liking it until we abandoned it. Emotions were also monitored. We were allowed to cry when she was sad, laugh when she was amused, but we couldn't take it too far. Joy felt too dangerous, too loud, too free, too unpredictable. I learned quickly that my happiness could draw her attention, and that attention could draw punishment.

Over time, I became skilled at erasing myself. I mirrored her voice, her opinions, and her expressions. I studied her moods like scripture, shaping myself into whatever version of "good" she needed me to be. But in the quiet moments when no one was watching, I felt a hollow ache I couldn't yet find words for. Looking back, it was the grief of losing myself before I'd even had the chance to exist. Sometimes, I caught glimpses of who I might have been, like when a song made me feel something real or a thought flickered that didn't sound like hers. But guilt always followed close behind, heavy and familiar. To want anything of my own felt selfish. To have an opinion felt sinful. I wanted to be good. I wanted to be loved. And so, I kept shrinking, shaping, silencing, until all that was left was a version of me that belonged entirely to her.

It's strange to mourn a person you never really met, but that's what it feels like. Grieving the girl I could have been, the one who might have laughed freely, dressed how she liked, and spoken her mind without fear. She never had the chance to grow. She became a shadow cast by someone else's light, fading at the edges until she all but disappeared.

5

Be Still And The Same

2010-2011 | AGE 13-14

***

2010, age 13

Mom and Dad decided to pick a fight again today. They are never home anymore; they leave early in the morning to do whatever missionary stuff they do, and then they don't come home till late at night. My older sister and I wake up in the morning, do our schoolwork really quickly, then wake the other kids up and feed them breakfast. We help them do their schoolwork, and then we just hang out with them in the woods or at home if the weather is bad. We feed everyone lunch and dinner, sometimes watch a movie or play a game, and then we get them all in bed on time. We clean the house as much as we can and make sure the dishes are done and there's food for Mom and Dad, and then we go to bed.

But tonight, they came into our room after we were already asleep, woke us up, and got us out of bed because we forgot to stack the firewood.

We told them we had caught up on all the laundry, done the dishes, and cleaned the bedrooms and bathrooms that day, but had just forgotten to stack the wood. We should've just kept our mouths shut because we got a yelling lecture about how much they *had done that day and how easy we had it. I could've predicted that would happen, so that was on me. I need to learn to just stay quiet. It was super dark and freezing outside, but we went out in our pajamas and snow boots, stacked the chopped firewood as fast as we could, and came back inside. Mom said she'd accept that for now, but she said we have to go out and restack it all tomorrow since we rushed it and it's not perfectly straight. At least it'll be a little warmer and lighter tomorrow, so we can see what we're doing. I wrote a list of everything we need to get done tomorrow so we don't forget anything again.*

***

During the summers, while campers were there, we were constantly busy. My older sister and I were teen leaders during certain weeks – we were called "Timothy's" because it was the "Timothy Program" because, in the Bible, Paul took Timothy under his wing and showed him how to be a missionary, or something like that. Usually, one or two Timothy's were assigned to the "camp kids" – these were all the younger children of camp staff, mostly the full-time missionaries, but there were also a few here and there who were kids of temporary staff, like a nurse or a cook. Since they had the kids, my older sister and I were able to fulfill our other responsibilities, of which there were many. We were in charge of our Timothy duties, which included a lot of cleaning, setting up the dining hall for meals, tearing everything down after meals, being a "junior cabin leader" of sorts, setting up chapel chairs, literally just running the camp, basically.

But we were also responsible for our house – Mom and Dad were never there, always doing camp missionary things, I guess.

Somehow, between all the camp duties we were in charge of, we had to find time to make sure the house was spotless before Mom and Dad came back at night. We obviously didn't do any schoolwork during the summers, but Mom would make a point of telling people that we were lazy and didn't bother doing our schoolwork during the school year, so we had to go home and do school whenever she wanted to embarrass us. Other parents and kids probably thought we were the most disobedient kids in the world, which was far from the truth, but Mom was pretty good at making it seem that way.

In the evenings, when the Timothy's were done taking care of the camp kids, we took over. We pawned the ones that weren't ours off on their parents, and we took ours back to the house. Usually, we ate dinner at the dining hall with all the campers, so they'd been fed already. All we really had to do was get them in bed. We were always in bed long before Mom and Dad ever came back to the house, so we were pretty used to going to bed without saying goodnight by then. Mom never did, but Dad used to come in and say goodnight to us when we were kids. That stopped when we moved to the camp, and they became missionaries and got too busy with other people's kids to worry about their own.

I remember other kids and Timothy's constantly telling me how lucky I was to have my mom, that they wished she were their mom. I honestly couldn't comprehend why they would wish that upon themselves, but then again, she acted totally differently with other kids than she did with us. She hugged other kids, told them she loved them, told them she was proud of them, and even smiled at them. She didn't do any of that with us. There were a lot of times when I'd be calling her over and over, she'd ignore me, and then I'd change my voice and call her by her first name, and she'd whirl around with a smile. Once she realized it was me, her smile was immediately replaced with a glare, and she'd snap at me for calling her by her name and also for bothering her when she was busy. But I knew if I had been any other kid, she would've been sweet as honey.

In the off-season, once summer camp was over, we had a lot of work to do around the camp. There was maintenance to fix things that had been broken during the summer, upgrades that the camp somehow found money for or had gotten materials donated, a lot of cleaning and winterizing, and just a lot of work. So, we still didn't do school in August and September. Over Labor Day weekend, we always had a Family Camp. We, of course, were responsible for a lot over the weekend, so we weren't always available to play with the other kids who came with their families. Once we got the younger kids in bed, my sister and I would go with the other kids to play games in the woods late into the night. We never got in trouble for being out so late because Mom and Dad never even realized we weren't home.

In November, there was a Fall Discipleship Camp, which was basically a retreat for teens and young adults that was nothing but chapel, devotionals, worship, Bible, prayer, and more chapel. It wasn't a "fun" camp, so not many people came, but it was my favorite because there wasn't as much for me to do. It was a much smaller group, so meals were easier to prepare, the dining hall setup and teardown didn't take as long, and the whole weekend was basically spent in the chapel doing God things and praying, so we kids pretty much stayed out of sight, out of mind unless it was meal time.

There were a few Snow Camps in the winter, and those were the "fun" camps – tubing, ice skating, elk feeding… all the snow activities. Camp kids were allowed to pick one activity to attend with the campers, while we were too young to be campers ourselves. But if we weren't attending the day's activity, we had a lot of work to do. There was a lot of mopping throughout the day since snow and mud got tracked all over the place, the bathrooms were disgusting, and that was all our responsibility, plus keeping our house clean and watching the younger kids, of course.

During the "school year" months, when there wasn't a camp or event going on, my older sister and I would homeschool ourselves and the younger kids, feed us all meals, entertain ourselves, and put the kids to bed at night. All while Mom and Dad were off doing whatever super important missionary duties they had. We hardly ever saw them, and we honestly didn't mind.

After a few years of living at the camp full-time, Mom and Dad called another family meeting and told us we were moving back down to the valley. They were quitting the missionary thing, Dad was getting a new job, and we'd be moving as soon as summer camp was over. That was the summer of 2011. Except they didn't tell us until the summer was already about half over. The family meeting was between camps on a weekend; the news seemed sudden to us, but they seemed like they'd had it planned for quite a while. I don't remember them giving us a reason, just that this chapter of our lives had come to an end.

We went through the last few weeks of camp dazed and confused, packing every evening and weekend, not telling anyone we were leaving. That was the most confusing part for me – I wasn't allowed to tell my other camp kid friends that we were no longer going to be at the camp, that we were moving away as soon as camp was over. I'd known these kids for years, mostly during the summers and winter camps, but still. I was really confused as to why they weren't allowed to know that I was leaving and that we had no intention of coming back next summer. I wondered if any of their missionary parents knew.

Camp ended, and, sure enough, we packed up and left about a week later. We didn't have a house in the valley anymore since we had sold our Boise house, so we moved into my grandparents' house – the same house we lived down the street from when I was younger. They had a much larger house than we'd ever had, and they had several rooms at the opposite end of the house from their master bedroom. Mom and Dad had a room, the girls had a room, and the boys had the largest room. We pretty much took over that entire end of the house. I don't remember how long we lived there, but it was at least several months before we moved into our own house. I hated every bit of it.

***

2011, age 14

I've been in bed since yesterday afternoon. I know Mom is going to come in any minute to make me get up; I wish I could just disappear into thin air. I'm usually so good at not crying now, but yesterday, Dad was screaming at me for so long that I started to cry, and I couldn't stop. Mom and Dad both yelled at me, even more, telling me to stop crying, and I just started crying even harder every time. I don't know why I couldn't stop; it was like something was choking me from the inside, and I couldn't even catch my breath. I was hysterical and couldn't breathe, and Dad just kept getting closer and closer to my face, just screaming so loud.

I guess Dad got tired of yelling because he suddenly grabbed my arm, dragged me to my room, and threw me on the bed. He told me to get under the covers, and then he pinned the blankets around my head with his arms so my head was stuck, and I was really struggling to breathe. I freaked out because I thought I was going to suffocate, and I just kept screaming. In hindsight, maybe if I had just stopped screaming, he would've taken the blankets off my face, but I guess that's on me. Now

I know for next time. I don't know how long it lasted, but I felt like I couldn't breathe for a really long time. He must have let go at some point, because I woke up to silence, a dark room, and my sisters sound asleep in their beds. Eventually, I fell asleep, but when I woke up this morning, my whole body felt so sore, almost like someone beat me up or something. I know I'll have to get up soon, but now I know that if he starts yelling, I should just stay quiet and wait till he's done.

I guess I didn't learn anything after all because it happened again yesterday. Dad got mad and started yelling. I tried so hard not to cry, but he was just tearing me down so much, and I felt so worthless and wanted to defend myself, so I talked back. He yelled more, and I ended up crying again. I'm so mad I couldn't just hold it together and stay quiet. After a while, Mom said she was getting a headache from all the yelling and told Dad to take me outside. He grabbed my arm again and dragged me outside to the front porch. Once he shut the door, he turned me around and held me up against the house by the front of my neck and kept yelling so close to my face I could feel his spit hitting me. I thought that maybe if I screamed loud enough, someone might come over and make him stop, so I just kept screaming, but the more I did, the harder he squeezed my neck, and it got harder to scream and even harder to breathe. After a while, he finally let go of my neck and slapped me full force across the face. My eyes watered immediately, my ears were ringing so loudly, my face felt like a million bees stinging me, my throat was still tight, and I wasn't quite able to breathe normally yet. I don't know how long that feeling lasted, but it felt like hours. He went inside, and I heard him yell, I'm guessing to Mom, 'I slapped her, and I'm not sorry about it.'

Then he came back outside, grabbed my arm, and dragged me to my room. Today is Sunday, and I still have huge red finger marks on my neck. I came out of my room this morning dressed for church, and Mom pushed me back into my room and found a different shirt for me to wear that would cover the red marks. It's a bright green long-sleeved turtle-

neck shirt. It's August. I'm so hot I'm literally already sweating, but Mom says if anyone sees the marks, I'll have to explain that I disrespected my parents, and I'll be in even more trouble when we get home. I'm obviously going to make sure nobody sees anything because the last time my youth pastor saw an injury and Mom explained I had gotten in trouble, he got on to me for disobeying my parents and therefore disobeying God, right in front of a bunch of other kids. It was humiliating, and I felt like a naughty little child.

I have the turtleneck folded once, so it's as high as it can go up my neck. My face still hurts; my throat is so sore it hurts to swallow anything, even just water, so I didn't eat my breakfast, which I know is my fault. Mom and my grandparents made me well aware that if I hadn't talked back yesterday and had to be disciplined, I would have been perfectly fine and able to eat my breakfast. My grandparents always tell me I need to learn to respect my parents so I don't get in trouble so much. I used to try to explain to them that I don't know what I'm doing wrong, but they don't listen; I think I'll just stop trying to defend myself or reason with grown-ups; they don't listen to kids. I'm really hoping none of my siblings tell on me at church or embarrass me in front of people; I don't think they will, though; we're all usually really good at staying quiet about what happens at home.

***

I hated living with Nana and Grandpa. I got in trouble for something almost every single day. Mom and Dad would constantly hit me, drag me around, ground me from going to church or youth group, and teach Nana to do the same thing. The first time she slapped me, I was shocked. I always knew Nana didn't like me as much as she liked the other kids, but I figured that was just because I wasn't like her. She liked flowers and plants, and so did my sisters. She liked painting and doing art, and so did my sisters.

I didn't like any of that stuff, and I think that annoyed her. My sisters would be happy as can be, sitting at the table painting flowers on paper plates, and I would get bored within minutes. She never really liked me as much as she liked them, and she sure yelled at me a lot, but she'd never hit me before.

After we quit the Bible camp and moved into her house, however, it was like she was an extension of Mom. If Mom was mad at me, Nana was mad at me, which was basically always. She never defended me when Mom or Dad was yelling at me or dragging me somewhere. She slapped me right in front of Mom, and Mom started laughing, so Nana started laughing. I had tears in my eyes from the sting of her slap, and they both started mocking me, saying I was crying like a baby and "maybe the little baby needs her blankie". They started throwing blankets at me, then pillows, then cups of water from the kitchen counter. I finally walked away toward my room, and they yelled after me, "Yeah, go take a nap like a baby." I pretty much knew then that nobody was going to defend me, ever. Nobody ever had, so that wasn't anything new. I guess I just still thought there was someone out there who would.

That situation happened a lot - Mom and Nana just seemed to find enjoyment in ganging up on me, screaming at me, mocking me, sneering, and laughing, etc. There was one time when Mom had tripped me and shoved me backward over the foot of a rocking chair, so I fell and landed on my back. Before I could get up, Mom and Nana were both standing over me, pouring water on my face and kicking my ribs and legs, all the while taunting and mocking me. Neither of them worked, so they could've found literally anything else to do, but no… inflicting pain for entertainment was their game of choice.

I really started to miss those years at the camp – not because I enjoyed living there, but because I enjoyed never seeing Mom and

Dad. They were never around. It was always just us kids for years. They weren't around, so we didn't get in trouble as much. We got so good at being out of sight, out of mind. We could escape to the woods, to the trails, or to the reservoir and just hide out there all day. We could come back at night and go to bed, never having laid eyes on our parents. I thought those were the "good times," but I didn't recognize that period for what it really was, which was just pure neglect. Looking back, I missed what we had, and I wish I'd recognized the freedom I had when I had it. But that freedom was a distant memory because I then found myself in extremely close quarters with a mom who didn't work and had all the time in the world to watch us, boss us around, get mad at us, mock us, degrade us, smack us... Really, just do whatever she wanted to us because we were in her sight 24/7.

We started going to a new church when we moved into Nana's house, and I hated going. Even still, grounding me from attending church on Sundays or youth group on Wednesdays was the worst thing Mom and Dad could do to me, and they knew it. After only a week or two of attending that church, I had already made some friends. I'd never really had friends outside the summer camp friends, so I loved making friends at church and being around kids my age. But whenever I'd get in trouble, Mom would make me stay home from church on Sunday or let my sisters go to youth group without me on Wednesdays. She knew I hated it, so she kept doing it. I know people asked my sisters where I was, and Mom instructed them to tell the other kids that I had gotten in trouble and was grounded again. I don't know if they did or not; we usually didn't rat each other out like that, maybe because we had always been taught never to talk about what happens at home, but also because I think a part of us just naturally tried to protect each other if we could. At least that's how it was with my older sister and me; we didn't talk much throughout some of our growing-up years, but we always sort of silently stood up for each other.

The details are fuzzy, but one day Mom said we bought a house, so we moved all our stuff from Nana's into the new house. A day later, Mom said just kidding, we didn't buy this house, and we had to move all our stuff out of that house back into Nana's and continue staying there. I remember something about it being a foreclosure, but I'm really not sure why they would give us the keys and have us move in just to have us move back out a day later. Needless to say, we weren't doing school while we were living at Nana's house. We were house-hunting and getting punished, and that was pretty much our lives for several months.

At some point, since my parents had absolutely zero dollars to their name, apparently, a man from the camp bought a house in Nampa and rented it to us. We moved out of Nana's and into that house, and we were there for a few years. I always knew we were poor our entire lives; I remember being on food stamps and WIC when we were little, and when we were missionaries, I remember Mom and Dad saying we could never quite get to 100% support. Sometimes they blamed us for that, and I remember being confused about why in the world it would be my fault that strangers wouldn't give us their hard-earned money so we could be missionaries and live at a camp for free. The whole "raising support" thing always seemed awkward and weird to me, honestly. Anyway, we were still poor in this new house; I remember overhearing that the guy wasn't charging us much in rent, and there was a lot of anticipation that my older sister and I would get licenses and jobs so we could start contributing to the household finances.

Once we were settled in the new Nampa house, we finally started doing school again. We had what I think was technically a formal dining room that we turned into a schoolroom. Dad had built each of us our own school desk while we lived at camp - painted in our assigned colors, of course - and they were all five crammed into the "school room" surrounded by bookcases and stacks of school supplies. I do remember actually doing school for a while during that first year, although it was still up to my sister and me to make sure the younger ones did their schoolwork. Sometimes, I filled out their workbooks for them when they didn't want to, just because I knew they'd get hit later if Mom looked through their books and saw they hadn't done anything. I always made sure I got one or two things wrong, though, so she wouldn't suspect anything.

Sometimes I had to do the same thing with my own school – get one or two things wrong on purpose. Mom always made everything a competition, and school was no exception. She always compared my older sister and me, even though we were a grade apart. She always said I was smarter and that my sister wasn't trying as hard, so then my sister would get mad at me. I would start getting some things wrong in my assignments, so she would have higher grades than me, and it worked for a little bit. But then I started getting in trouble because my grades were declining, so I really couldn't win either way.

Mom and Dad's hatred of my older sister became pretty extreme after we moved into that house. They would both taunt and provoke her to the point where she would be crying hysterically. They would stand there talking about her as if she wasn't there, but she'd be standing right in front of them. They would say things like, "I don't know what we're going to do with her," and basically talk shit about her while she was a few feet away, and they did it on purpose. A lot of times, one of them would grab her wrists, squeeze and twist them, which caused her to scream more, and often yank her by the wrists and slam her down on the floor, and just hold her there while she screamed. This was a daily occurrence for quite a while. Sometimes, Dad would take her outside because Mom didn't want so much screaming in the house, as it gave her headaches.

One time, my sister tried to walk away, so Dad dragged her by her wrists out the back door, which Mom was holding open for them. He dragged her across the deck, and her head hit against the deck so hard I could hear the crash from inside the kitchen. She looked really dizzy, and her eyes were rolling all over the place, and she has no memory of what happened after that to this day. I'm not sure if she blocked out the memory or if she actually got knocked unconscious. After she hit her head, Dad kept dragging her across the deck, down the steps, and around the yard while Mom watched through the screen door and laughed. She turned around, saw me standing in the kitchen, and screamed at me to go away, so I took the other kids and went to another room. I'm not sure how that incident ended, but my sister had pretty bad marks on her wrists afterward, and she seemed super dazed and out of it.

Another time, the same wrist thing was happening, and Dad took my sister outside again. That time, he told me to open the back door, but I refused because of what I saw the last time, thinking he'd just stay inside this time. But he yelled at me and opened the door himself. I think he lost his grip on her because he was also opening the door, and she got away for a second. She had really long hair, and it was in one long braid at the time, so he grabbed her braid as she was running away. She got yanked and fell backward, hit her head on the porch steps, and then he dragged her pretty far across the yard by her braid. I remember Dad washing blood off his hands when he came back inside. My sister's wrists had marks again, and her face was beet red since she'd been crying and screaming while completely out of breath. I remember feeling like the whole situation was my fault because I had refused to open the door for him; like maybe if I'd just opened it and let them both outside at the beginning, it wouldn't have escalated that much.

Life pretty much consisted of school, getting punished, yelling, walking on eggshells around Mom, and making sure the younger kids stayed out of her way. Unfortunately, that usually meant my older sister and I were always IN her way, because of course we were. I really wanted to throw someone else under the bus every once in a while, just to have a break from always being the target, but I always felt bad and could never go through with it. However, if someone else was already getting in trouble, I got to the point where I'd just let it happen; sometimes it was easier to simply walk away and be thankful it wasn't me than to intervene, try to help them, and just get myself in more hot water.

At the end of the day, we were all the same, anyway, so I guess it didn't really matter who got in trouble when. We were all targets, just of varying degrees based on Mom's mood or whim that day. But we were all just kids – a bunch of bodies she was burdened with and had to deal with every day. There was nothing special about any one of us in particular, and she made that pretty clear. None of us was an individual, and we knew it. Our sole purpose on earth was to obey our parents, give perfect Christian performances whenever anyone was watching, memorize more Bible verses than any other kid at church, and never ask questions. "Shut up and obey your mother" may as well have been framed on our wall.

We hadn't even lived in that house for a full year before Mom and Dad apparently decided we didn't have enough kids. Because why not – let's just add even more people to our fucked up family.

Key Characteristic #5

INTENSE SECRECY

Secrecy was sacred in our house. What happened inside those walls stayed there, sealed tight beneath layers of fear and performance. We all understood without needing to be told that the family's image had to be protected at all costs. To the outside world, we were faithful, close-knit, and obedient. We smiled in public, said the right words but only when spoken to, and we played the part she scripted for us for fear of what might happen if we didn't. At home, however, we knew the truth, and we knew it could never get out. A crack in her carefully crafted facade could mean extreme punishments the next time she was alone with us. I learned early how to lie with a straight face or a smile, and how to explain away bruises and cuts in ways that seemed natural and entirely possible. The appearance of perfection and holiness mattered more than anything else, and protecting her reputation was our unspoken duty. Betraying that illusion, even if by accident, was the worst sin of all.

The rule of silence governed everything. Secrecy became both a cage and a strange kind of comfort; it kept us safe from her rage but trapped us inside her story. We lied like it was second nature to us, we were seen and not heard, we smiled and laughed, and went home exhausted from our performance. We were the perfect Christian children: obedient, quiet, polite, and devout. The fear of exposure lived just beneath the surface; we wanted the truth to be known, but, simultaneously, the truth coming out was our biggest fear. Telling the truth wasn't an option.

Living in that silence split me in two. There was the version of me that the world saw – the polite, smiling, faithful daughter – and the one who lived inside, who was fearfully watching and waiting. The longer I kept silent, the harder it became to tell what was real. I second-guessed everything: my own memories, my emotions, my pain, my personality. If I cried, I wondered if it was really justified. If I felt angry, I convinced myself it was sinful. I carried confusion like a second skin, trained to look composed while I was crumbling quietly underneath. The silence that once kept me safe eventually swallowed me whole, until I wasn't sure where the lies ended and the truth began.

6

Thou Shalt Not Tell

2012 | AGE 15

***

2012, age 15
I tried to kill myself today. It didn't work.

***

According to Mom, I was always a failure. I would never amount to anything; I would always mess up, and I probably wouldn't go anywhere in life. I could never do anything right growing up; nothing I did ever measured up to her standards. Her standards kept moving, though, and they were impossible for anyone to meet. I got to the point where I figured Mom's life might be better without me in it. I seemed to be causing her so much trouble, always having to deal with me and punish me and discipline me... I figured she'd probably be happier without me.

I started being silent. I noticed a few times when the "out of sight, out of mind" thing really worked. I decided to do an experiment to see how long she would go without speaking to me. I woke up, did my schoolwork in my room, came out to do my chores when she was occupied, and went back to my room without crossing paths with her. It seemed like a good way to live until Dad came home on the third day and asked where I was, and Mom said, "I don't know, and I don't care because she's just been horrid all day." I hadn't even seen her that day at all, so I didn't know how I could've been "horrid", but Dad always believed her. I got in trouble with him for making Mom's day miserable. It never really mattered whether any of us had been good or bad; if Mom told Dad we'd been bad, he believed her and dealt with us accordingly. We could never win.

I went through phases where I'd try different things to please Mom. Sometimes I just wouldn't care, wouldn't try, would do my chores sloppily, and just wouldn't put forth effort in general. I'd get the screaming from her; then I'd get it from Dad. Then, I'd do the opposite and try extra hard. I'd do my entire week of school in one day, I'd do my chores and then just continue to clean the entire kitchen from top to bottom, I'd help the kids with their school and chores, I'd do everything in my power to make sure Mom had a perfect day, and she'd still tell Dad I was awful when he got home. And then I'd get the screaming and yelling and punishment, etc., just as if I had been a brat. It never mattered. One time, after I cleaned the entire kitchen, Mom started screaming at me for putting everything on the counters away, and now she couldn't find anything. I thought I had helped, but, as usual, I'd somehow made her life worse. Again, I could never win.

That's part of what led me to the realization that her life really would be better without me. When I stayed in my room for three days and never saw her, she didn't seem to have any issues except when Dad came home and asked about me. Which, let me be clear, was on the third day of staying in my room; he didn't ask about me the first or second night, so clearly his life might've been better without me, too. Seeing as he didn't really care where I was or what I was doing. When I did nothing, her life was miserable. When I did everything, her life was miserable. Therefore, maybe if I were just *gone,* she'd be happy.

I tried to kill myself for the first time at fifteen, and it didn't work. I failed, and I knew Mom was right. She always said I was a failure, and I even failed at killing myself. I had swallowed a mixture of about 30 or 40 different pills from our medicine cabinet, and all that happened was that I got really sick. I probably ended up puking most of it up, unfortunately. I felt like such a waste of breath. I wasn't good at anything, not even suicide.

I had even prayed, too; I'd prayed that God would allow me to be successful, that He would let me die so Mom could have a better life without me, and I would just be out of the way. Everyone always told me "God answers prayer," but clearly, He does not. Anyway, I figured I'd just chosen the least successful method, and I'd just need to come up with something better for next time. Next time it would work, I promised myself. Next time I won't wake up; next time I won't be a failure; next time Mom will come in and find my body, cry for the cameras for a day, and then be happy for the rest of her life now that she won't have to deal with me. She'd probably get a lot of attention for having a dead daughter, too, which I knew she would love. She likes it when people are focused on her.

Did I tell anyone I tried to kill myself? Hell no. Why would I? Who would I even tell? Nobody would believe me either; that's the problem. I couldn't tell anyone what went on at home, and I couldn't tell anyone about the full-on war waging in my mind. I tried to confide in my youth pastor once, and he told my parents. I got it pretty good when I got home, so thanks a lot, Pastor Rich. No, the adults in my life seemed to enjoy failing me every chance they got; they didn't listen, so I stopped talking.

***

2012, age 15

I don't understand why I feel so numb. I can't feel any emotion. Nothing makes me cry or laugh anymore, and I can't feel happy or sad even if I try. I don't think I can even feel pain anymore. I've been cutting and burning myself, but I don't feel anything. Not physically, and not emotionally. I thought it might be "depression," but I told Mom about how numb I feel and asked if I could go to a doctor for it, and she yelled at me and got so mad it was crazy. She said depression isn't real; it's just something teenagers say to get attention, and it's just a fad. She also said suicide is the most selfish thing a person could ever do. I'm never talking to her about my thoughts again because that did not go well. Instead, I wrote about my thoughts and feeling numb in a journal, but that was also a bad idea because Dad found it and read it, and he got mad at me, too. He yelled at me for making things up and trying to get attention. He found my sister's journal once, too, came into our room, and read the whole entry out loud, and told her she was never to write anything like that ever again because it was all lies. I'm pretty sure she's feeling similar to how I'm feeling, but we don't talk about it.

***

During that time, I often cut myself with a pocketknife and burned myself with lighters. Mom had allowed me to buy a knife at a gas station, so I had a folding pocketknife that I kept in my room. I never went too deep – I didn't want there to be a lot of blood or big gashes – I just wanted to feel something. I couldn't feel a thing, even when I ran the blade into my arms. Nothing. I thought something was wrong with me, and I was immune to pain somehow. I just wanted to feel pain again – or feel anything, for that matter.

We had a 17-year-old foster sister come live with us for a few months; she had lighters because she would smoke whenever she left with her mom or her friends. That's how I got a lighter. The knife wasn't working, but I figured I might just be too used to it. I started using the lighter to burn my hands and arms, but again, I never felt a thing. I really did think something was wrong with me, but I had no phone or computer to look things up. We had a family computer, but it was only to be used by Mom and Dad, or when we legitimately had to do research for school. All our schoolwork was Amish or Mennonite, so I doubted Mom would be okay with Google searches about self-harm and feeling numb. That didn't really fit with the Christian behavior I was supposed to be exhibiting. I obviously couldn't talk to someone outside the family – that would get straight back to my parents.

After bringing up the subject with Mom and striking out, and after Dad found our journal entries, I was pretty much done thinking I could ever confide in them about anything. Mom used any information to her advantage, even if that meant embarrassing or humiliating us kids in public or in front of other church parents. She liked to do that a lot. Dad used any information to prove how ungodly we were and took every opportunity to spit Bible verses in our faces and yell at us that he'd pray for us and say we'd better pray for ourselves as well if we want any chance of forgiveness or Heaven.

From then on, I just kept my thoughts to myself; I didn't confide in my parents, my older sister, youth group leaders, friends, my youth pastor... nobody. Friends my age wouldn't know what to do, and adults would tell my parents. Survival had always been up to me before; I figured that would just never change. It would be up to me to get myself through life, and that sounded exhausting. I didn't have the energy for it. I also couldn't bring myself to care very much either. I got to the point where I really didn't find enjoyment in anything; I didn't look forward to anything; I didn't take pride in anything I accomplished... I just didn't seem to care about life anymore. So again, I was a waste of breath. A waste of space. I couldn't find a reason to still be living, especially when nobody around me really seemed to care if I kept living either. Why bother trying to survive if nobody wants me to – not even myself?

I kept cutting and burning, partly to see if anything felt different day after day, and partly because it had almost become a habit, I guess. I saw it as a progress report – if I did it every day, then as soon as I could feel again, I'd know. Well, my older sister figured out what I was doing and took my lighters away. I still had my knife, but I decided I'd better stop cutting before she took that away too. I found other ways to try to feel pain, though; I still have a three-ring scar on the back of my hand from our coiled stove burner. In the right light, you can still see it, and it sort of makes a smiley face.

I also tried to break my wrist on purpose and, as I anticipated, I never felt a thing. When my arm started turning every shade of black and purple and was becoming difficult to hide, Mom said she had to take me to the doctor to get an X-ray done. Sure enough, there was a compression fracture at the base of my thumb. I purposely faked falling out of the van the day before she noticed the bruising to create a cover story for my wrist once I realized the bruising was getting a little too wild. To this day, Mom thinks I fractured my hand by falling out of the van. That's the story I've always told, too, actually; come to think of it, I don't think I've ever told anybody what I actually did to break it. But that's how lies can survive – if nobody besides me knows the truth, nobody else can slip up. And I know for a fact I'd never slip up on my own lie. The fewer people in on the lie, the better. If the lie survives, I survive.

My older sister and I still talked during that time; we lived in the same room for a while before Mom moved her to the basement to make room for more foster kids in my room. She didn't know what I was going through, and I didn't know what she was going through, but we talked about Mom and a little bit about how we felt at the time. We both said it felt like we were wearing masks whenever we left the house. Whenever we went to church, AWANA (which is sort of a Bible club), youth group, a rare day at a friend's house, or anything else, we put on a mask and pretended to be happy, to have fun, and to enjoy life. When we got home, we'd take off the mask and go back to reality, completely drained and exhausted from acting like someone else all day. We knew there would be consequences if we allowed ourselves to remove the mask in public.

We also talked about how Mom always wore masks. She had a mask she wore at church that portrayed the mother of a perfect Christian family. She had a mask she wore for the social workers that portrayed "supermom" and a woman who had millions of kids and did it all herself – Wonder Woman basically. She had nice masks for neighbors, teachers at the foster kids' schools, the bus drivers… all portraying a perfect mother with a perfect family who is all-knowing and more Christian than all the other moms. And then there was the version of Mom we got at home, and that one had no mask. She was the unfiltered, raw, callous version who was like a crazy, kid-hating witch, always yelling, always screaming, never satisfied, never happy, dragging kids around the house, shutting kids in rooms and holding the door shut if it didn't have a lock, leaving babies in cribs to scream till they got tired of screaming, and it seemed like she never got weary of handing out punishments. She thrived on it, actually. It was like her battery recharged every time she handed out a chore, administered a punishment, ordered a kid to run laps around the backyard, or just made a kid miserable in general. She ate that shit up. She loved it.

7

A Quiverful

2012-2014 | AGE 15-17

***

2012, age 15

We're doing foster care now. Mom and Dad got approved to adopt a kid through an adoption agency, but I guess for some reason, they're giving up on that route. Mom said it's going to be easier to adopt kids from foster care, plus it's free to adopt if you already have them as foster kids. So, I guess we're doing that now. I'm not sure why we need to, because we clearly already have more kids than she can handle, because my sister and I do everything around here already. We help the kids with their schoolwork, do the chores, and cook the meals... our youngest is 10 now, though, so maybe she's getting bored with just having older kids? I don't know. Anyway, now we're just going to be responsible for a bunch of foster kids, too, in addition to the ones we already have.

***

While we were still living at the camp, Mom and Dad decided they wanted to adopt another kid. We had one or two kids that we were supposed to adopt, but they each fell through for whatever reason; I'm not sure. That whole thing is a blur to me. I remember them asking us if we were okay with adopting another kid. I said no, and I think someone else said no as well, but then we got in trouble because Mom and Dad had already decided we were doing it and had already done all the paperwork. I remember asking why they wanted more kids – I mean, we already had five – and they got mad at me for that too, saying they couldn't believe I didn't want to give a poor, unfortunate orphan child a loving home. They always made me out to be the bad guy, so I guess I was used to it by then.

I did know that having a lot of kids was godly; God wanted people to "be fruitful and multiply," which, apparently, meant "have as many kids as you can even if you hate them." Mom never said this outright, but I got the impression that the more kids you had, the more godly or holy you were. She judged families who had fewer than five kids; one of the other camp missionary families "only" had three kids, and Mom said it was probably because they weren't good enough parents and three was all they could handle, and that they weren't quite as Christian as we were.

That family wasn't as Christian as we were for a lot of reasons, actually; they let their daughters wear tank tops and mid-thigh shorts, they had their ears pierced, the mom wore makeup sometimes, and they said bad words like "crap" and "darn." There were other abominations just as horrible as these, but I'll spare you.

I remember getting asked if we were Mormon a lot growing up, and I didn't know why. When I asked Mom, she said it was because we had a lot of kids. She said Mormons believe more kids will get them to higher levels of Heaven, so a lot of Mormon families have tons of kids. She said Utah was where an important Mormon temple was, so there were a lot of Mormons in Idaho since it was only one state away. She said they were wrong, delusional, and not real Christians because there aren't different levels of Heaven. She said their leader, Joseph Smith, was one of the false prophets the Bible warned about.

Anyway, we never ended up adopting anyone through that agency while we lived at the Bible camp. Then, once we moved back to Nana's, they started talking about foster care and foster-to-adopt. Apparently, if you adopt a kid from foster care, not only is it free, but they even pay you. Adopting a kid from another agency required us to pay, so clearly foster-to-adopt was the better option, I guess.

They did the thing where they asked if we were okay with it again once we were in the new house, and again, I said no. Again, I was the bad guy for not wanting to take in unfortunate young souls in need of love and affection. I just thought we had enough kids, seemingly too many for them to handle as it was. My sister and I did everything for the kids we already had, so I was pretty sure it would be no different with foster kids. Just more kids for me to take care of. Not surprisingly, they'd already applied, completed training, and done whatever else, so the decision was already made. I'm not sure why they bothered "asking" us at all.

We started doing foster care in March of 2012. Our first placement was a 17-year-old girl and her 1-year-old son. She slept in our room, so we had four girls on two sets of bunk beds, plus a playpen for her son, all in one room. Mom hated her because she dressed provocatively, had tattoos and piercings, said bad words, dyed her hair, had a smartphone, had a boyfriend, had a different baby-daddy and also a child, and went to public school. Every single one of those things was a sin, of course. Mom said we needed to pray for her every day and witness to her, so she'd see the sinful path she was on and repent. It was absolutely imperative that we - my sisters and I - convert her to Christianity. She was only going to be living with us for three months, so Mom said we had to hurry and convert her quickly so she would be a Christian when she returned to her mom's house. That was basically our #1 priority for those three months.

I remember one night she was asking questions about Christianity. The three of us sisters were answering everything and "leading her to Christ," and she prayed "the prayer" and became a Christian that night. We immediately went across the hall to our parents' room and told them she had accepted Christ. Mom glared at us and said, "So? Go back to bed." We figured she was just tired, so we told her again the next morning after the girl had gone to school. Mom still didn't seem impressed, proud, happy... nothing. She didn't really have a response at all, other than her daily glare. I remember thinking that was confusing since we had always been taught to always be leading other people to Christ, but now we had, and Mom wasn't responding at all. Dad congratulated her and gave her a hug before she left for school, but that was it.

That girl turned 18 in June and went back to live with her mom, but then we got a 3-month-old baby girl almost right away, and we had her for about three months before she was reunited with her parents. I didn't really mind foster care up until this point; first, I actually liked the teenage girl we had, so that wasn't so bad. The baby girl was a super chill baby, and it was kind of fun having a baby in the house, but it pretty much went downhill from there. We had sibling sets coming in all the time, onesie-twosies coming in on weekends for respite or emergency placements, and we always had anywhere from 8 to 14 kids in our home at any given time. And guess who was in charge of them all...

I think having so many kids all at once was a status symbol for Mom. She liked the attention, she liked the praise, she liked the superhero complex, I guess. She collected kids like baseball cards and wanted everyone to know exactly how many she had. The more she had, the more praise and attention she got. We were a status symbol. We were only there to lift her up on her Super Mom pedestal.

At one point, we got a set of three brothers, all autistic. I don't remember their exact ages, but they were all three between five and eleven, I believe. The oldest boy, who was probably eleven, was a little bit more autistic than the younger two boys, although I'm not sure if that's the correct way to word it. I think "lower functioning" might be the right term; the younger two brothers were a little bit "higher functioning." Anyway, that was my first encounter with autistic children, and I had no clue what it meant.

Mom said they were slower than "normal" kids, and they weren't as smart. They reminded me of one of my own brothers, and I've always wondered if he was autistic as well; Mom refused to get him tested because she didn't want her kids labeled or something. Anyway, she didn't have anything good to say about autistic kids. They were stupid, dumb, slow, basically brain-dead; she complained a lot that she wasn't getting paid extra for having to deal with them.

The oldest boy had an extreme aversion to Spider-Man. I remember not understanding it at the time; I just knew he hated Spider-Man toys, clothes, posters, photos, plus anyone mentioning Spider-Man. He would start having a meltdown - Mom said it was a belligerent tantrum. He would squirm and scream and be absolutely hysterical; looking back, I wonder if it was more of a severe anxiety or panic attack than a tantrum. Mom enjoyed taunting him by talking about Spider-Man or showing him pictures of Spider-Man on her phone to get him to start freaking out. She'd chase him through the house till he was cornered and had no choice but to look at the phone screen, or she'd block him in a room so he couldn't get away from her.

One time, she bought Spider-Man pajamas and tried to force him to put them on. He kept squirming and flailing, and she wasn't able to get them over his head. She got duct tape and taped his hands together, then taped the pajama shirt and pants to his torso and legs so he couldn't get them off. He was screaming and crying and absolutely freaking out; hysterics, panic, all the above. She sat in a chair blocking the entrance to the living room so he couldn't escape, and she kept taunting him, singing, "Spider-Man, Spider-Man... Spider-Man's gonna get you... Spider-Man's gonna eat you." That just made it worse, and he worked himself up so much he actually couldn't calm down.

I remember the rest of us kids sitting at our school desks watching the whole thing, trying to talk to the boy and help him. We weren't allowed in the living room while this was going on, but we were telling him, "Hey, just stop screaming, and maybe she'll stop." That had been my theory growing up - if I just stayed still, stayed quiet, didn't move, maybe Mom would stop. It didn't always work, but it usually seemed like the best option. We told him the same thing since that seemed like the only way we could help the situation. Mom yelled at us and told us we weren't allowed to talk to him anymore, so we just had to sit there watching the whole thing unfold. It lasted for several hours.

Dad came home from work and Mom was still at it; she told him to take her place so she could start dinner, and she instructed Dad not to take the pajamas off of him until he calmed down. Mom didn't make dinner - that was always our job - but I think maybe she just got bored and wanted to get up or had to go to the bathroom or something. Dad sat down, and Mom left the room.

The boy calmed down when Dad came in; none of us - foster or bio kids - were ever quite as afraid of Dad as we were of Mom, but he could still do some damage since he just obeyed Mom's orders, so we were still wary. Since the boy had calmed down, Dad went over to him and started taking the tape off. I went over to help since Dad didn't know Mom had told us to stay out of it. We got the tape off, but it left red marks on his skin, and it seemed like it hurt pretty bad coming off. I ran to throw away the tape and sit back down at my desk before Mom came back, and Dad didn't rat me out, thankfully.

When Mom came back in the room and saw that the tape was off and the boy was calm, she got super mad at Dad. She started yelling at him that she'd told him to just watch the boy, but Dad said the boy had calmed down, so he figured the tape could come off. Dad had to apologize to Mom for basically disobeying her, and the boy had to sit in time-out for quite a while, if I remember correctly.

I guess this is as good a time as any to mention that Mom was one of the primary trainers for the foster care certification classes in Idaho. The required classes that prospective foster parents had to take to get certified. She taught them. She was also a keynote speaker for several virtual trainings and courses, as well as conferences in and out of state. She taught a variety of topics, including fostering with biological kids in the household, balancing attention between foster and bio kids, trauma-informed parenting, foster-to-adoption, post-adoption, special needs parenting, including autism, godly parenting, appropriate discipline methods for foster and bio kids, handling children who had been abused… You get the idea.

Wealth of information. Expert in her field. Highly sought after. Foster care legend. Number one resource. Everybody knew her. And me? Well, I was the daughter of a legend. "You're —'s daughter?! You're so lucky! You must be so proud! I wish she was my mom! I'm so jealous! You've got all her expertise at your fingertips! What a lucky daughter you are!!" Again, you get the idea.

I sat in on some of her trainings from time to time, but I didn't even recognize her. People came up to me afterward and shook my hand. Gushed about Mom. I smiled on the outside and died a little bit more each time on the inside. Every person who loved Mom was another person who would never believe me. Every fan of hers was an enemy of mine. Mom made sure she had everyone in her corner, leaving my corner empty - exactly how she wanted it. Not that I would ever say anything. I wasn't actually convinced that Mom wouldn't kill me one day; that is, if I didn't do it myself first.

***

2012, age 15

We've had several foster kids come and go now, and it's been made abundantly clear that Mom and Dad don't want anything to do with us "old kids" because they only ever pay attention to the new kids we get from foster care. My older sister is getting her driver's license soon, and I have my permit, so Mom and Dad are pretty happy about that because we'll soon be able to drive foster kids to appointments, school, and visits, and go grocery shopping or run errands for her ourselves. We obviously babysit all the time, plus do our own schoolwork, plus cook and do all the chores, but Mom never notices. Also, whenever Dad comes home and there's a load of laundry or dishes that haven't been done, he yells at us for not helping Mom all day because she does so much, and we're just a bunch of lazy kids who can't lift a finger to help. They joke all the time that they only had kids for the manual labor and chores, but I'm not so sure it's a joke.

***

By the time they stopped fostering, I remember Mom saying we'd had over 250 kids in our care over the years. I honestly don't know if that's accurate, but I also wouldn't doubt it. We had a lot of fucking kids through our doors. A lot.

In 2013, we got a sibling set of two girls, ages 5 years and 5 months. The 5-year-old was super delayed, assumed to have been on drugs at birth, starved and malnourished, and only sort of potty trained. The 5-month-old was almost grey, detoxing from a bunch of drugs and alcohol that were in her system at birth, but also in the breast milk she continued to get from her mom. I think we had just said goodbye to another sibling set, so I believe they were the only kids in our house besides the five of us at that point. Mom hated the older girl. *Hated* her. She said she was dumb, stupid, gross, disgusting, never listened, always defiant, etc.

My memory of her from those early days was that she did baby talk and she wasn't quite potty-trained, but that was largely due to how much she'd been neglected since her mom was an addict. She was really sweet, though, and very small. She looked more like a toddler, loved being picked up, loved piggyback rides, loved playing with us older kids, and loved going to school since she had never been to school before. She was very playful and outgoing, and she made friends easily at school and church. She was just a sweet little kid, and I really didn't mind having her around. For privacy, I'll call her "T."

The baby was so tiny, and she was quite clearly detoxing, so she was agitated sometimes and just absolutely still other times. Overall, such a chill baby, though. As the year dragged on, it became pretty clear that the bio mom wasn't going to be able to get the girls back. As I recall, she just couldn't stay clean, couldn't establish stable housing, couldn't meet the standards set for her by the court. After about a year and a half, I think, her parental rights were terminated, and the social worker was looking for a permanent option for the girls. I'm assuming they went through any family members or next of kin first, but it was sort of assumed they'd ask us if we wanted to adopt them. I remember standing in my parents' bedroom talking to Mom about it. I asked her, if we were asked to adopt the girls, would we say yes? She said, "I'll say yes to the baby, but unfortunately, they're keeping them together, so we have to take T, too."

I asked why she didn't want T so many times. The answer always had to do with the fact that T is so behind, she needs too much help, she's stupid and dumb, she'll never amount to anything, we'll be shackled down for the rest of our lives because she'll never be able to live on her own, since she's just so stupid and dumb. Mom said she'd likely put T in a group home once the rest of us were out of the house, just so she wouldn't be tied down by her for the rest of her life.

***

2013, age 16

I didn't want to go to church last week. I'm on the youth group worship team; I play guitar and sing, and it was my off week when I wasn't scheduled. I know it can't be the depression because Mom said that's not real, but something just felt off, and I didn't think I could summon enough energy to be around people that day. Mom was super mad about it and was forcing me to go to church, but finally, she said I could stay home as long as the house was spotless by the time they came back. And it was spotless, as spotless as a pig sty house can be. Dishes and laundry were done; everything I could clean was clean, but of course, it wasn't good enough for her. Whatever.

But this week I did go to church, and everyone was looking at me weirdly. A bunch of adults came up to me saying they're praying for me, but I couldn't figure out why. A bunch of the youth group teens were acting weird around me, too. One of them asked if it was true, and I had no clue what she was talking about. Then she said, "Oh, we heard you're pregnant". WHAT! Not sure how I could be pregnant when I'm not even allowed to have male friends, let alone date one.

I asked Mom why in the world people would think I'm pregnant, and she just said people were wondering why I wasn't at church last week, and that must have been their conclusion. I don't think the entire church would just come to that conclusion on its own. I feel like someone must have started that rumor. I asked Mom why she didn't just say I wasn't feeling well and stayed home, because that was literally the truth. She told me I put her in a horrible position of having to explain why her own daughter is going off the deep end and rebelling against God. I haven't gotten a clear answer on whether Mom started the rumor that I'm pregnant, but I'm pretty sure it was her. I hate this. I just want to disappear.

***

While we were fostering the girls, we got another foster baby in February of 2014. We got a call about a newborn baby boy who was left at the hospital after his mother gave birth. Mom said she knew he was going to be born with drugs and alcohol in his system, and she knew he would be taken from her like her other four children were, so she just had him and left. I'm not sure if that's true or not, but it's what I was told. The hospital was not allowed to release him until he was 48 hours old, so Mom and I went to the hospital to wait so we could get him as soon as he was able to be discharged. The nurses didn't think he'd make it past about a week, so we were told to just make him comfortable until he passed away.

I remember looking through the glass window at all the babies in bassinets with little name tags, wondering which one he was. Then a nurse walked out with the tiniest baby I'd ever seen, wrapped up in a little blue and white hospital blanket. He was dark-skinned, clearly not white. I remember Mom looking at him and saying, "Oh… he's brown." At the hospital! In hindsight, I know I wasn't totally educated on racism at that point, but I still knew her comment wasn't quite appropriate to be said in public, especially about a newborn baby she was supposed to be taking care of.

She didn't reach out to take him, presumably because he was brown, so I took him from the nurse. He weighed nothing. He had perfectly tan skin and the darkest hair – everywhere. He had a full head of hair, his arms were hairy, his back was black with thick hair, and he even had little tufts of hair sticking up on the tops of his ears. I thought he was perfect.

The nurse told us his name, and I'm wondering if we looked confused or something. She explained that he's Native American, I'm guessing, to explain why his name may have sounded a little different. After that, Mom was all about him being brown. Apparently, if he were Black or Hispanic, that would have been horrible, but because he was Native American, she wanted to shout it from the rooftops. She told everyone she had a Native baby. I guess she thought that was cool.

After that, she started getting really into Native American history, thought of herself as an expert on the Shoshone-Paiute tribe, and bragged to everyone that she was finally reconnecting with her Native American ancestry. As far as I know, we *might* be like $1/1{,}000^{th}$ Native American – we're white… like really *white.*

The baby boy was about six months younger than the baby girl we already had, so we had the five of us bio kids, a 5-year-old, and two babies in the house. That kid saved my life. I was still so numb, couldn't feel emotion or pain or literally anything, but holding him somehow made me feel something. I was the one getting up with him at night. I fed him, rocked him, held him while I did homework in the middle of the night... he kept me alive. Exhausted, but alive.

***

2014, age 17

I'm so exhausted today. I was up all night with the baby again – I don't know why Mom and Dad can't get up during the night with their own kid, but at least he's a pretty chill baby, and I was able to get some homework done. He's still detoxing from all the drugs he was born on, and he's also basically nocturnal. He sleeps all day and stays awake all night, so someone has to be up with him.

My older sister and I have been taking turns lately because Mom and Dad need their sleep, I guess. I had classes and work yesterday, came home, and watched the kids while Mom did who knows what in her bedroom; I made dinner for everyone and told Mom it was ready, but she never came out. I have no idea what she does in her room, but she's literally in there 24/7.

I helped everyone do their evening chores and get ready for bed, and then I was able to sleep for, like, an hour, maybe, before the baby woke up and Mom came and got me to stay up with him so she could go back to bed. He's a happy little guy, so I actually love spending time with him. It's just that I get no sleep, then have to get to classes at 8 am, work in the afternoon, and come home to do it all over again.

The only time I have to do my homework is during the night while I'm up with the baby, but I also have to feed him and keep him occupied since the night is basically his daytime. I'm so tired; I don't know how much longer I can do this.

***

8

Culture Shock

2015 | AGE 18

In Idaho, you can go through driver's ed and get your permit at fourteen and a half; I was fourteen when I got mine in the spring, and I turned fifteen a few months later. At the time, you could then get your license at sixteen, but Mom and Dad made us wait till we were seventeen. They said we needed more time driving with them before they sent us out on our own. But once we were seventeen, they didn't waste time; I'm pretty sure Mom took me to the DMV to get my license within a day of my seventeenth birthday. As soon as I had my actual license, I had to start paying for whatever gas I used, plus the car insurance for the minivan, which was the primary vehicle she had me drive. To do that, however, I needed a job.

Mom said we had to get jobs as soon as we could drive so we could help contribute to family bills and finances. She had me start applying while I was still sixteen so that I'd have a job lined up as soon as I got my actual license. I applied to Maurices, Old Navy, and a bunch of other retail stores, tons and tons of daycare centers, and a few receptionist positions, even though most required either a degree or a high school diploma, and I was still in high school. But she was very adamant: I was not permitted to apply to any fast-food place or any restaurant where I'd be a server, or anything to do with food service. She said those jobs were for low-life scum who weren't good enough to do anything else or didn't have any valuable skills. She said other parents who allow their children to work in food service clearly don't care about their kids and don't have high hopes for their futures. Basically, if I worked in food service, I would be a deadbeat.

I ended up getting a job at a daycare center in the basement of a church; we knew people who attended that church, so Mom let me accept the job offer. I had turned seventeen in June that summer, and started the job in July. I made around $8.00 an hour, worked from noon to 6pm Monday through Thursday, and from 8-6 on Fridays to accommodate my school schedule. In August, I started taking classes at the local community college. Mom said that since I was a senior, I could do dual enrollment at the college, since it was half price for high school students, and it would end up being cheaper than the curriculum she would have had to purchase for me that year. Plus, most of the curricula we used didn't go past 8th grade since they were predominantly Amish or Mennonite. I took four classes – two on Mondays/Wednesdays, and two on Tuesdays/Thursdays – both in the morning, which is why I worked afternoons and all day Friday.

I made about $260 per week, and Mom charged me $150 per week for rent, groceries, bills, and whatever else. That was over half my paycheck. With what was left over, I had to pay for gas, which I understood, and I also had to pay for the car insurance on the minivan since it belonged to them, but I was using it to go to school and work. Mom always said she would lessen my rent if I helped around the house more. I was in school four mornings a week, at work the rest of the day, and all day Friday. I had homework and chores in the evenings, made dinner almost every night after I got home from work, helped around the house on weekends, and stayed up all night with the babies and babysat whenever she needed me to. I'm really not sure how much more I could have helped, but she never lowered the rent. And whenever I asked, she said she honestly should be charging more, so I needed to be grateful for what she let me keep.

On Fridays and any day that I was out of school and could work the full day, my boss allowed me to take a 30-minute lunch. We had physical time cards that we hand-wrote our in and out times on, and they were turned in for payroll each Friday. One Friday, I was there pretty late since a parent hadn't come to pick up their kid yet, and I was making sure my time card was good to go before my boss collected them. I noticed she was editing my lunch times to be 60-minute unpaid lunches, but I was only taking 30 minutes.

I was young and naive, and too scared to confront her because she clearly hated me and treated me horribly, so I went home and asked Mom about it. Dad said that was a crime, and I needed to address it, but Mom said I was probably just wrong, like I was usually wrong about everything else, and I should just let it go. I didn't have the courage to do anything about it back then, but I've always wondered how much money my boss cheated me out of over the year that I worked there.

During my senior year of high school, when I was taking college classes, my older sister was also taking college classes as a freshman at Boise State. There were many times when we would both be doing homework, and Dad would turn off the Wi-Fi.

Usually, I had some sort of assignment due and needed the internet to finish it, but he and Mom never cared. I think they thought it was funny that my sister and I were groveling, begging, promising to do anything if they would just turn the internet back on so we could finish our homework. I would typically have to leave to go to a coffee shop, McDonald's, or the library to finish my assignments.

One time, he turned it off in the middle of my final exam – and they both knew I was taking the exam. It had been a big deal because I'd had to find someone else to watch the babies while I took an exam with a time limit that was due at a certain time. When the internet went off, I obviously got kicked out of the exam and, of course, I only had one attempt. I had to email my professor and meet with him in person to explain what happened. Thankfully, he allowed me to redo my final for the class. I did it at school before going home. Another time, when this happened to my sister, Dad took her keys and blocked the door, preventing her from leaving. The keys he took were to the car that she owned, bought with her own money, not a vehicle she was borrowing from them.

When I first started at the community college, my first few classes were English and Math, and I remember feeling like I was in way over my head. I had flown through books like it was my job ever since I'd learned how to read, so I thought I would be okay in a college introductory English course. I did do okay grade-wise - I finished the class with an A+, but I felt so lost.

The excerpts we were reading were not Biblical, so I had no idea how to write a response. We were given non-Christian essay topics, and I had no idea how to do that either. All my English books growing up had been Biblical, so writing about other topics was foreign to me. Mom also read every paper I submitted; she said she was still my teacher since I was still in high school, even though I was taking college classes. She insisted that I include a Biblical worldview in each paper, so I had to add a Bible verse and explain how it related to the required topic. Other students said words I had never heard - cuss words - and I didn't know what they meant or what to say in response. They referenced current events and pop culture a lot, and I felt like they were speaking a different language. The professor even had us write about a current event for one assignment, and I had no idea what to do. I ended up using the school library computer and searching "current events," thinking that would be enough. I was so lost.

The math class wasn't any different. Students using bad words, talking about movies I'd never seen and songs I'd never heard, discussing current events in the world that I didn't know were happening. I struggled with the math assignments, too. I had done math every year growing up, but nothing like that. I'd done Biblical story problems like Joseph had 40 sheep, types of things. I'd done basic algebra and geometry, but it still didn't prepare me very well for a college math class. I aced that class, too, but only because I was so determined to work hard and do well, plus I had Mom breathing down my neck that I would get 100s and nothing less. She told everyone she met that she'd done such a great job homeschooling her children that we got better grades in college than the public-schooled students did. I had to do well so her narrative would be correct, but I felt like I was so far behind everyone else.

That first semester, I also had sociology and psychology 101 classes. The student aspect was the same - talking about things I'd never heard of - but the classes were so interesting to me. I was learning about society and people, why they did what they did, what made people tick. In the most basic manner, of course, as these were introductory college courses, but they were like a whole new world to me. I loved those classes, but every time I went home and gushed about something new I'd learned, Mom acted like she already knew and said they were teaching it wrong. I believed her. Who wouldn't believe their own mom? I still enjoyed those classes for the rest of the year, but I felt guilty enjoying them once I knew Mom didn't approve of the lessons.

I had to take a humanities course the second semester, so Mom chose Music 101. She said music class was important and that I'd be the best student in the class since I'd been playing piano since I was three and guitar since I was ten. Oh yeah - Nana was, apparently, a professional pianist, so as soon as we were around three years old, all of us girls were required to take weekly piano lessons from Nana. I was playing Beethoven and Mozart at six years old, hating every minute of it.

The music class, however, was not what Mom probably thought it would be. It was more of a music history class, so we were listening to artists from decades past, all genres. So... non-Christian. I'm not sure what she was expecting, but it wasn't a Christian college, so, naturally, the class wasn't going to be about Christian music. I had to look up songs and listen to them for homework assignments, but she said I wasn't allowed to do that at home unless they were Christian songs.

Thankfully, there was a girl in my class who was also in another class with me the previous semester, so we became friends and studied together between classes. She had a cell phone, so she searched for the songs, and we got our homework done after class before I went home. She had a pretty unique Bible name and went to church, so I figured Mom would be happy I'd made an acceptable friend, but Mom said she was pronouncing her name wrong, and she didn't like the church she went to. Friendship not approved.

During our time at this house - the one rented from a family friend for a low price because Mom and Dad were financially illiterate - we got another foster sister. She was fourteen when she came to live with us, and we were supposed to be her "forever home." She had been bounced around between family members and foster homes her whole life, so we were supposed to be the last stop. I remember asking Mom why that would be decided for her before she even got to our house and knew if she even liked our family, and Mom said the girl didn't have a choice; she was staying with us till she aged out regardless. We were her last stop.

I remember the day she came because I had gotten pulled over that evening on the way home from work. They were doing construction on our road, so both ends of our street were closed off. People living on our street had to drive around the signs and cones to reach our houses. I was coming home from work, drove around the "road closed" sign, and the car behind me turned out to be a cop. I pulled over, and I could literally see my house across the field. I gave him my license, explained that I lived right over there - pointing at the house - and he was nice about it and basically just said: "Have a good night." I got home, walked in the door, and found the social worker standing in the entryway with our new sister. Mom gave me a glaring look that told me she'd seen me and the police car, and I could tell she was livid.

After the social worker left, I was absolutely screamed at for getting pulled over in plain view of the house so the social worker could see me breaking the law. Apparently, Mom had answered the door, saw me pulled over from the doorway, and was mortified that her perfect family facade was cracked. I was trying to explain that I didn't do anything wrong, I didn't get a ticket, I simply drove around a construction sign to come home to my own house, and the police officer checked my address and let me go, but she wasn't listening to anything I had to say. All she was worried about was that her daughter was seen being pulled over, and she wasn't able to present a picture-perfect family. Anyway, welcome home, new sister. We all love it here.

Mom hated the new sister from the very first day. She made that pretty clear, too. Dad was mostly indifferent, but Mom despised her. Mom treated her like crap, always talked down to her, called her fat, tried to put her on diets because it was embarrassing to be seen with a fat daughter, and criticized her for not being able to speak Spanish even though she was Mexican... she just didn't care about her at all. And the sister reciprocated those feelings; she despised Mom, and I didn't blame her. To this day, I don't blame her. She was tossed around from family to family, ended up at our house, which she was told was her last stop regardless of whether she liked it, and walked through the door of a house full of hate and control. She hated Mom, didn't like Dad, and didn't really like any of us siblings. Again, I don't blame her.

I was already doing college classes and working a job, and my days were mostly spent outside the home by then, so I really didn't get to know her very well. She slept in the girls' room, but we didn't spend much time together. I stayed up late either doing homework or taking care of the babies, and she had a strict bedtime enforced by Mom, so she was asleep by the time I went to bed. I didn't have any issues with her, I just didn't force a relationship. It was clear she didn't want to be in our family, and I knew she was being forced to be adopted by my parents, so she just sort of grouped us all together and disliked everyone. Understandable. I defended her a few times when Mom was being ridiculous, but it never actually worked, so I stopped after a while.

I couldn't defend anyone anymore by that point like I used to; Mom was unhinged, and there was no point arguing with her.

You couldn't use reason or logic with her - it was like she didn't understand facts. Dad didn't argue with her much anymore either. He sort of just went along with anything she said or did. If she was yelling at our new sister and looked to Dad for assistance or support, he'd just start yelling at her, too. That went for everyone, really. If she was mad and Dad wasn't supporting her anger, she'd stare at him or yell at him until he sided with her. We would just stand there, listening to both of them yell and berate us, waiting until they got tired of yelling. It was pointless to defend each other, but even more pointless to attempt to defend yourself. It just amped them up and made the situation worse. If we walked away, that incited an even bigger rage, and the verbal assault turned physical. If we talked back or tried to reason with them, things would, again, turn physical. The best way to avoid the physical stuff was to stand there, listen to the yelling, wait till they were done, apologize and grovel, and then let it go.

At some point during my senior year, we moved a few miles down the road to a new house – one that we weren't renting from a friend. There were four bedrooms besides the master, so my older sister got her own room, the rest of us girls each shared with someone, and the boys shared a room. It was a much larger house than any of our previous houses, but it still felt so incredibly claustrophobic because of all the crap that was absolutely everywhere. With the exception of the Boise house, where all our stuff stayed in storage while we lived there, every house we ever lived in was an absolute hoarder's house. There were pathways from the front door to the stairs, to the kitchen, to the master, to the bathroom... but each of our bedrooms had to be spotless. I'm not sure why Mom even cared whether our rooms were clean when the rest of the house was a pig sty, but it was a well-known rule that your room should never be cluttered. Mine was always clean – well, my section was, at least. I always shared a room, so whatever space belonged to me was always spotless. I couldn't function if it wasn't.

I graduated from high school with 31 college credits from the community college. I had to attend the Idaho homeschool Christian coalition organization of Christian homeschoolers or whatever it was called, just like my older sister did the year before. Christian Homeschool Organization of Idaho State? Maybe that was it. I think the acronym was "CHOIS," so that might be right. Whatever it was called, it was a group of 50 fellow teenagers who'd all been homeschooled in Idaho and were, you guessed it, Christian. There was actually one person who was kicked out of the graduation because they were Mormon, and the "board" decided that wasn't Christian. It was a pretty judgmental group of people.

I knew about four or five fellow graduates because of church, AWANA, or graduate get-togethers. It was like they were trying to be a real "senior class" like in public school. We had a movie night, a bowling night, and some other activities during our senior year so we would have pictures for the yearbook. Oh yeah – we had a yearbook, and I was on the yearbook committee. Mom said I had to be. We also had a junior/senior banquet – the "prom" of the homeschool community, basically. We did English group dances and line dances, the parents all had to attend as well, there were prayers and sermons, father/daughter and mother/son dances, and it was just all very *Christian.*

The only saving grace was that our littlest baby brother – the Native American one who saved my life – was also in attendance. He had his little baby tux on with his little baby bow tie, and he was the date of my dreams. He was only a few months old the year before – my junior year. I attended that year's junior/senior banquet as a junior, and my sister was a senior. Baby boy had an even tinier tux with an even tinier bow tie, and he was the dream date of everyone in the room. The love I have for that kid is insane. He made life worth sticking around for.

When he was about three months old, he was diagnosed with eye cancer in both eyes called retinoblastoma, or cancer of the retina. He did a six-month round of chemo and lost all his gorgeous black hair, but he was still the most beautiful bald baby ever. He ended up doing another round of chemo after he turned one - I don't remember the timeline of all that. Around eighteen months, he had one eye removed since the cancer had spread into the optic nerve. If the eye hadn't been removed, the cancer could've spread into the brain, and it would've been nearly impossible to stop after that. He had plastic eyes made; he thought it was the coolest thing in the world, and he would pop out his eye from time to time, and we'd have to put it back in. He thought that was pretty funny.

One time, he took his eye out at church, in front of a group of his fellow two- or three-year-old kids. I had the pager that parents were supposed to keep during the service, and it started buzzing, so I headed back to his classroom. He was standing there grinning, while the other kids were huddled in a corner staring at him. The teacher said something like, "Um... he took his eye out?" I looked at him and said, "Where's your eye?" He smiled and pulled his plastic eye out of his pocket. I washed his eye and put it back in, but I honestly couldn't help but laugh. He was such a funny kid, always being silly and stealing more and more of my heart every day.

Anyway, the graduation was a very Christian, very homeschooly affair. The parents of each graduate pre-recorded a message to their graduate to be played as the graduate crossed the stage. My parents said some bullshit about how they were so proud of the godly woman I was becoming, and they made sure to sound more Christian than any of the other parents. They did a good job, I'll give them that. It sounded lovely to everyone; it was fake as fuck to me, though... I actually laughed listening to it as I crossed the stage to get my make-believe diploma. The only reason I was able to get into Boise State University that fall was that I had a real transcript from the community college, so I came in as a transfer student. That homeschool diploma meant nothing, and Mom's Word document homeschool transcript with cooking and babysitting on it meant even less.

***

2015, age 18

Mom has always compared us to each other, and it's getting really annoying. She says things like "why can't you be more like her" or "she never did that when she was your age," and I think she does it to make it seem like one of us is better than the other. She also compares us to herself, like I have a 3.94 GPA in college right now because I got a B in Political Science. She said she graduated from college with all As, a 4.0 GPA, and always aced every assignment. She says if I wanted to get As, I would, so I'm obviously being lazy and not trying hard enough. I'm taking 21 credits this semester, plus working 13-hour night shifts at the homeless shelter, then coming home to help watch my siblings and our foster kids, but she said I'm just making excuses because she worked all through college and never had any trouble getting perfect grades. I don't think I can ever live up to her expectations.

Somehow, Mom found out that my older sister and I are taking the exact same course in college – different days and times, but the same professor and the same course. I think she saw the same textbook in both of our rooms or something; I'm not sure, but she's making it a competition, and I hate going to that class now, even though I was really enjoying it. Every time I come home, she asks me what grade I got on a test, a quiz, an assignment, or literally anything, and then she asks my sister what she got. When we took our midterm exams, I got a higher score than she did, and Mom made such a big deal out of it, calling her dumb and comparing her to me, saying I was more academically inclined, and I think it's making my sister hate me. I hate when Mom compares us to each other, but she always seems to find something to compare and then makes a big deal out of it, like she's trying to make us hate each other. I think it's working because I haven't spoken to my sister in months, even though our bedrooms literally share a wall.

***

Mom always created academic competitions between my older sister and me throughout our entire lives. I was more academically inclined and loved reading and doing schoolwork, and she was more interested in the outdoors, animals, plants, insects, etc. She was still smart and did all her schoolwork, but I found the work easier, I guess, and would speed through it. Mom always told us things like my sister is dumb and I'm smart, she and I would probably end up graduating together even though I was a grade lower, and a bunch of other stuff, just to pit us against each other. My older sister graduated from high school in 2014 through that same Idaho Christian homeschool organization of sorts. I remember Mom telling me that she was actually graduating at a 10th-grade level because it was all she was capable of, but that I would be graduating at a college level since I was so much smarter and ahead of everyone else my age.

My older sister worked at a daycare for years – probably starting in her junior year, well into college. Mom told me that's all she would ever amount to, and that all she could do well was take care of kids. Mom said she would probably just get married, have kids, and only know how to be a mom because she's not smart enough to do anything else. In 2014, I also got a job at a daycare. I figured Mom would say the same things about me, that it was all I knew how to do, but instead, she made it another competition between me and my sister. Who was in charge of more kids, who was being paid more, who worked more hours, who taught more educational stuff versus just being a glorified babysitter... It was exhausting, and I never wanted to talk about work when I came home because I knew I'd be compared to my sister. Even though I was usually the one compared in a "good" light, I hated it because Mom was driving a wedge between me and my sister, and she knew it.

9

A Proverbs 31 Woman

2015-2016 | AGE 18-19

In 2015, we adopted the kids. There was the sibling set of two girls who came in at 5 weeks old and 5 years old, the Native American baby, and the Mexican teenager. The younger three were adopted at the same time, and then later the teenager, but I can't remember the exact dates. I also don't know how we - a super white family - were able to adopt a fully Native American child when his entire family was registered on the reservation. The story Mom told me was that the tribe's social services liaison lawyer person just so happened to be the baby's biological aunt; the lawyer-aunt person was so happy with how Mom was raising her nephew that she signed off on a non-Native, non-tribal family adopting him. I don't know if that's true at all, because I feel like that's not how that works. The Indian Child Welfare Act requires that tribal members, Indian extended families, and licensed Indian foster homes be prioritized, and it was literally created in response to a ton of Native kids being placed in non-Native homes. I know

Mom fought to keep him because she got a lot of attention for having a Native American son, but I wasn't part of those conversations, so I have no idea. I love the kid - he literally saved my life - I just think something fishy happened there, and now he has zero ties to his heritage because Mom has completely cut him off from his tribe and biological family. Anyway...

The courtroom adoption ceremony for the three younger kids was a pretty big deal; it took place in November during National Adoption Month. The news and media were there, speakers were there, a room full of refreshments and tables was set up - it was a pretty big deal. Mom invited her parents, families from church, and other foster-care connections, so the courtroom was pretty full as well. We had been scheduled to finalize the adoption of those three kids months prior, but Mom had asked to delay the court date so we could do it during the National Adoption Month party thing. I'm pretty sure she just wanted to do it when all the cameras were there and more people could give her attention.

I think it might have been a few months later when she scheduled the adoption court date for the new teenage sister. Mom didn't invite anyone to that adoption. There was no party going on, no news cameras, etc. We all went into the courtroom, finalized the adoption, and went home. The teenage sister was with us for the previous adoption ceremony, so I can only imagine how she must have felt about her ceremony; I'm sure she compared the two. I don't think any of us were surprised, though; Mom hated her. Mom also hated T, the older of the sibling set, but that adoption was also for the babies who drew people's attention because they were cute.

Also, we were the only family who already had five kids, were adopting three more, and had another adoption ceremony scheduled a few months later. Mom was supermom; she was praised, people took pictures with her, and she was in her element. People kept coming up to us kids, telling us how lucky we were to have her as a mom. We were so used to hearing how amazing our mom was; I think it just didn't faze us anymore. We smiled and nodded, being the polite and silent children we were always supposed to be. It was always just easier to be quiet and let her have the spotlight.

In the summer of 2015, I quit my toxic daycare job and started working 13-hour night shifts at the Boise Rescue Mission - a homeless shelter for women and children in Boise. It was a Christian shelter, and we knew one of the directors, so that's how I got the job. I worked from 7 pm to 8 am, took a nap upstairs in one of the shelter rooms, went to class at Boise State, then took another nap at the shelter, and clocked back in at 7 pm for my next shift. I did that four days in a row and went home the other three days. Mom didn't like that I was barely home, but I couldn't really figure out a better option since I was so tired after working all night and still had to be at my 11 am and afternoon classes. She said I needed to figure something else out for the next semester because she really needed my help at home with the kids.

The next semester, I took as many online courses as I could. There were still a few I had to take in person, but I tried to make those weekend or evening classes as much as I could. I was feeling like the walls were closing in on me at home more and more. I was feeling almost claustrophobic, and also spread too thin with my work, school, and babysitting schedules. I had no time to myself; even when I was at home doing homework after everyone had gone to bed, I usually still had a baby on my lap.

I got to the point where I didn't tell Mom which nights I was working, so I could just be gone that night and she'd think I was at work. I picked up a lot of extra shifts for people anyway, so it was pretty normal for me to tell her I was working that night and just leave with little advance notice. Usually, I met up with a friend I'd met at one of the churches we'd attended. Her brother and his friends worked at Taco Bell, which closed at 2 am. She and I would drive around all night, then meet the guys at Taco Bell when they were closing. They'd usually prop a door open so we could get in, and we'd take any leftover food and drinks, then hotbox the car. I'm pretty sure my boss knew what I was up to, but I never had to do any random drug tests. A lot of my coworkers constantly got pulled for random drug tests, but I never got pulled the entire time I worked there. In hindsight, I think she suspected some shit was going on at home, and maybe she was trying to help me out.

When my older sister was eighteen, Dad gave her a purity ring. Therefore, when I was eighteen, I got my purity ring. When she got hers, I remember she didn't want to talk about it, and she said the whole thing had been really awkward. I was dreading getting mine because I figured it would probably be the same. Dad took me to Fred Meyer, a grocery store, and we picked up a slim rose-gold band at the in-store jewelry counter. He took me to Dutch Bros, a coffee shop, and he gave me the ring as we sat at a table outside.

In case you're not familiar, I'll explain it to you. A daughter's purity belongs to her father. Her purity is her virginity. A daughter's virginity is owned by her father. When the father approves of a man for the daughter to marry, he will hand over ownership of her virginity to the man at the wedding. Then, her purity - virginity - belongs to her husband. The ring is typically worn on the wedding-ring finger; the father takes it off the daughter as he gives her away at the altar, and the husband then puts the wedding ring on in its place, symbolizing the transfer of authority.

I knew all this already, as it had been drilled into our heads by both our parents and church leaders, but also because all the teenage girls I knew already had their purity rings. Some families did it at fifteen or sixteen, many did it as soon as the daughter got her first period, as she was officially a woman, and others did it upon graduation from high school, since the daughters were officially going to be out in the secular world. But everyone I knew had one, so I was well aware of what it meant long before I got my own.

Dad didn't explain much since he assumed I already knew what the ring was for, so he just said, "I hope you'll save yourself for marriage," and gave me the ring box. I opened it, put it on my finger, and we had awkward small talk till we went home. I was so uncomfortable.

From church, I already knew that my purity was not just about not having intercourse with someone (yes, they said intercourse; "sex" was a bad word). It was also holding hands, kissing, flirting, or having impure thoughts. I was to refrain from all of those things until Dad was able to give my virginity to my husband at our wedding.

I remember feeling so awkward that day with Dad; we never talked about sex in our home as it was a taboo and sinful subject. Sex was sinful. Even the word itself was sinful and not to be spoken aloud. I didn't actually know what sex was - like how it was done - but I knew the concept, I guess. I knew it was between a man and a woman, only after marriage, and it was for the purpose of having a child. Therefore, I knew that sex before marriage was a sin, and a child out of wedlock was a sin. I also knew the fault was always on the woman for seducing the man or causing the man to stumble.

Throughout my teen years, I remember all the girls at various churches we attended showing off their purity rings. You could always tell which families had more money, which ones had a family heirloom, and which families (like mine) got their rings from a grocery store. It was like a bunch of people getting engaged at the same time and all showing off their new bling, judging which ones were more expensive, larger, brighter, better.

Girls wore their purity rings with pride; they were women, they were godly, they were pure. The goal was to be a "Proverbs 31 woman" - Proverbs is a book of the Bible, and chapter 31 outlines what a woman ought to be. Wise, faithful, virtuous, capable, compassionate, generous, strong, confident, beautiful, supportive wife, loving mother, devoted to God and her husband.

Every church I ever attended had youth group nights where the girls split from the boys, led by female and male leaders, respectively. The girls had deep discussions about being a Proverbs 31 woman, being faithful to God, our fathers, and our future husbands, saving ourselves for our future husbands, praying for our future husbands, talking about purity, virginity, and abstinence, and causing boys to stumble, crying and praying together for hours. I was told that any impure thought - such as thinking a boy was cute - was a personal attack on my future husband. Many girls ended up sobbing and confessing to similar impure thoughts, afraid they'd ruined their chances of finding their future husbands. Those were always extremely awkward, uncomfortable, and emotional nights. Meanwhile, the boys played basketball in the gym.

There wasn't a lesson for the boys - the onus was on the girls to guard our purity, our thoughts, our clothing, and guard the boys from themselves. A girl's body was a moral battleground while a boy's body was simply a body. Boys weren't warned or held accountable, nor were they burdened with the weight of temptation. If they were tempted, it was the girl's fault for tempting them.

Looking back, I think it's a bit odd to literally put a "virgin" label on teenage girls. Whoever is still wearing a ring is still a virgin, and the ring is like a public notice of their virginity status. It all just seems a bit icky to me now. A bit pervy, too. Grown men don't need to know which young girls have never been touched.

I also believe, now, that this extreme religious idea that the responsibility is on women and girls is extremely detrimental, not only to societal progress, but also to women' s mental health. The imbalance of responsibility is a worldview that damages everyone who grows up within it. When a faith-based tradition teaches that girls alone are responsible for purity, morality, and self-control, it reinforces a cultural script that has already been brutal to women for generations. It tells society that women are the gatekeepers of sin, the guardians of men's behavior, the ones to blame when anything goes wrong.

In that framework, men learn too little responsibility while women learn too much shame. Whether they realize it or not, I feel like many Christians keep fueling this divide, strengthening a world where women are still judged more harshly, punished more quickly, and forgiven more slowly. Purity culture didn't shape only my childhood; it has helped shape an entire society that struggles to see women as full, autonomous human beings instead of moral caution signs and sexual objects. Women simply exist for men's pleasure, but when something sketchy happens, it's the woman's fault.

Growing up inside the purity culture framework leaves deep marks on a woman's mind. When you're taught that your body is dangerous or something to be ashamed of, your desires are sinful, and your worth hinges on staying "pure," you learn to distrust yourself long before you ever trust anyone else. Shame becomes second nature. Anxiety becomes a survival skill. Every choice feels weighted with moral consequence, and every mistake feels unforgivable. Women raised in purity culture often carry this invisible burden for years - chronic self-doubt, fear of judgment, hypervigilance, and a fractured relationship with their own identity. It doesn't shape what we believe; it shapes how we think, how we feel, and how we move through the world. Simply put, it destroys us.

***

2016, age 19

Even though going to college is mandatory for us, I actually kind of like it. I like school, I guess, and I think I'm decent at it because I always get As and only one B so far. Mom says we have to go to college, and she also says we have to do a Social Work degree, nothing else. Social Work is the only option, and then we'll be foster care case workers upon graduation. She's already planned our futures for us. My older sister got her associate's and didn't continue on to finish her Bachelor's, and Mom was absolutely pissed about it. She did the competition thing again, basically saying my sister was dumb, not smart enough to get a "real" degree, and that she would never amount to anything. I want a master's and maybe a PhD someday, so I'm finishing my Bachelor's, but I don't want to do Social Work. I changed my major a month ago without telling anyone – it's my degree, so I figure I can choose which one I pursue. I still act like I'm in social work classes, though; it's just easier to let Mom believe I'm doing what she wants me to be doing so she doesn't get as mad.

That didn't last long, though. Today, I got a letter from BSU in the mail, and she opened it while I was at work, of course. She always opens all our mail before we even know about it. Birthday cards, bank statements, credit card bills, health insurance bills, and college stuff. She opens it all and sometimes forgets to give it to me, so I'll be late paying a bill or something. I'm pretty sure she does that on purpose. Anyway, she opened a letter from the college that was basically a confirmation of my change of major, outlining which classes I have left and how many credits I have left to complete the new degree. I got home from work today, and she was absolutely furious.

I barely walked inside, and she's waving a paper in my face, demanding an explanation. I know what it is, but I act like I don't; I ask to see the paper so I can see what it is. She puts it behind her back and says, "I think you know exactly what this is." I still say I don't; I don't feel like dealing with it right this second. I figure she'll tell me eventually; I probably don't have to wait long. Once she latches on to something, she doesn't let go easily. I go about my evening, changing clothes, helping with the kids, helping with dinner, doing homework; all the while, she keeps saying, "Is there anything you want to tell me?" Not really, honestly; I never want to tell her anything. I only talk to her about stuff when she finds out, but I must be getting pretty good because she doesn't find out about much anymore.

My older sister and I don't have much of a relationship, but we do have a sort of mutual understanding. We are both perfect daughters to Mom's face, talking shit about each other since that's Mom's favorite thing to do. She badmouths my sister to me, and badmouths me to my sister. And then we tell each other when necessary. It's crazy that Mom can be so naive as to think my sister and I are so dumb that we don't see what she's doing – always trying to pit us against each other and also get dirt on us that she can use against us later. We barely speak to each other, but we'll take the time to shoot a quick text as a warning when Mom does or says something we may need to know about. Anyway, that's how I know what the letter is. My sister texted me while I was still at work, saying that Mom had opened my mail, that there was a college letter confirming a new major, and that Mom is furious. I had hours to prepare, hours to stop freaking out about how I was going to explain this one, and hours to calm down and realize that this is my college degree, I'm personally paying for my own education, and she can deal with it.

Now, that's not how my brain naturally works; I normally take hours to get there, and it's never easy. Naturally, my brain says that I must obey my mother at all costs, and I must never stray from her plan for my life. It's like I'm scared for my life if I don't. I knew I'd have to deal with this at home tonight, but at least I had time for my brain to catch up. Thanks to my sister, Mom didn't catch me off guard like she thought she did. I could tell my lack of reaction was making her even angrier. Whatever, she can stew.

After I get all the kids to bed, I come down to the living room to continue my homework. I'm not allowed to have my laptop – that I paid for – in my room, so I have to do my homework on the living room couch. Mom is sitting there, expectantly. I ignore her. Eventually, she says, "So, you changed your major without asking me?" I don't even look away from my laptop. My heart is pounding so hard, I'm certain she can hear it from across the room. "Yes," I reply, hoping I sound nonchalant. I really don't want this time to turn into a yelling match like it usually does. I just want to do my homework and go to bed. She asks why. I tell her I don't enjoy social work; I am more interested in criminal justice, so I changed my major. She harps on the fact that I didn't get her approval first and that I did it behind her back. She says criminal justice is a dead-end degree, and I'll never be able to do anything with it. She says I'll be a failure, but that's what I get for not getting her approval before making a decision on my own. She's saying I lied to her, I deceived her, and I'm making her look like a fool because she's already told all the foster care case workers at the department that I'll be joining them for my internship next year, and now she'll have to tell them I won't be.

I don't see how that's my problem, but my brain still tells me I'm responsible. I apologize to Mom – that's all I really can do. I've learned by now that I can't actually explain my reasoning to her or justify a decision; she doesn't hear me when I do that. She is sometimes placated, however, by groveling and incessant apologies. I owe her now. I did something without her permission. She's mad. I apologize. It's not quite enough. Now I owe her. But that's nothing new – I've always owed her. Ever since I was born, I've owed her. Nothing I do is ever enough, and I know I'll owe her forever. A never-ending debt for... something. I'm not sure what. But I'll never be able to pay it off; that much is clear. She owns me. She's always owned me. I can make-believe I have control by committing small rebellions, like changing my major without telling her, but in the end it won't matter. She owns me, and I know freedom isn't actually possible. I don't even know what it would look like.

***

My older sister and I weren't really speaking to each other. Our relationship was all but nonexistent. Mom had pretty much succeeded in placing a wedge between us; we still helped each other out, when necessary, though. I'm not sure why; looking back, I wonder if both of us just sort of understood that we were both stuck in a mess we didn't create, and there was really no good way out. We were never meant to get out.

Mom started talking to me about kicking my sister out. Mom had found out my sister had friends who were male and also non-Christian. Both of those traits were cardinal sins. Mom told me in secret that she was going to kick my sister out, but she wasn't going to give her any warning. She told me not to say anything to my sister because it would be so funny to watch her flounder around on the sidewalk with all her stuff and nowhere to go. I laughed and agreed with Mom.

Then I told my sister. She really didn't know where she was going to go; she had friends, but no situations where she could rent a room or anything like that. I had a coworker at the homeless shelter who was closing on a house but still had her apartment and was looking to break her lease. I put my coworker in contact with my sister, they did all the paperwork blah blah blah, and my sister took over the lease on a one-bedroom apartment in what was actually a halfway decent area. The apartment complex was gated, too, so that was something. Neither of us mentioned any of this to Mom.

The day came when Mom was going to kick her out. My sister came home from work, and Mom turned to me and said, "Watch this," with a devilish grin on her face. My sister got to the front door and walked inside, and Mom and I were standing in the entryway. Mom said something like, "Oh, what are you doing here? You're no longer welcome in my home; find somewhere else to live." She absolutely expected my sister to break down, freak out, and go crazy. Instead, my sister was like, "Okay," took a few friends she'd brought with her upstairs to get the last few things she had in her room, and left. Mom was stunned. It was honestly hilarious – she always had perfectly crafted reactions to all situations, but this time she was the one who was caught off guard. She was *never* caught off guard; even if she sort of was, she recoiled quickly and acted like she knew the thing all along.

She went upstairs to my sister's room and stood in the doorway absolutely shocked. The room was empty, except for the bed. My sister and her friends had moved all her stuff to her apartment over the past several weeks, so when the "kick-out" day came, she didn't have much left. I had coordinated with her to let her know that when Mom was away from home, she and her friends would come get things, and Mom would be none the wiser. I think Mom figured out pretty quickly that I had been the one to warn my sister, or at least that's the route she chose to follow in her head. She was so livid, probably because her plan didn't work and she didn't get the satisfaction of seeing my sister struggle.

Key Characteristic #6

MANIPULATION THROUGH GUILT OR FEAR

Mom's voice ruled me at all times, even when I started working and earning my own money. I was becoming an adult, but not in her house, and not in her world. Every decision still needed her approval, and every opinion still had to pass through her filter. I thought that getting a job might give me some freedom, but it only became another battleground for control. She reminded me constantly that I'd fail without her, that I wasn't ready to face the world alone, and that no one would care for me the way she and Dad did. Her words – whether real or inside my head – were heavy with warning and guilt, wrapping themselves around every moment of progress like chains disguised as love.

Her manipulation was like second nature to her. When she wanted obedience, she often spoke in catastrophe: You'll get hurt, you'll lose everything, God will turn His back on you. When she wanted compliance, she used guilt: After everything I've done for you, after everything I've given you, this is how you repay me? I learned to fear her disappointment and attempted to anticipate her moods before they turned into punishment. I thought I was keeping the peace, but I was actually slowly surrendering my soul to her.

Even as I began taking college classes, I never felt free. I'd sit in a classroom with people my age who talked about plans and futures and possibilities, and I'd feel the invisible tether pulling me back home. I knew my future had already been planned for me, and I couldn't bring myself to dream about any alternative ideas. My body might have been on campus, but my thoughts still belonged to my mother. Every thought came paired with her judgment, reminding me that independence was pride, and curiosity was rebellion.

The emotional toll was constant and crushing. I went through cycles – there were moments when I tried to prove myself, make her proud, and bridge the invisible distance between us, and other moments when I gave up, feeling guilty and ashamed of even wanting more. I kept trying to earn her approval, as if love could erase fear, but it never worked. The rules always shifted, and the target always moved. No matter how hard I tried, I was always somehow wrong, ungrateful, or disappointing.

I didn't realize then how completely her voice had replaced my own. I thought I was making choices, but I was actually just reacting; I was shaping my life around her expectations, not my own desires. My thoughts weren't safe, my emotions weren't mine, and my silence became a survival instinct. I lived under her roof, caught in her web. Even when I was alone in my bed at night, her voice was there in the corners of my mind, whispering reminders of who I was supposed to be. Still, somewhere deep beneath the noise, a quiet knowing began to stir; a desperate, forbidden thought I could barely admit to myself. I wanted out. I didn't yet know how or when, only that if I stayed much longer, there'd be nothing left of me to save.

10

Guilt Trip

2017-2018 | AGE 20-21

***

2017, age 20

I joined the Navy today. I filled out all the paperwork and did the medical screening last week, and Mom and Dad had no idea. I knew they'd try to stop me if they knew, so I just didn't tell them. I swore in today, though, so I told them yesterday that I joined and invited them to my ceremony. Dad didn't come. Mom came with one of my sisters and both babies, who wouldn't stop crying and being loud, so they kept disrupting things and stepping out, and I'm honestly not sure why she even came. She didn't congratulate me or take any pictures; she wasn't proud, and she left immediately after she reminded me that I'm watching the kids for her tonight.

My sister took one picture of me swearing in, so at least I have that. Mom and Dad were so pissed when I told them I joined. They said war and murder are against the Bible, that women don't belong in the mil-

itary, and that my place is at home helping Mom. She said I'm really putting her in a bind by leaving and that she'll have no help. She said I clearly didn't think about anyone else before I made this decision and that I'm being extremely selfish by leaving her to deal with everything at home by herself. She still has all the other siblings who can help her, so I'm not sure why it's such a big deal. I just need to leave. I need out. I feel like I'm suffocating here. I can't do it anymore.

***

In the summer of 2017, I felt like all my life choices had already been made for me. I had changed my major in college, but somehow Mom still found something social work related for me to do. She used her connections and found me a position at a juvenile detention center; I was supposed to start right after graduation. I only had one semester of college left; I had taken summer classes, weekend classes, evening classes... basically as many classes as I was allowed to take at a time just to finish faster. I don't know why I was in such a hurry - I think I was convinced that if I finished faster, I could prove to Mom that I was smart, intelligent, etc. I was always trying to prove myself to her, so I'm sure that's what was driving me to finish college so quickly.

I had taken enough summer and weekend classes that I only had one semester left, and I would graduate with my bachelor's and associate's, plus two certificates, in December of 2017. I felt like the walls were closing in on me. I would graduate, start the job Mom had found for me, continue to live at home and help with the kids when I wasn't working, move out only when she permitted me to, marry someone she found and approved of who agreed with her religious opinions, have children, quit working to homeschool my children, and always live within a short distance of her house. Let's be real, though - there probably never would have been someone she actually approved of for me to marry. But that was the correct role for a woman and the plan for my future, and I felt like it was all happening too fast. I felt like I hadn't even done anything with my life yet, other than a few overseas mission trips that weren't my idea. Ireland was great, but I was telling kids stories that I wasn't even sure I believed myself.

I had to delay the plan, I had to get out, I had to find some other thing to do that would prolong the inevitable. I met with the department chair of the criminal justice master's program at BSU. She pre-approved me to start the master's program in August of 2018 - I guess they only took new students in the fall semester. I would have had to fall into Mom's plan from January to August before even starting a master's program. When I brought it up with Mom, she wasn't happy. She asked why I needed a master's and what I planned to use it for. She said I was being ungrateful - she had found me a job using my bachelor's, and there I was, always wanting more. I had thought she'd been happy that I wanted to pursue more education since education and academics had always seemed to be so important to her. But no - apparently a master's was too far. She didn't have a master's, so maybe that's why she didn't want me to have one. It sort of felt like she saw me as her competition, and she couldn't allow me to be better than her.

A friend of mine from church had joined the Navy and had tried to convince me to enlist as well. I looked up the different branches and the differences between active duty, the reserves, and the National Guard. I looked up the different jobs I could do and the process to join. I landed on the Air National Guard as the best choice for me. I wanted to go on active duty - I wanted to leave home and just never come back. But the baby had cancer; I didn't know how long he'd be alive, and I didn't want to miss anything. I didn't want to be somewhere and not be able to come back if something happened.

I visited the Air Force recruitment office in Boise between work and class one day. They told me I would enlist, sign a contract, and then choose my job. I told them I felt a little wary about that - not knowing what job I'd be doing until I was already locked into a contract - but they said that was how it worked. I said I'd sleep on it and come back.

I talked to my Navy friend, and he assured me the Navy is not like that. You choose your job, then sign your contract. I had no interest in joining the Navy, though. Ever since the river incident at the summer camp, I'd stayed away from dark water, and I had no intention of changing that. He said there were tons of jobs that had nothing to do with boats or water, and that I could still do an air job like I'd wanted in the Air Force. I agreed to at least go talk to a Navy recruiter.

I ended up taking the ASVAB (Armed Services Vocational Aptitude Battery - basically an SAT/ACT for the military) the first day I walked into the Navy recruitment office. I got a high enough score that the recruiter said I could basically have my pick of jobs - other than nuclear stuff, which I had no interest in anyway. I chose an "aircrew" rate (a job working on airplanes), went to MEPS (Military Entrance Processing Station) for the medical screening, ended up taking the ASVAB a second time because I was told they had lost my original score, and enlisted. Then I told Mom and Dad, and that went about as well as I'd expected.

I couldn't see any other choice. I couldn't come up with any other options that would allow me to at least delay the inevitable plan Mom had for my life. I just wanted out, even if it was just for a few months. I joined as a reservist, so I knew I'd come back after boot camp and school, but at least I'd have some time away from her. I was suffocating.

I completed my last semester at Boise State, graduated in December, had a graduation/going away party, and left for boot camp in February of 2018. There was so much yelling at boot camp, which wasn't really much of a change compared to what I dealt with at home, but the difference was that they weren't yelling specifically at me. It wasn't only targeted at me. They yelled at everyone. The other difference between home and boot camp was that my entire job was to focus on myself. All I had to do was follow the rules, obey the instructors, fold my clothes, and pass my exams. My responsibility was to take care of *me*. To get *me* through boot camp. I wasn't responsible for anybody else's success. It also wasn't my responsibility to keep other people out of trouble. Everyone worried about themselves, obeyed the rules, learned the material, and got themselves to graduation. It seemed so easy, like I got a break.

After boot camp graduation, everyone else in my division was getting airline tickets to their schools. I was sent to a holding unit - they told me I was on a medical hold, but nobody would explain why. I had passed all my medical stuff throughout boot camp, and I had even passed all the extra medical screenings required for my aircrew job. After a few weeks in holding, I was finally told that I'd been disqualified from aircrew because I'd had asthma when I was seven. I never told them that, so I wasn't sure how they found it, and I also didn't see how it was relevant, but the decision had been made. I had to select a different job.

When I went to meet the guy to select a new job, he said I had three options. I could choose between a corpsman (nurse), a boatswain's mate (work on a boat), and a construction equipment operator. I faint at the sight of needles, so nurse was a no, and I hate dark water, so boats were a no. Equipment operator it was. I was pissed. I had no interest in operating construction equipment, and I was livid that I'd been through all of boot camp only to be unable to choose my own job after all. I may as well have joined the Air Force and gotten a mystery job there. I went through a series of emotions ranging from "why the fuck did I join the military" to "maybe operating equipment won't be that bad" and everything in between. Then I was off to A-school at Fort Leonard Wood, Missouri. Those who have been there often refer to it as "Fort Lost-in-the-Woods," which I'd say is pretty accurate.

I went into A-school mad at the world, pissed at the job I got stuck with, wanting to just quit and go home. I had Mom's voice in my head the whole time, reminding me that this is what happens when I make my own decisions without her help. I felt like I should've just listened to her. She was always right, right? She knew best. She'd already formed a plan for my life, so I should've just gone along with it, and I wouldn't be here operating construction equipment in the dirt in the middle of summer.

By the end of A-school, however, I'd pretty much decided that operating equipment was actually pretty fun. I enjoyed every piece of equipment we operated, and somehow I was pretty good at it. I made a few friends, but I made sure to keep my distance from most of the people there. Most weren't Christians, so I knew Mom wouldn't like me being friends with them. There were a few homosexual people too, and I knew she wouldn't like that, either. I hung out with them, too, but I just made sure not to mention that to Mom when she called.

They had brought me my phone and laptop after boot camp, so I had communication again, but they didn't do a good job of keeping me in the loop. I knew there was some drama with a few of my sisters, but nobody would fill me in on what was going on. Something about a boyfriend, I gathered, but I didn't really know. The baby was doing well, though, or at least they didn't say otherwise.

They'd gotten more foster kids since I'd been gone, and Mom said they'd probably still be there by the time I came home. Every time I was on the phone with Mom, she made sure to tell me she was really struggling with all the kids since I wasn't there to help - I thought maybe that was a compliment, but I knew better. She was reminding me that I'd left her to deal with everything by herself, that I'd been selfish, that I'd be right back to babysitting as soon as I got home. And I was done with college, so I'd have nothing better to do than help her at home.

***

2018, age 21

I flew home from basic training and A-school today; it's the first time I've been home in almost six months. Mom coordinated with me to pick me up so I could surprise everyone, but she took me to a gas station. All the kids were buckled in the van and weren't allowed out, so it wasn't much of a homecoming. She also told me on the way home from the airport that they sold the house and we're moving to North Carolina. I've lived in Idaho my entire life, born and raised, and suddenly she just decided to move to the other side of the country? She could have given me a heads-up while I was in training – I've had my phone for the past four months.

I walked into the house for the first time in six months and immediately had to pack up my room and help load the storage units because, I guess, we're leaving for NC in a month. Mom said she rented three 26-foot U-Haul trucks, each pulling a car trailer, and she needs me to drive one since Dad will already be out there starting his new job. She also said I could stay in Idaho or move with them – my choice – but where am I supposed to go? It's not like she gave me much of a heads-up or enough time to get an apartment or a job. I guess I'm moving to North Carolina. I already wish I'd gone active duty, not reserves. I should've just stayed away.

***

I was home for about three or four weeks before we left for North Carolina. During my first week home, I was still deciding whether I wanted to move with the rest of the family across the country or stay in Idaho and figure out work and housing. I didn't have much time to prepare, but I knew the first step was to get a job. I contacted a temp agency and got a job loading boxes onto semi trucks. I hated it. Nobody gave me any training. I was brought to a conveyor belt that ended right in front of an open semi-trailer and told to load the boxes from the conveyor into the trailer as neatly as possible and also as quickly as possible. The boxes on the conveyor belt were already so backed up that they were falling into a pile on the floor, and the conveyor belt had stopped completely. Oh, and I was responsible for six of those conveyor belts, putting boxes into their respective trailers. All six belts were backed up already, so no matter how fast I worked, I could never catch up. Nobody spoke to me; everyone took a 30-minute lunch break at the same time, and everybody shut down their conveyor belts at the end of the day. We had a short meeting in the office and then went home. Back the next day to my same six conveyor belts. Hated it. But it was a job, and the only one I could get within a day of coming home.

I worked that job for one week, and Mom told me I had to quit so I could help get everything prepared for the move. We were taking loads of boxes and furniture from the house to a storage unit down the street - three storage units, actually - because we had to be out of the house before we were actually leaving

Idaho. We ended up living at my grandparents' house and in our RV travel trailer for a minute at the very end. Mom rented those three 26-foot U-Haul trucks, and each one was pulling a car trailer. We backed two U-Haul's back-to-back by the three storage units and started loading. Once those two trucks were full, we moved them to make room for the third truck. The third ended up being mostly full by the time everything was out of the storage units. So. Much. Shit. I've honestly never understood how our family accumulated so much stuff, and I felt like we got rid of a bunch while we were packing, too. Mom should've been featured on an episode of *Hoarders*; she probably would've loved the attention.

Three trucks, each towing a car, plus our 15-passenger van towing the RV. Mom drove the van, which had all the kids in it, and my grandparents and I each drove a U-Haul. The trip from Idaho to North Carolina took about eight days; we only drove in the daylight because, apparently, Nana didn't like to drive in the dark. We never got on the road before 9 am, and we always stopped by 4 or 5 pm. Not a lot of progress each day. Nana also drove extremely slowly, and we were all supposed to stay together and not get too far ahead, so she slowed us down a lot. Most of the drive consisted of me cruising down the freeway at 45mph. My brothers started going stir-crazy in the van with the younger kids, so they'd take turns riding in the truck with me. Or they'd ride with me when Mom got mad at them for something. Usually, the boys got frustrated with the kids, tempers flared, Mom got mad, and the boys got in trouble. Eight days in a van with Mom would make anyone go insane, honestly.

Mom made sure to stop at any historical site along the way; she said it was part of the kids' homeschooling during the week. She was always able to justify nobody doing actual schoolwork by claiming whatever they were doing as a "subject" or a "class," even if it was just seeing Route 66 and reading historical signs along the highway. When afternoon came, Mom looked for an RV park, KOA, campground, or truck stop for us to stay at for the night. No matter where we stayed, my grandparents were never able to park the trucks or back them in anywhere, so I had to park my truck, get out, park another truck, then get out and park the third truck. Mom was always mad every single night that I hadn't parked the trucks fast enough and that other people in cars or RV's had been lined up behind me.

One night, mid-trip, I snapped at her that it wasn't my idea to stuff half of Idaho into a bunch of trucks and caravan across the country. My patience wore thin that entire trip, and I just couldn't deal with her anymore. I was banned from the RV that night and had to sleep in my U-Haul. Honestly, I preferred that; we were cramming six adults, three kids, and two cats into a medium-sized RV. The two youngest kids shared a bed with me, so I actually slept better in the cab of the truck.

When we finally rolled into North Carolina, we had to stay one more night in the RV since we weren't able to get the keys to our house until the next day. Oh yeah, they'd already bought a house. Or I should say Mom did. Mom shopped for houses, found the one she wanted, and went ahead with the purchase without Dad having any say at all. Then again, that's how she bought all our houses through the years. Dad didn't get to have a say; Mom would find the house she wanted, and they'd buy it. With Dad's money, of course; Mom never worked. He made the money; she spent the money. He had to have permission to spend $5 on a burger if he forgot to bring lunch to work.

When we got all moved in, I immediately started applying for jobs. Immediately. I had construction equipment operator experience from my Navy training and a criminal justice degree, so I applied for jobs in both areas. Correctional officer and construction worker, sheriff administrative assistant and traffic flagger... and everything in between, including retail, food service, you name it. I wanted to start working as soon as possible, save my money, get my own place, and get out of my mother's house. Whatever job reached out to me first, that's the one I'd take.

I ended up getting a job through a temp agency testing prototype construction equipment on the night shift at a construction company. I worked ten-hour shifts, five to six days a week, 4 pm to 3 am-ish... or something like that. I literally got to work, went to my assigned machine, ran it all night, parked it, and went home. By far the easiest job I've ever had. If I had an excavator, I would dig trenches and fill them back in all night. If I had a roller, I would flatten a dirt field all night. I listened to music and played in the dirt for $13 an hour. Not a bad gig.

The shitty part of life was living at home. I worked nights, so I needed to sleep during the day. But I couldn't sleep all day because I had to help Mom with the kids. Obviously, because why on earth would a mother ever take care of her own children? That would be crazy.

I got home around 3:30 in the morning, slept for a few hours, then got up to watch the kids so Mom could "get stuff done" before I had to leave for work. What she was "getting done," I had no idea. To this day, I still have no idea. She would go into her room as soon as I came downstairs; she'd shut the door, and she'd stay in there for hours until I banged on the door, telling her I was going to work. I loved hanging out with the kids, but I was always so tired and never quite got enough sleep between shifts.

There were several days she'd ignore me or yell at me to just leave, so I'd leave for work, and the kids would just be hanging around the house unattended with Mom still locked in her bedroom. When we were younger and she did that, she always told us she was "balancing the checkbook," but then we got older, balanced our own checkbooks, and realized it doesn't take six hours a day, every single day, to balance a checkbook. I honestly have no idea what she was doing in there.

My older sister and her husband stayed behind in Idaho while we all drove to North Carolina, and then they drove out about a month later. One of my younger sisters stayed in Idaho with her boyfriend for a year or so; I believe they got evicted from their apartment. Nana said they couldn't live with her, so Mom bought them both plane tickets, and they moved to North Carolina in 2019. At that point, we had thirteen people living at the house, along with three 26-foot U-Hauls worth of *stuff*.

11

Unequally Yoked

2018-2020 | AGE 21-23

***

2018, age 21

We've been in North Carolina since the first week of October. I spent Thanksgiving at home with the family, then drove 13 hours down to Mississippi to visit some Navy buddies from A-school for the weekend. I never should've gone. The guy I thought was my closest friend decided to keep me hostage in his room and rape me all night, and I was too drunk to fight him. I kept saying "no," but guys don't listen to that; they think "no" means "keep going," I guess. Anyway, now I just drink myself into oblivion, and it seems to work. I work nights, come home at 4 am, drink till I pass out, and go back to work at 4 pm.

It's a good cycle – I don't feel anything at all. I did wake up this afternoon still in my clothes and work boots with a speeding ticket in my hand... I have no memory of being pulled over, so I'm not sure how that happened, honestly. I'm pretty sure Mom was screaming at me for it, but who knows. Everything sounds foggy these days, like people are talking to me through a double-paned window, and the words don't really register. I don't remember much, and I'm not sure I'm mentally present half the time. Whatever, I'll probably be dead before the traffic court date anyway – if all goes well, I won't even wake up tomorrow. Fuck it. Fuck life. Fuck rapists. Fuck the world. I'm done.

***

I lived in a fog for months. When people talked, they sounded like they were far away. I never remembered the drive to and from work. While I was digging holes in the dirt, I either operated in complete silence or blasted music as loud as it would go. To this day, I don't remember getting that ticket. I hid bottles in my closet and started drinking when I got home from work until I passed out. I couldn't feel a thing. I woke up in the afternoons and went downstairs to watch the kids, but I couldn't get myself out of the fog to be present with them. I put on movies for them, mostly.

The only thing that made me feel anything at all was when I held my baby brother. He wasn't really a baby by then; he was four years old, but he was still my baby brother. Always would be. He and I seemed to have a different bond than anyone else in the family. Maybe it was because I'd stayed up with him so many nights when we first brought him home… I don't know. He was my buddy, though. He was the only person who could make me smile, make me sad, make me feel anything. I got up in the afternoons for that, I guess. Then I went back to work, digging holes in a daze.

I didn't have any friends in North Carolina. I never had a chance to meet anybody. We moved, I got a job, I worked at night and slept during the day. Where was I supposed to meet anyone? I had no hobbies, no events to attend, nothing to do, and nobody to do anything with. I drilled in Raleigh one weekend per month for the Navy, and there were some people there, but nobody I cared to know out of uniform. I found a gym in town, so I started working out, but it was at 4 am, so nobody else was there. I created a routine that included work, gym, sleep, repeat, but it was only marginally better than the work, sleep, repeat routine.

When I did try to be present at home on the weekends, I could never do anything right. I was always in trouble with Mom for something - always. She decided that the $ 300-per-month rent I was paying her didn't cover meals, so I had to start buying my own food. I only kept a little bit at a time and made sure I barely took up any room in the fridge, but she said I was hogging the entire fridge, so I started buying more shelf-stable stuff. I kept that stuff in the pantry, but, by golly, I took up too much room in there, too. I labeled my food clearly, and she'd feed it to the kids or eat it herself because it was all they had since nobody had watched the kids long enough for her to go grocery shopping. That was, therefore, also my fault. I couldn't win.

I felt like I didn't even know who I was anymore, not like I'd ever actually known in the first place. I felt like I was losing myself, but I didn't have the motivation to get myself back. I was fading away, but I didn't care. I wanted to fade away completely. Wouldn't that just be easier? I got to the point where I didn't want to save myself. I didn't want anyone else to save me, either. I was being slowly erased, and I couldn't wait until I could just be gone completely.

Jack was becoming my best friend. Jim and Johnnie, too. I drank when I was home, then I took some with me to drink at work and in the car. At 3-4 am, when I was driving home from work, there was no one else on the road. The only person I could hurt was myself. But, somehow, I always made it home safely, unfortunately. I always pulled into the driveway, put my car in park, and failed to remember the entire drive home. Did I imagine it? Maybe I did finally die. No, I made it home again. Didn't I? I did... Dammit.

***

2019, age 22

I reported my rape just after the New Year; I confided in a Navy buddy, and he encouraged me to report it. I did, and I feel no different. I did an unrestricted report, so there will be an investigation and all that, but I really don't expect it to go anywhere. Male abusers tend to get away with things. I don't see why my case would be any different. Anyway, back to the bottle...

When I was in high school, I used to pray that God would make my suicide attempts successful. He never did. I guess prayer doesn't really work after all. If you want something done right, you really do just have to do it yourself. Thanks for nothing, God.

***

Around August of 2019, I got tired of the fog. I got tired of not remembering anything, not being able to hear people when they spoke, and not being able to feel. I poured all my bottles down the bathroom sink. I knew I needed to stop, and I also knew I wouldn't stop if the bottles were still there. I didn't want to be an alcoholic. I didn't want to be someone who couldn't cope without alcohol. I didn't want to be dependent on it. I didn't want to be addicted to it. I wanted to stop, or at least I tried to convince myself of that. I don't think I actually wanted to stop numbing myself to the pain, but numbing the pain was numbing everything else, too. I wanted to feel again, I wanted to laugh again.

Throughout that year, I had gotten with whatever guy wanted me. I didn't care. I figured I'd already been raped; what's the worst that could happen? There really wasn't anything worse than that, right? Fuck it.

I got tired of that, too. Once I stopped drinking and a little bit of clarity entered my brain, I cut off the guy I'd been seeing. I didn't want to do that anymore. I felt gross. I felt like I didn't have control of anything anymore. I wanted to take back control, and that needed to start with my body. What happened to me in November was out of my control, but that didn't mean I couldn't be in control moving forward. I wanted to figure things out so badly; I just didn't know where to start.

In hindsight, where I definitely should not have started was with one of my instructors from A-school. He messaged me on Instagram, and we got to talking. He knew the guy who'd raped me since that guy had also gone to my A-school, so I figured he was a good person to talk to about it. I didn't want to talk about it, but people kept telling me to, and that talking would help. I told him about it, and he said he was sorry it happened, but that it was about time I just got over it.

He was about to be stationed in Virginia - only a few hours away from me. We talked for several months until he moved, then I went up to Virginia to see him. After that, I drove to Virginia almost every weekend for another couple of months to stay with him. He did a lot of things I didn't love, but I tried so hard to make it work; it was a real relationship, wasn't it? Shouldn't I be trying to make it work?

Any time I brought up my assault, he said he didn't feel like talking about it, or that I should just get over it, or that enough time had passed that I should be able to move on. I figured he was right - it'd been over a year; that was enough time to get over a rape, right? He didn't want to call me his girlfriend, either. He reprimanded me when I referred to him as my boyfriend, but we'd been "together" for four or five months, so I thought we were dating. Maybe that was my mistake.

In the mornings when I would stay at his house in Virginia, he didn't like that I woke up with messy hair and a tired-looking face. He told me he'd prefer if I got up, washed my face, brushed my hair, and got back in bed so he wouldn't have to be disgusted by me every morning. He said it was the least I could do. I profusely apologized, and every morning, I got out of bed and fixed myself up before he could wake up and see me looking like I'd just been sleeping. I felt so ashamed that I'd let him down or upset him; I really should have been a better girlfriend. Well, not girlfriend, but... whatever I was.

In February of 2020, I had one-month orders to Mississippi, and he didn't like that. He said I didn't value our relationship because I didn't go to visit him for a month. He was literally in the Navy also - that's how we met - so I figured he'd understand that I had to go on orders out of state and wouldn't be able to see him for a bit. He started ignoring my calls and texts, and when he did respond, it was always something backhanded or rude. Several girls I was on orders with begged me to break things off with him; they overheard our phone calls and read his messages, and told me he was toxic. I felt like if I broke up with him, I'd be failing. Mom always said I was a failure, and this is yet another thing I seemed to be failing at.

Thankfully, I had a good group of girls with me in Mississippi who were right about him. They explained that you often can't see your relationship for what it is in the same way someone on the outside can. I felt weird breaking up over text, but it was impossible to reach him by phone. He refused to call me or answer my calls. I finally got him on the phone when I got home, and I ended things as nicely as I could, and he basically said "okay" and hung up. Afterward, I wished I'd been a whole lot less nice. I swore off guys at that point. I had nothing good to say about any of the guys I'd been with, so I came to the conclusion that I didn't need one. The pursuit seemed pretty worthless and, quite honestly, a waste of my time. I decided to focus on myself for once. Crazy concept, I know, but I'd never done that before.

In March of 2020, I had another set of orders to Mississippi, but they got canceled due to COVID. I had another set of orders scheduled for April, but they got canned, too. I was pretty pissed, honestly. I had thrown myself into work and the military, and COVID was throwing a wrench in my plans.

On April 1st, I was at work when I got a text saying all orders were canceled for the foreseeable future until COVID was over. I remember I was operating a front-end loader that day, and I had posted a story on Instagram - something about being an "essential employee" while everyone else worked from home due to the pandemic. A mechanic from the shop replied to my story, and we started chatting about COVID and how we couldn't really do anything but still got labeled "essential employees" and still had to be at work. No parts were being shipped from overseas, so the mechanics couldn't really work, and I was working in the warehouse sorting parts most days, so that also meant I didn't have any parts to sort.

The mechanic came over from his shop to the warehouse from time to time to get parts for the few things he could still work on, and we got to talking. He started coming over to the warehouse more often with some excuse that he was looking for something, had to make a hose, had to locate a part... Whenever I was running equipment, I'd take it to his shop and tell him I heard a weird noise or that some sort of fluid needed to be refilled or that I thought something might have broken. He always dropped whatever he was doing to come "help" me.

We started hanging out after work every Thursday. By then, I had left the temp agency and got hired by the construction company, so I was working four 10-hour shifts and only worked Monday through Thursday. We went to Bojangles the first time, and Don Betos for tacos after that. We got the same order every time - three tacos each, al pastor, cilantro and lime. We couldn't dine in since everything was closed due to COVID, so we ate in his truck.

Eventually, we started taking the tacos back to his house. I'd stay at his house till super late at night, and then go home. Somehow I convinced Mom that I'd made friends at work and that we were all going to one of their houses to have a campfire. All the time. We had a lot of "campfires." There were some nights I didn't get home till 4 am - the campfire went late, and we were having too much fun.

I know a lot of people say they fooled their parents, but in reality, the parents knew the whole time. In my case, I actually did fool them. Mom was so convinced I would never be so "sinful" that I would sleep overnight at a house with a man while I wasn't married. She was so convinced that I still embodied all her religious beliefs that she never suspected a thing. She wasn't thrilled that I was with males and also, presumably, non-Christian friends, but I told her there were a few girls and also a few Christians. Dad said that was actually a good thing - I could witness to the non-Christians. Therefore, the campfires were a good idea; they were a mission field.

If I haven't made it clear by now - there were no other friends and no campfires. Actually, we did have a campfire once, and a few of his friends were there, but that was only once. The rest of the time it was the two of us watching Jim Carrey movies, Adam Sandler movies, or *Too Hot To Handle*. I didn't actually stay the whole night at his house for several months. The first time I did, I played the classic "I'm staying at my friend's house" move. It wasn't entirely a lie - I was staying the weekend at my girlfriend's house to celebrate my birthday, but I stayed the first night at his house, then we both stayed the weekend at my friend's house, along with a bunch of his friends. A half-truth, if you will.

Mark was perfect. Still is. The first time we hung out together outside of work - at Bojangles - somehow, I knew I was going to marry him. He was listening to Tyler Childers in his truck, and that was my favorite artist at the time. He was like a breath of fresh air after so much fog. He was clarity instead of confusion. He was so easy to talk to. He wasn't trying to show off or be a know-it-all like every other man I'd ever met. He actually listened when I spoke. He was real. He was kind. He was "the one," and I knew it.

***

2020, age 23

I moved out for good today. I took a shower in the bathroom I share with my sisters. After I took my entire shower and was getting out of the tub, I noticed a camera on the counter that was on and recording, facing the tub straight on. I realized immediately it had just recorded me undressing, taking my entire shower, and getting out of the shower naked. I unplugged it and turned it upside down, got dressed as fast as I could, walked out of the bathroom, threw it down the stairs, and was screaming my head off as I packed a quick overnight bag.

I ran downstairs and was yelling at Mom that she had just recorded me taking a shower. I asked why there was even a camera in the bathroom at all, let alone facing the bathtub, and she said it was so she could supervise T taking a bath while Mom was downstairs. I was still so mad and told her that it didn't even make sense, because I'm not sure why you need to supervise a 12-year-old taking a bath, let alone put a camera in the bathroom to record her. I asked Mom where the video went, and she said it was on both her and Dad's phones. I told her to delete all the footage because they both now have nude videos of not only an adult, but also a minor, on their phones. And I said I was going to call the police. She was yelling at me and chasing me as I ran out of the house, begging me not to call the police. I got in my car and drove straight to Mark's house.

While I was driving, Dad called me over and over, and I just kept ignoring his phone calls, but I did finally answer. He was begging me not to call the police, said they would delete all the footage, and he said Mom didn't mean to leave the camera in the bathroom after T was done with her bath; she just forgot. I told him the camera had no business being in the bathroom anyway, but he insisted it was imperative so they could supervise T taking a bath. I said someone could have just been physically in the bathroom with her if she really needed to be supervised, but he said Mom is so busy she had to use the camera while she was downstairs with the other kids. He told me that if I called the police, all the kids would be taken into foster care, and I might never see them again.

I'm pretty sure that's true, and I'm really scared that Mom might do something to the other kids or me if I do call anyone. I really want to report them because I feel like that has to be some sort of crime, but I know it's safer for the kids if I just let it go and leave things how they are. Mark said he really wants to call the police, but I begged him not to because I know it would destroy my family, and I can't do that. Mom would destroy me somehow, I just know it.

***

I called Mark on the way to his house and told him everything. He had met my parents once, and it was like he immediately knew everything about them. He wasn't fooled at all. He saw things in five minutes that had taken me years, if not decades, to see. Through the phone, I could tell he was pissed, but he spoke very gently, calming me down so I could drive to his house safely. I never stayed another night at Mom's house; I went back with Mark to grab some things, but I refused to be there without him accompanying me. I just felt safer with him, like everything would be fine as long as he was with me.

That all happened in July, and I left for orders in California in August, so I really only lived with Mark for a few weeks before leaving. All the rest of my stuff was still at Mom's house; she said I could leave it there until I got back from orders since they didn't really need the room for anyone else. I was in California for two months, then ended up flying straight to Mississippi in October for another set of orders. I was scheduled to return home in February, 2021.

Once I found out I was going to be gone another four-ish months, I checked with Mom to make sure it was still okay for my stuff to be at the house. She again confirmed that she didn't need the room and that my stuff would remain untouched so I could pack it up when I got back. I knew I was going to be living with Mark, and I made Mom and Dad well aware of that, too. They weren't pleased since it's against God's Will for me to live with a man when we're not married. Oh, they also said we were "unequally yoked" since I was a Christian and Mark was not. They also said he was sinful because he had tattoos. Dad told me he wanted me to be happy, but that he was either going to pray that I would meet someone else who was a Christian, or pray that Mark would confess his sins and give his life to Christ.

The entire time I was in California, I was convinced Mark was going to leave me. Out of sight, out of mind, I figured. I didn't have any friends from my childhood - nobody stuck around for very long, let alone a boyfriend. I just knew he was going to realize sooner or later that I was too much. I had too much baggage; my family was crazy religious; I was going to be gone for several more months plus another year on my upcoming deployment... I was just waiting for the other shoe to drop, basically. It was all too good to be true. I wasn't the girl who got the perfect boyfriend. I didn't deserve how he treated me. And yet, ever since April 1st, when he replied to my Instagram story, not a single day had passed without him contacting me. We called as much as possible, and when we couldn't call, we texted. We dealt with the time difference and figured out the best times to talk. We made it work, but it was like we didn't even have to try very hard. It was so natural and easy. But I was still so scared it wouldn't last.

In October, Mark came down to Mississippi to visit me. He got a new position at the construction company, but had a few weeks off in between quitting his old one and starting the new one, so he was able to stay with me for several weeks. The day after he arrived, he proposed! I figured we were going to get married eventually - I knew he was the one - but I thought he would propose when I got home in February. I obviously said YES, and we made quick work of calling all his friends. His oldest friend joked that he should get ordained online and marry us, and we all laughed. We made some other calls and also FaceTimed my soon-to-be in-laws. They knew about the ring and proposal, of course, but they were so happy and supportive. We discussed wedding plans with them, figuring we'd wait until after I returned from my upcoming deployment to set a date. I believe it was Mark's dad who basically said, "Why wait?" Good point...

We called his friend back and said, "Soooo... would you actually get ordained online and marry us?" He thought we were joking, of course. We weren't. We made plans for him and two other friends to fly down to Mississippi, I invited two of my girl friends who were already in Mississippi on orders, and we got married fifteen days later on the beach at sunset. We all wore blue jeans, boots, and flannel shirts, and we headed to Texas Roadhouse afterward to celebrate. We all got drunk, walked back to our hotel, and passed out. Best wedding ever.

Mark had to go back to North Carolina not long after our impromptu wedding, but he surprised me by flying back down for Thanksgiving. I had bought microwavable mashed potatoes, mac n' cheese, stuffing, ham, and rolls, and I was going to put together a little hotel room meal for myself. I talked to him on the phone a day or two before Thanksgiving, and we were just chatting when someone knocked on my hotel room door. I was annoyed because I just wanted to chill and talk to Mark that evening, so I irritably said, "Hold on, someone's at the door." You guessed it - Mark was at the door. I'm pretty sure I started crying immediately, still holding the phone to my ear. Best Thanksgiving ever.

While he was there, we went to the dollar store and got a cheap Christmas tree and some decorations, and we made my hotel room look as festive as possible. He could only stay for the weekend, but he made plans to come back for Christmas. We made a rule that we would only get each other three gifts, but then I found something else, so it was four each; then he found something else, so we changed it to five each... We ended up with an obscene amount of gifts for two people. When he came back, we watched *Christmas Vacation*, opened gifts, went to dinner, and just enjoyed being together. Best Christmas ever. He was able to stay until after New Year's - best... Well, you get it.

In January, I only had a few weeks left until I flew home, but I guess Mom couldn't wait that long. She asked if she could pack up all my stuff in my room because she suddenly decided she did need the room. I specifically asked her not to - I said she could put all my stuff in the walk-in closet if she needed to use the room, but I said that I wanted to pack up my own things. She said okay. Then, about a week later, she showed up at Mark's house with loads of boxes and bins. She had gone through all my stuff, thrown it in boxes, and dropped it off at Mark's with no warning.

Mark obviously told me about it, so I called Mom and asked what was going on. She said she just couldn't wait any longer, and my stuff had to go. She also said she had another load of things that Dad was going to bring over, so I had to coordinate a time with Mark when Dad could come by. The entire living room was full of boxes; I didn't have that much stuff, so I was sure it couldn't all have come from my room. Sure enough, Mom had been going through other stuff at the house, and she brought anything she didn't want to Mark's. I only had six weeks between getting home from Mississippi and leaving for deployment, so I already knew those six weeks would be spent going through all those boxes and throwing most of them away.

Oh, and she also told me she had been charging me $200 per month as a "storage fee" since I had left my belongings in her home; she just forgot to tell me. Since I'd been gone for six months, I owed her $1200. Great. Whatever. She had always come up with more and more things I owed her money for. She liked charging us for anything she could think of. Rent, meal assistance since we ate her food, utilities since we used her washer and dryer, storage fees, late fees, etc.

I also got a call from an attorney saying the trial for my sexual assault case had been scheduled for the week I got back. I would literally leave Mississippi on Friday, finally be home after six months of being away, and leave again on Sunday to be in Pensacola,

Florida, for court. I had previously been told that I would be consulted before a trial was scheduled to ensure I was available. Well, nobody consulted me; I was simply told a date and location. Mark booked his own flights immediately so he could come to Florida with me. It had been over two years since the assault, and I just wanted to get the entire thing behind me, so I didn't argue. I'd go home for a day and fly right back out again if that's what I had to do.

Key Characteristic #7

LIMITED CONTACT WITH THE OUTSIDE WORLD

Isolation followed me like a shadow even when I thought I had escaped it. My mother's voice and rules were no longer physically surrounding me, but they still shaped the strict boundaries of my world. I was in my 20s, married, and supposed to be building a life of my own. Yet every step away from her felt like stepping into enemy territory. I married someone who did not subscribe to her faith, and I was met with immediate judgment. They said I was rebelling, turning away from God, following a path of sin, being led astray by a non-believer. I was "unequally yoked." To my mother, love only counted if it was approved, controlled, and sanctified under her definition of obedience. So, even in marriage, I carried a guilt that didn't belong to me. My husband became my only confidant; he was the only person who actually cared to know what I was going through. I shared my trauma with him, but kept it from anyone else because secrecy had been bred into me.

Deployment came, and I tried to convince myself it would be a sort of freedom, not from my husband, but from everything else. Distance, oceans, time zones – I thought all of it would finally loosen my mother's hold on me. But isolation has a way of finding you, even in the desert. I was surrounded by people and yet felt completely alone. The unresolved pain, guilt, shame, and quiet war inside me finally collided. I unraveled in ways I didn't understand; sleepless nights, waves of panic, and the sense that I was disappearing into myself consumed me.

It wasn't just the trauma of the sexual assault that broke me; it was the years of conditioning that told me I had no right to feel broken. I had been taught to endure, to pray harder, to never need help. So, I feared reaching out. I resisted help because somewhere inside, I still believed that suffering in silence was holy, and asking for help was weakness. I recognize now that deployment was not my breaking point – it was my awakening. The isolation I'd been stuck in my whole life had followed me across continents until there was nowhere left to run from it. My mind finally began to fracture under the weight of everything I'd been made to carry alone. And in that breaking, something in me finally whispered the truth: this is not what love was meant to feel like.

Her isolation was never just about keeping me apart from the world; it was about keeping the world out of me. She didn't have to lock doors or take my phone to ensure obedience. She had already built a system in which trust beyond her was betrayal, every outside influence was an evil threat, and love was safe only if it came from her. Even miles away, even when wearing a uniform that bore a new name, I was still living in her small, constructed world. That was the genius of her control; she didn't need to be present to keep me confined. I carried her voice inside me, her fears disguised as faith, and her rules disguised as righteousness. I had mistaken isolation for safety for so long that connection felt dangerous.

It would take me years to understand that the loneliness I felt wasn't proof of my failure, but proof of her design. I learned that the final act of rebellion wasn't running away, surviving deployment, or standing up to her. It was learning that I was allowed to be seen and heard, and that I could let the world in and still be whole.

12

Verdict

2021-2022 | AGE 24-25

***

2021, age 24

COVID has caused a million delays with the court process, plus someone lost the recording and half the transcript from my NCIS interview. Typical. Supposedly, I have a victim advocate assigned to me, but I have no idea who it is. Mark said he'd come to court with me, so we flew to Florida for an entire week just to find out one of the jurors' wives had COVID, so the whole thing got rescheduled for a month later. Now I'm sitting in my hotel room waiting for my turn to take the stand; I don't want to do it. I feel like I should want to; a lot of women don't get the opportunity to tell their story and be heard, but that's the thing – I don't think I'm going to be heard. He's a man. Men get away with things. But I'm here; I'm testifying today; I'm not lying, so I don't know why I'm so nervous. He'll be there, obviously, and I don't want to see him. Mark couldn't get another week off work, so I'm down here alone; I just want to go home.

***

I returned home from Mississippi and immediately left again for Florida, but this time, Mark came with me. We were there for a week; the first few days were jury selection, and my testimony would likely be on Wednesday or Thursday at the latest. On Tuesday, I was notified that a juror's wife had COVID, so the entire trial was postponed one month. I was so upset - I would get to go home for a few more weeks but have this on my mind the entire time; then I'd have another full week in Florida, two weeks at home, then deploy for a year. I just wanted to spend every spare second with Mark, but I had to plan for another trip to Florida, and he didn't have enough leave to come with me a second time. I'd be on my own.

We decided to make the most of the rest of the week - our flights weren't until the weekend, so we figured we may as well have some fun. We explored different bars, restaurants, and stores. We tried to make it feel as much like a vacation as possible.

The day we flew home, Mom had scheduled a family photo shoot at a fire station. We got off the airplane, drove home to change clothes, and met everyone at the fire station for photos. That was my first time meeting my niece in person; she had been born while I was in Mississippi, and I'd only seen pictures and videos. Mom said I wasn't allowed to hold her without a mask on - Mom was really obsessed with masks during COVID. I wasn't sure why she was making the rules about who held the baby when it was my sister's kid, but I wasn't about to start any arguments.

The family photos were so cringy and irritating. Mom wanted everyone spaced six feet apart, and not ironically, either. She truly believed that each family should not touch anyone else since we lived in separate homes, and especially since Mark and I had just been on a plane. Everyone had to stand with their spouse or kid until it was their turn to be put in place for photos. Also, everyone had to wear a mask.

We had received a two-page document prior to the photo shoot with detailed instructions for each couple or sibling. We were to park and remain in our vehicles until we received a text from Mom to enter the building. She texted us each a few minutes apart so we wouldn't risk walking in with someone else and being contaminated. Once we entered, we were pointed to specific spots where we would stand with our spouse or kid and wait. Mark and I were first, so we took off our masks, did our couple photos, put our masks back on, and went back to our standing spot. Each of my siblings did their individual or couple photos, then we did the group photos. Each sibling or couple was led to a spot six feet away from anyone else in any direction. We were all staggered, and we kept our masks on for the photos. I complained, and Mom allowed us to do one group photo without masks, but we had to put them right back on. I was so ready to leave as soon as we'd started. Welcome to family photos with my family, Mark.

After the photos, Mom told everyone to leave the building, again, one at a time, so we wouldn't run into anyone else on the way out. We all got in our cars, and I texted my sister. She said we could come over to her house to properly meet my niece, so we did that the next day, I believe. We didn't tell Mom - I'm sure she wouldn't have approved, especially since my sister didn't make me wear a mask while I held the baby. I decided pretty quickly I'd give my life for that kid.

I flew back to Mississippi for the trial a few weeks later, by myself. To this day, I've never told my parents about the assault, the trial, or any part of that entire experience. Their opinion of sexual assault victims is so convoluted and toxic, and I knew they would blame me for what happened.

"Why were you drinking?"

"Why were you hanging out with *boys*?"

"What were you wearing?"

"I told you so..."

I navigated the emotional aftermath alone; I did my interview alone; I talked to lawyers alone; I signed forms alone... The only real support I had was after Mark came into my life. Before him, I did all that shit by my damn self because there was nobody in my life that I could trust, that would believe me, that wouldn't judge me, and that would genuinely support me.

The first few days of trial consisted of jury selection, plus there were a series of motions presented, and I was testifying by mid-week. I started journaling in a Word document on the last day of court when I got back to my hotel after the verdict. I added more entries here and there throughout deployment; I wasn't consistent with it; I just added to it when I remembered or felt like writing. I've added all those entries to this book since they portray my thoughts and emotions in my own words, fresh and in the moment.

***

Excerpt from journal

March 12, 2021

My abuser was just found "not guilty" today and walked out of the courtroom as a free man. No consequences. No punishment. Nothing.

Somehow, even up until the very end, a small part of me was still so hopeful the jury would come through. There was still the smallest sliver of hope that I would hear the word "guilty" and that he would be held accountable.

I don't know what I thought I would feel. Maybe I would be relieved? Maybe I thought I would finally feel closure? I wanted justice to be served, and it wasn't. I wanted him to pay for his actions, and now he won't have to. He's a free man, accused of rape but found not guilty.

He was acquitted by a jury of eight men. MEN. No women. Nobody who might have actually understood sexual assault from my perspective. Men who haven't had to live their entire life constantly skeptical of strangers. They haven't had to fear while walking alone at night or getting gas by themselves. They're privileged. Because they are men.

How could they possibly have judged my case fairly? They were only looking at it from a man's perspective. They can't understand how scared I really was, or why I tried to deny what happened and delayed my report because I was trying to process the incident and act like nothing happened. Like everything was normal. I was trying not to draw attention to myself or act any different than usual while I struggled with what just happened to me.

I tried to forget it on my own, but I couldn't. I had to eventually accept that it happened, and I knew I had to report it. The defense made my delay in reporting look like I simply felt guilty about it – about him cheating on his girlfriend with me. They made it look like it was consensual, and then two weeks later, I just decided I wanted to make a big deal out of it. They made me look like a liar.

The defense attacked me so meticulously that when I walked out of the courtroom, I felt like I had been reduced to absolutely nothing. It felt like they tore my entire existence apart and threw the tiny pieces in a pile on the ground. I can't even describe how incredibly worthless I felt. As a person in general, but mostly as a female. I felt like I didn't even belong there, like a sore thumb. A woman trying to convince a roomful of men that I was telling the truth. That I was actually assaulted. That he was guilty of rape.

It's almost laughable, isn't it? They were never going to convict him. I feel like they all just went through the motions because they had to – because it was procedure. They knew all along my story would never win. He's a man, and I'm 'just' a woman.

I don't know how I'm supposed to process this. I've been dragged along for over two years waiting for closure from this case, and now it's over. Completely over. He's free, and I'm left to pick up the pieces of myself. He gets to live his carefree life, and I have to figure out how to go on with my life and put this behind me.

So many people have told me to be proud of what I did, that it's hard to get up on the stand and tell a room full of strangers every tiny detail about the worst night of my life. I'm told I was extremely brave to face my abuser and tell him what he did to me. I'm told I should be grateful to have "had my day in court" and that many women don't get this opportunity.

I understand, and I know these people are all trying their best to help me through the aftermath of this case. But as of right now, as of today, I don't feel very thankful that I 'got' to testify in court. I don't feel proud, I feel humiliated. I feel dehumanized and completely worthless. There is nothing else I could have said that would have changed the verdict, so why was I even there? Why did I even report in the first place? All it did was constantly remind me over the past several years that I still had an open case, and I was continuously asked to recall details that I so desperately wanted to forget. I was miserable for years while he was just living his life.

During the first six months after it happened, I was drinking myself into a hole. I never remembered driving to and from work, I couldn't remember conversations, and I even woke up one morning with a speeding ticket in my hand and no recollection of getting it or even being pulled over. I couldn't see the point in being sober because all my memories would just come flooding back, so I made sure I just wasn't sober. It seemed like a logical plan to me – an easy fix!

Over time I started wishing I could enjoy things again. Family time, coworkers, my job, friends, movies, music... everything just sort of seemed to 'exist' and I was indifferent to it all. About 9 months after the assault, I decided I needed to stop drinking. I poured all my alcohol down my bathroom sink and successfully remained sober for about six months or so. During that time, I poured myself into anything that would take my mind off the case. I took a month-long EMT course for no apparent reason. I poured myself into work and the military, spent a lot of time on orders, and just tried to generally distract myself.

Then I met Mark. We worked together, started out as friends, and he quickly became my best friend. I thank God every day for giving me Mark, and I will forever feel that I don't deserve him. Once I was with him, I didn't feel like I needed to specifically distract myself because I just felt safe with him, like I was finally home. I felt like I belonged, and he never made me wonder if I was enough. I guess I just had everything I needed, and I didn't have to worry about the case every day.

Once I found out we were officially going to trial, and I would actually be testifying, I was anxious. I wanted it to be over with, but I also wanted to know he would have to pay for his actions. I went through all the preparations, I practiced answering questions and being cross-examined, and I was as prepared as I could be. When the day came, I completely broke down in tears. I sat there in my dress blues trying to act professional, but I couldn't stop crying for the entire two hours I was on the stand being questioned. I relived every single detail over and over. I told complete strangers what happened that night, hoping and praying they'd believe me. The defense made their argument, accusing me of lying about every single individual detail. Tearing me apart in front of the entire courtroom, denying that anything traumatic ever happened to me that night. And they won. He was found not guilty, and they all went home. It was over.

What the heck would be my motivation to lie about this? I wasn't getting any money; there was no benefit for me other than closure and justice being served. I had nothing to gain from lying. Why would I go through all the trouble to make up a horrible story, stand by it for over two years, agree to testify in court, fly to another state, and tell that same horrible story to a bunch of male strangers?! I would have much rather stayed home and spent time with my husband. In no way did I actually want to be in court. And yet, a group of eight men still decided that my story was just a story, and that he was not guilty of sexual assault.

I can tell you this – if anything ever happens to me again, I would never in a million years report it.

***

After court, I went back to my hotel room. I had an online training session that evening for deployment, so my flight was one of the last out that night. I was so distracted during the training that I didn't actually retain a single thing. Packed up, I headed out to my rental car. Flat tire. Of course. I checked the trunk - no spare. I called the rental company - no answer. The rental pamphlet mentioned AAA, so I called them, too. They could come out in about three hours. I didn't have that kind of time. I finally got someone from the rental company on the phone, and they said I could just leave the car at the hotel, and they would take care of it. Cool. Just had to get a cab, then.

I had to download the Uber app, and three drivers in a row accepted my ride, got within two minutes of me, and canceled. I downloaded Lyft. Same thing. I couldn't get a driver to actually show up before canceling the ride. I googled local taxi companies and called some of them. They could come get me in an hour. At that point, even if I left the hotel right that second, I'd still miss my flight. While still trying to get an Uber or Lyft to accept my ride and actually show up, I was also calling the military travel booking line to book a different flight. They put me on hold.

By the time my flight was boarding, an Uber driver had finally picked me up. There was so much traffic, and he was in no rush, so the drive took twice as long as it probably should have. Meanwhile, I was still on hold with the travel line. I'd been texting Mark that whole time, tears streaming down my face ever since noticing the flat tire until arriving at the airport. I hadn't realized I'd been crying until I was in the cab. I'd gotten a "not guilty" verdict, and then all hell had broken loose. I had nothing left in me - no sense of urgency, no motivation. I wanted to give up, curl up at the airport, and just cry for hours. But I also wanted Mark. I wanted to go home. I just had to get myself home, then I could cry.

The travel line got me on the absolute last flight out of Pensacola that night, and I arrived home well into the early morning hours. Mark had picked me up at the airport, driven me home, and then just held me while I cried myself to sleep. I felt drained. I felt exhausted. I felt so, so empty.

The next week, we used my Hilton points from my stays at hotels in California and Mississippi to book a room in downtown Nashville, Tennessee. We drove out and spent a week sightseeing, touring the Jack Daniels distillery, trying different bars and restaurants, and just having fun together. Just the two of us. It was a much-needed distraction, plus a good memory to take with me when I left.

In the week before deployment, I was attempting to say all my goodbyes. I wanted to see all the kids before I left, but Mom wouldn't let me come to the house with Mark unless I scheduled a time. I had used all my leave for the few weeks I was home so I could spend as much time with Mark as possible, so I wasn't working and had all the time in the world to come see the kids. She was being so difficult to work with, though, and I knew if I just "showed up" with Mark, she wouldn't let me in since I hadn't made an appointment. I could go by myself, but I didn't want to do that.

A few days before I left, I still hadn't seen the kids. Mom gave me a 30-minute window to say goodbye. She said she had appointments that morning and errands to run that afternoon, so I had to make it quick. I showed up with Mark, which she didn't like, and she made us wear masks inside the house. There was nowhere to sit since all the couches and chairs in the living room were covered with laundry, and there were pathways carved through the shit that filled the entire house. Nothing had changed. I shoved some laundry to the side to make room for Mark and me to sit; I'd been doing that my whole life. Mom said I wasn't allowed to hug the kids due to COVID. I said I was about to be gone for an entire year and that I'd really like to hug them, but she refused to let me. She left the room for a minute, and I gave the kids bear hugs, making sure to let go before she got back.

April 4th, 2021, Easter Sunday, I hopped on a plane and headed back to Mississippi. We had several months of pre-deployment training and things before we flew overseas. Since it was still mid-COVID, I had to quarantine in my hotel room for two weeks as soon as I arrived. I had all the time in the world to sit by myself, alone with nothing but my wandering thoughts and emotions to keep me company.

13

Deployment Begins

2021 | AGE 24

***

Excerpt from journal
April 12, 2021

It's been a month. One whole month since that day at trial. The day when I felt like the most worthless person in the world. I went home to my husband and just hugged him – that's all I wanted to do. I felt safe there, in his arms, like nobody could touch me and nothing could hurt me. I wanted to stay there forever. He told me I wasn't worthless, that he loved me, and that everything was in the past. I think he understood that even though the case was over, it was far from over in my mind, but he constantly made sure I knew he would help me for as long as it took to get past it. I now have to figure out how to live with the fact that I lost, and the other guy won – he walked away a free man. That part still hurts.

I remember very clearly sitting there in the courtroom, waiting anxiously to hear the verdict. The president of the jury stood up and read from his paper, and it was as if the words "not guilty" were in italics, all caps, and underlined all at once in size 60 font. They seemed to echo in my head, and I don't remember hearing a single word that was said after that. My entire story seemed to crumble in front of me; the faint hope that I might actually get to see justice served was obliterated. It was over. To this day, I cannot think about that moment that seemed to last forever without breaking down in tears. Everything inside me just seemed to break, and I felt like just a shell of a person; there was nothing left to fight for, so my heart just gave up. It was over.

I told my husband that I had wanted it all to just be over for so long, and now that it actually was over, I instead just wanted it all to be gone. Gone from my mind, erased from my memory; I wanted someone to snap their fingers and wipe the whole thing from my brain.

I no longer have the burden of the case, the trial, and testifying. Those chains were released but replaced with seemingly stronger chains, dragging me ever downward into a feeling of worthlessness and depression. Further than the darkest place I have ever been.

My lawyer was amazing. It was her job to take my case, but I nearly forgot that based on how she acted and how she treated me. She was a friend, a confidant, and the greatest comfort to me during that time. She told me I was not alone in feeling like women have no say and that we are lesser than men.

If I were to make a list of the women I look up to and respect, she would be first on that list. She made me feel human and told me my voice mattered. That I mattered. She has no obligation to keep in contact with me now that my case is over, but she does anyway. She has checked in on me periodically, making sure I'm alright. She gave me books to read, some fun and fictional, others more similar to my situation. Accounts of other survivors. I tried to read one and got through just a handful of pages before I had to stop. Everything the woman was saying was just too familiar; it was like I was reliving all the feelings and emotions I thought I had gotten past. I'll finish reading it someday, just not right now.

About a week ago, I left home for deployment. I've buried myself in fitness, walking or running 8-10 miles every day. I've started and finished reading two books already. I listen to music and podcasts and watch sermons online. I'm afraid that if I don't stay busy, my mind will take me back to a month ago, or even worse, that awful night several years ago. I don't want to fall into a pit of depression again. I don't want to drown myself in alcohol again. I don't want any of the feelings of guilt or loneliness or mental exhaustion to resurface. I want to be normal again; I just want to feel whole.

Someday, I hope I can feel grateful for the opportunity to tell my story. I hope I can feel proud to have had my day in court. Right now, I just can't bring myself to see it that way. I still feel like I failed. I wish the world were different, and women's voices mattered. I wish we weren't looked at as inferior to men. As long as I'm wishing for stuff, I wish men respected women more! I know some things never change, but I truly hope this does. I want to have a family someday, but I dread the thought of bringing a daughter into this world as it is today. Society is not kind to women; that's just a fact. It's a man's world, and it always has been. Women are to be seen and not heard, and when we are heard, we are not believed. It's a messed-up system, but I don't know how to fix it.

***

I spent the next four months going through the motions, putting on my uniform and showing up to work with a smile. I tried so hard to just be normal. I tried to make friends, but failed every time. I never wanted to hang out on evenings or weekends. I went to dinner with people a few times, but I started to notice I always sat in silence at the table, dissociating and staring off into space. I just wasn't good company. I stayed in my room and kept to myself outside of working hours.

I talked to Mark daily, but rarely called home to Mom or Dad. They didn't know about the sexual assault, the investigation, the trial, the verdict - and if I had my way, they would never know. They wouldn't care. Whenever we heard about a sexual assault, Mom always said it was probably the girl's fault because of what she was wearing, how much she had been drinking, or where she was walking. Mom said if a girl was walking alone in a parking garage at night and got assaulted, it was her own fault. I knew she would have the same opinion about my situation. I had been drinking, so I knew she'd say I'd asked for it. I wasn't wearing "immodest" clothing, though; Mom said girls who dress provocatively are just asking to be raped. Well, I was wearing jeans, boots, and a hoodie, so what was I asking for then?

I wanted to talk to the kids, especially my baby brother, but Mom wasn't too keen on that. She'd send pictures here and there, but I didn't get to talk to him on the phone very much. I felt like I was fading away again, and Mark was the only person keeping me grounded. But he wasn't there. When I was talking to him, I was fine. Then I hung up the phone and felt completely alone. I knew that was irrational, but I couldn't seem to control my own emotions. I was pretty good at gluing on a smile during the workday, doing my job and following orders, but the smile and facade came off as soon as my uniform came off. I cried all the time, then got mad at myself for crying. I was stronger than that, right? Maybe not.

***

Excerpt from journal
June 13, 2021

I never realized till about a year ago, but now I know I have anxiety and depression; however, I have no idea how to manage them. I always used to just bottle up everything I was feeling and never let anyone see any pain. Nobody knew what I was dealing with inside because I never let them know. Now that I have my husband, things are different. He is the most patient and caring person I have ever met, and he is always trying to make my life easier. Whenever I'm with him, it's like my anxiety goes away, I have nothing to be depressed about, and all my problems are solved. But when I'm on my own, I can't seem to handle things by myself. I don't know what to do. I've been deployed for nearly 3 months now, with about seven more to go, and thinking about that makes everything worse. I'm trying to go one day at a time, but then I think about just how many days are left without him, and it's daunting and overwhelming. I get off work every evening and hide in my room. I stay in my room all weekend with most of the lights off. I like it because it's calm and quiet, but then that calm and quiet allows my mind to wander.

Yesterday was June 12th, exactly 3 months after he was found not guilty. When I'm alone, that's all I can think about. I see his face in my head all the time, and I can still hear his voice. I was alone all day yesterday, and my husband was busy back home, so he didn't text much. I tried watching movies, I scrolled through social media, I checked every email account I have, and I even did some homework for next week just to keep myself busy. But any time I wasn't actively engaged in something, I found myself in tears. Tears because my brain brought back every detail of that day in court, tears because the one person who could make everything instantly better isn't available, tears because I know I need to learn to deal with stuff, but I just don't know how...

This weekend was mostly spent lying on the couch, wrapped in a blanket, staring off into space in a dark hotel room. I didn't feel like eat-

ing, but I was absolutely starving, and I barely drank anything at all. I left my room once to walk to the store - I bought ice cream, thinking maybe it would either cheer me up or drown my sorrows, but that plan fell through. I don't know how to make this better. I don't know how to get past everything that's constantly running through my head. I want nothing more than to look back on all this someday and see it as an experience that I stood up and walked away from with my head held high. I want to be able to do what my lawyer said - to be proud that I had my day in court and got the opportunity to tell my story. Right now, I don't see any of that happening any time soon. I can't even get through one day without depression and anxiety being the main characters in my day. I want to be normal.

***

We had a four-day weekend for the 4th of July, and Mark drove down to stay with me. I felt like I'd been resuscitated and I could actually breathe again. That was the last time I'd see him for another seven-ish months, so I spent every second of that weekend glued to his side. I didn't care to hang out with anyone else; I just wanted to be with Mark. When it came time for him to drive back home, I loaded up any extra stuff I'd accumulated over the previous months so I'd have as little as possible to carry overseas.

I tried my best to spend the next few weeks focused on nothing but the military. Work, class, training, packing, studying, nothing else. Oh, and I started a master's program online because I felt like I needed more things to fill my spare time with. I didn't want any extra time on my hands that might cause my mind to wander.

***

Excerpt from journal
August 6, 2021

More time has passed, but I don't feel like I'm getting any better at managing anxiety, depression, feelings of worthlessness and insignificance... I would love to just flip a switch and have everything be okay and just be normal. I guess that's wishful thinking, but I still have hope that someday I'll be okay. Or at least more okay than I am right now. I'm still deployed – over in the Middle East now – and still struggling. I still have several months left till I can go home, but I know that when I do, and I see Mark, I'll be a whole lot better. I feel like I can deal with anything when I'm with him, but I somehow can't do anything when I'm alone.

I started my master's program in May... partly because I have the opportunity to use tuition assistance, but also partly because I felt like it would be one more thing to add to my plate, keep me a little bit busier, and give me something to focus on and distract myself with. However, I sit down and focus and have all my homework done for the week before the week even starts, so then I have nothing to do for the next six days. So that was a great plan. Maybe once I get out of quarantine and get into the groove of my work schedule, I'll be able to fill my time more. I hate sitting around with nothing to do because my mind always wanders.

Lately, I've been wondering what I could've done differently. What if there was something else that I could've said in court that day that would've made a difference. What if I had been more confident or answered the questions better. Or, what if I just hadn't reported it. He walked away free anyway, so if I had simply never reported it, it would have had the same outcome either way. Free man. Not guilty. I guess I would have always wondered what might have happened, though. I probably would have kicked myself for not going through with it just on the chance that he would be convicted. Instead, I went through over two years of crap and recounting the story and phone calls and emails and three different lawyers and two weeks of court.

I've also wondered if I could have requested females on the jury. I don't know if that's even allowed, but it seems fair, right? My entire jury was men who have probably never experienced sexual harassment or assault in their entire lives. I would bet that if there had been a jury full of women, all of them could have told at least one story about how they had been harassed or assaulted. Guarantee it. It's just a thing; women are objectified by men and always will be. A guy whistling at you is harassment, and yet they just do it whenever they want. Unwanted touching, assuming consent, making you feel guilty for not giving them what they want, inappropriate jokes or comments – this stuff literally happens every single day to women, and we just have to deal with it. If I reported every time I got sexually harassed, I would have so many cases. And I would have lost every one of them. Why? Because I'm not a guy. I hate that the world is like that. I hate society. And I hate that I had an all-male jury.

***

Deployment days were three times as long as regular days, I was convinced. I had to quarantine again for another week as soon as we got to Kuwait. I was one of the few who hadn't gotten the COVID shot yet - we had to quarantine while all those who'd gotten the shot already were fine, apparently. We worked nights for the first month or so because the temperature was too high to work safely during the daytime. Our leadership didn't agree with that, though, so they quickly switched us from nights to days. It was pretty fucking hot, but Mark had mailed me about a gallon of sunscreen, so I was fine.

My in-laws mailed me a care package every single week, each box containing different snacks, activities, food, and necessities such as tuna and mac n' cheese. I looked forward to those boxes; I never expected them to do that, especially since they barely knew me at that point, but those boxes were the highlight of deployment. My mom sent me one box. It had a Bible, a few snacks, and some coloring pages from the kids. I put the pages on my wall and let the Bible gather dust on the bookshelf I'd built. Oh yeah, I built a bookshelf. It was pretty cool. I signed the back of it, so if anyone sees a bookshelf with my name on it in Kuwait, that's probably it.

Just like in Mississippi, I put on a game face during the workday and hibernated in my room every evening. We had Sundays off, and I usually didn't leave my room at all if I could help it. I talked to Mark every day, messaging or calling, and I looked forward to those moments. With the time difference, we figured out the best times to call that fit with both of our schedules. I'd never in my life met a person who gave a shit about me as much as he did. I'd never met someone who actually put effort into maintaining a relationship with me.

I had stopped fearing he would leave me, but that fear was replaced by the thought that he didn't miss me. That he liked having me gone. Irrational, I'm aware. But those chemical imbalances in the brain sure do a number on your thinking capabilities. As deployment wore on, I had started feeling like everything I was bottling up and pushing down inside of me was about to burst soon. I felt like an explosion was imminent, but I wouldn't be able to control it once it started. I felt like my grasp on my emotions was slipping. I'm not sure if I ever actually had a good grasp on my emotions to begin with, but whatever control I'd had was slipping away, and I didn't know how to get it back. I think I was rapidly approaching my breaking point. How does one prepare to reach their breaking point?

14

Excerpts

2021 | AGE 24

* * *

Excerpts from journal
October 5, 2021

Every time I sit down to write, I wish I could say I'm better and that everything is back to normal. I wish I could say my mental health is perfect and I'm doing better than ever. Maybe someday I'll be able to write that, just not today. Today I'm sitting in my room during working hours because I got a concussion three days ago and can't return to work yet. Three days of sitting by myself in a quiet room with no distractions, which is the perfect opportunity for my mind to dig up all the memories I keep trying to bury. I would be lying if I said I didn't think about it every day – that awful night, the court date, the verdict... It seems to permanently occupy a section of my thoughts, and nothing I do can get it to leave. I know it will always be a part of my past, but I keep being told to learn from it instead of dwelling on it. I'm trying. I really am trying.

I had a meeting with my senior enlisted leader yesterday regarding the concussion incident, and the verdict got brought up. I know he didn't mean to upset me, and I know he was trying to be understanding, but it's usually just something that I think about in my own head. I'm not used to hearing other people talk about it because I never tell anyone about it. My upper leadership had to know, of course, but I haven't been spoken to about it since that day at court. I guess I was hoping they all forgot. I started crying in the middle of the meeting. Why can't I just forget about it?

I've tried to read other women's stories and how they dealt with it, but in order to get to the part that would help me, I have to read the part about what happened to them. Most of them are just too similar to my own story, and I don't want to read them. I don't like reliving that night, and I don't like reliving those days in court. I still see his face so clearly in my head, I can hear his voice, I can hear the defense attorney's voice tearing me apart and calling me a liar, I can hear the jury member reading "not guilty" off his piece of paper, I can see the smirk he gave me when he realized he was free... I hate that I can't get those images and sounds out of my head. I wish our heads only had space for a certain number of memories, so I could just make new ones to replace the negative ones.

We are six months into deployment, with about four more to go... hopefully. I want nothing more than to be home. I only had two weeks with my husband and family between court and deployment. That's not enough time to deal with anything. I hope that when I'm home, everything will start to calm down in my head, and I can get into a routine and learn to enjoy life again. Right now, all I can think about is anniversary dates.

October 23 – Mark proposed last year, and we got engaged

November 7 – Our 1st wedding anniversary

November 23 – him. That stupid night.

I hate that I can't be with Mark for any of those things. The first two are happy anniversaries; things we can celebrate and be thankful for. I wish we could be together for our 1st anniversary, but I just keep telling myself to remember that there will be so many more, and we can make each celebration better than the last. But the last anniversary... I wish I were with Mark, but for different reasons. I don't want to be alone on that day. I know I think about it every day, but I know it'll be stuck in my head even more on that day, and I know Mark would be able to help me through it. He always knows what to say, and his hugs seem to fix anything. Next year, though. Next year I'll be home. Next year, it'll be another entire year of healing. Maybe by next year, I can write that I'm better. That I got past it. That it doesn't bother me anymore. Next year needs to get here faster.

***

October 7, 2021

Hate is a strong word. My mom always told us to use "strongly dislike," and we weren't allowed to use the word "hate" in the house. But right now, there are a few people that I hate. I don't strongly dislike them; I hate them. Thirteen people. All men.

Nine jurors.
Two defense attorneys.
One lying witness.
One rapist.

I hate them all.

I've hated the last one for years now, and for what I would say are very good reasons to hate a person. The others I hate almost the same amount, but for different reasons. For lying about what happened; for twisting the story; for making me feel worthless; for not listening to me;

for not believing me; and for letting my abuser walk away as a free man. I think those are some pretty good reasons. Maybe one day I'll lessen it to a "strongly dislike," but not today. Today it's hate. I've never actually hated a person before; I know, as kids, nearly everyone yells that they hate their parents or their siblings or a friend, but it's usually due to immaturity and not in seriousness. I never actually legitimately hated another human being before. Someone would've had to do something so unmistakably atrocious to me to cause me to hate them. That's exactly what someone did. And I will continue to hate him and his twelve accomplices for however long I choose.

***

October 16, 2021

We had a unit-wide mandatory training yesterday on Sexual Assault Prevention and Response (SAPR). I didn't think it would be an issue, but as soon as the training started, I found myself fighting back tears. Throughout the entire video portraying a young woman getting too drunk and being taken advantage of, the slides showing the exact process of what happens when you make a report – a process I know all too well – and the conversation afterward about reporting and preventing assaults. I fought back tears the whole time, and my head was throbbing by the end.

Some of the information they shared was incorrect, which I only knew since I'd just been through the whole process, and I wanted to let someone know that they shared misinformation. I pulled one of my chiefs aside – the one that I trust implicitly – and tried to explain to him that they simply gave wrong information and told him how the process actually works. I couldn't even make it through one sentence without getting choked up. Clearly, he noticed I was struggling, and he went back to a previous conversation we'd had and encouraged me yet again to seek out help. To go to therapy, or counseling, or a chaplain... to get treatment for my deteriorating mental health. He said that if I can't even make it through an annual training, I clearly have unresolved pain that needs to be healed. I know that's true, but I don't want to go to therapy. I really don't.

He asked if I would allow him to reach out to some people and get information on what resources are available for me, and I said yes. I made sure he knew I didn't want to be locked into anything yet or commit to weekly sessions, but I was willing to look at available options. He said he would get back to me.

Today, after work, he called me back to the office and we sat down along with a female chief. They explained the options available, or at least a few first steps I could take, and explained the importance of getting help. I was told again that therapy is not a bad thing; therapy can really help people heal from past trauma and find ways to cope with triggers and daily life without breaking down. I don't want to go to therapy. I don't want to tell a stranger my story and bring up all the horrid details that I tried so hard to bury and forget. But I'm constantly being reminded that you can't heal from mental and emotional trauma without talking about it. Apparently, talking is healing, which seems opposite to what I would have said. To me, talking is opening wounds that I worked so hard to cover. But I guess that's just it, I've covered them instead of healing them.

I know I need help. I know I can't keep living every single day in the mental state I'm in right now. But that means seeking help from a stranger who is paid to listen to people's problems. Do they really care? I don't know. Are they actually invested in my issues and genuinely seeking to help me heal? I have no idea. I don't trust easily, but I guess I'm going to have to learn to trust a stranger with the deepest personal stuff I have. The stuff I'd rather just bury deep inside and never have to see again. Unfortunately, I've been trying to bury it for years, and I haven't been successful thus far.

Who knows, maybe a therapist will be good. Maybe they'll actually have helpful things to say and good things I can work on to get past all this. But I can't stop worrying that it'll do the opposite of its purpose. Maybe it'll make things worse. Maybe by bringing all those memories back up I'll just keep spiraling down even further. What if I don't get better? What if it doesn't help?

Mark is supporting me 100%. I just wish he were here. I wish he could come to therapy sessions with me, sit next to me, hold my hand so I could know I'm okay... if he were just in the same room, or even just in my line of sight, I would be okay. He'd be there, and everything would be fine. He makes everything okay. But I know I can't just always lean on him all the time. I know I must learn how to cope with things on my own, without him. He is my comfort and my safe place, but I need to be able to survive on my own as well.

He said he's more than willing to go to therapy himself, for the purpose of learning ways he can help me at home. I thank God for him daily – he literally wants to see a therapist to learn how to help me heal. I feel like the luckiest human in the world to have him in my life. I just wish he could be with me on Monday. I'll have to see the chaplain by myself, start therapy for the first time by myself, talk about the most painful topics by myself... I would feel so much stronger if he were here.

Since meeting with the chiefs this afternoon, I haven't been able to focus on one thing for longer than half an hour without crying or at least fighting back tears. I'm so anxious and scared, and I'm dreading Monday. I don't know what to expect, I don't know who I'll be talking to, I don't know what questions they'll ask... I don't know anything, and I must do it all alone. I just want it all to be over. I want the memories to be gone and the trauma to disappear. I just want to feel whole again, like I'm worth something. Right now, I just feel like there's something wrong with me because now I'm going to see a therapist. Mental health doctors, therapy, treatment plan... I feel like people will think I'm not mentally stable, and I'll be judged. Mark said I went through something traumatic, so of course, I won't be perfectly fine. He said he'll go to sessions with me when I get back. I can't wait for that.

***

October 18, 2021

Chief took me to see the Chaplain today. I stayed up way too late last night, afraid to sleep because I knew that with the morning, there would come a conversation I didn't want to have. I got to talk to Mark for a while, but I promised him that I would at least lie in bed and try to sleep. I was so anxious and nervous about meeting with Chaps – I didn't know what to expect, I didn't know who I would be talking to, I didn't know what he would want me to tell him... I didn't want to go.

When we got there, Chaps immediately took me into his office and shut the door. Chief said he would come in if I wanted him to, but I just wanted as small an audience as possible. I've already had to tell my story to way too many people. He waited outside while we talked. Chaps asked me a little about myself, about Mark, about what I'm struggling with recently... he waited a while before asking me to tell him what actually happened that night. He had a box of tissues and set them in front of me before we even started talking, which I was thankful for because I probably used half the box.

I told him my story. I told him about reporting it, about how long the case took, about court, and about Mark and how he has been my biggest comfort ever since I met him. I told him how worthless I felt during the defense's closing arguments, how they reduced me to absolutely nothing. How I walked out of the courtroom feeling like a few specs of dust. I told him about having an all-male jury and how much that upset me; I will forever wonder if the outcome would have been different if there had been a few females on my jury. He seemed shocked when I mentioned it – he agreed that, as a female, I definitely should have had females on my jury and those representing me should have taken it upon themselves to ensure that happened. But I can't go back, so I have to live with the outcome decided by men.

Chaps talked a lot about forgiveness. The power of forgiveness... he said that whenever I'm at the point where I can forgive him, I will finally be able to let go and heal. I told him that, in my head, to say "I forgive you" is almost like saying "it's okay". I know they're different, but they seem the same right now, and what he did was not okay and will never be okay. I want to heal, and I want to feel whole again, but I don't see myself forgiving him any time soon. Maybe someday, but not right now.

He also talked about finding the positives. I explained that my lawyer had said something similar, telling me I should be thankful I got my day in court and had the chance to tell my story, and that most women never get that opportunity. Again, not ready yet. I can't do that yet. The guy who held me hostage in his room and raped me got away with it – how can I count myself lucky to have told my story? How can I be thankful that I got to go to court that day and be completely mentally and emotionally torn apart by a bunch of men? Maybe someday. Hopefully someday.

We talked about Mark a lot – how he is my comfort and my support and my safety. I told him I feel so much stronger and more confident whenever I'm with him; I feel like I'll be okay because he's there. But I fall apart when I'm on my own, and I know I need to figure out how to cope and deal with things on my own, and I can't always rely on him. But Chaps said that what we have is actually perfect. I was feeling so guilty for leaning on Mark so much and not being able to handle things myself, but Chaps told me that there's something called the "spirit of presence". Simply being present can be extremely healing and comforting – it can be something as simple as a hug, sitting on the couch together, holding my hand – just simply being present. He told me that Mark being present for me is the best thing he could do for me, and having that person that

I trust implicitly and love unconditionally just being there for me can be better than any fancy treatment. He said I do the same thing for Mark without realizing it – if Mark is struggling with something and I'm simply sitting with him or giving him a hug, I can serve as a comfort to him and help him through his problems without even saying anything. I want nothing more than to be home right now with him... I know he would make things better just by being there.

Chaps asked if I've been having nightmares – the question sort of took me by surprise because I have been, but I assumed it was due to lack of sleep. I've been having them for quite a while now, but I've been stressed and busy and not sleeping well anyway, so I just disregarded it. But he said they are more than likely due to past trauma, and apparently, that is quite common. He said that I am probably scared or afraid of something in my subconscious, and that causes nightmares. I never remember what they were about when they wake me up, but I do know that I was always either running from something, trapped, or in imminent danger for some reason. I guess that makes sense now. I just wish they would stop.

Chaps wants me to start therapy, but the only person in the mental health place here is a male, and he said he would prefer I be assigned a female due to the nature of my trauma. He said I need someone more sympathetic and gentle. I guess I appreciate that because, after all, a bunch of men didn't believe me in court, so I probably wouldn't trust a man to believe me in a therapy session. Chaplain is a man, but he seemed different. He was so easy to talk to and made me feel heard and understood. He never judged me; he was so soft-spoken, and he never interrupted me. He let me finish whatever I was saying, and then he would offer me something – advice, a piece of wisdom, or just simple feedback that made me feel validated and heard. He made sure I knew that I did nothing wrong, and that my not being okay after a trauma like that is completely understood. He said I shouldn't feel guilty, ashamed, or anything else for seek-

ing help. I clearly haven't been able to heal on my own, and I've accepted that I need outside help, which is the first step, he said. When I get home, he wants me to see a non-military therapist. Someone outside of the regimen and the ranks. Someone outside this so-called "family".

I submitted my request for reenlistment last month – I'm supposed to swear in for another six years in a few weeks. Some days, I wonder why the heck I did that. It was someone in the military who hurt me so badly that now I need therapy. It's the military that made me spend nearly the entire first year of my marriage away from my husband. I want to go home. I dread the thought of deploying again, and I never want to see half these people again. And yet I want to stay? It makes no sense when I think about it like that. There are positives – lots of positives – but they're hard to see right now. That's why I submitted the request. I know that once I get home and things calm down and I'm back to "normal" life, I'll remember all the good things about the military, everything it's given me, all the great opportunities, the fact that it led me to Mark... I'm not in a great state of mind right now, so I know that if I make a huge decision while I'm so messed up mentally, I will most likely come to regret it later. I know in my heart that I don't want to get out, no matter how much I want to right this second. It's hard to see the light when I'm in such a deep hole of darkness.

Today was hopefully the first day of a healing process – I don't feel any different tonight than I felt last night, but I made the first step. I'm hoping it was a good step. I know I can't keep this to myself anymore, and I know that trying to forget things hasn't worked. I have to deal with everything, and I need to do it before it takes over my entire life. I've been warned that my mental health could affect my relationship with Mark, my marriage, my future kids, other relationships, my job, my military career, and literally everything else, apparently. I don't want any of that to happen – I want to fix it, but fixing it is going to hurt, and that doesn't sound super great. But I know I want to be the best version of myself for

Mark, I want our marriage to continue to be amazing, and I know I have to heal if I want that to happen. I can't keep putting all my burdens on Mark and letting him carry me through life. I lean on him so hard, and I know he wants me to, and he wants to do everything in his power to help me and make my life easier, but I can't keep doing this to him. I have to figure out how to cope on my own.

***

October 20, 2021

I was doing an assignment today for a class about ethics in criminal justice, and the topic of an essay I had to write was regarding how forgiveness plays a role in our criminal justice system today. Sort of ironic, seeing as the Chaplain just mentioned forgiveness to me two days ago. The textbook was saying that forgiveness can serve as a "check" for anger, so that we can feel the proper amount of anger for a period of time, but ultimately overcome a desire to cause harm to the offender by forgiving them instead. So, if I do forgive him, I can still feel angry toward him, but I would be able to express that anger appropriately and not wish him more harm.

I hope I can get to that point someday. Right now, I still wish court had gone differently and that he were behind bars right now, registering as a sex offender, serving time, and regretting his stupid choices. He deserves that – he deserves to be punished for what he did and suffer accordingly. I believe that. But he's not... instead, he's just living his best life, probably relieved he was found not guilty and hating me for dragging him through the whole thing. I don't care if he hates me. I did what I thought was right, and I tried to let justice be served, but it wasn't. He walked out of the courtroom free as a bird, and I'm left to pick up the pieces of myself, and now I'm supposed to forgive him?! Again, maybe someday – but not today.

***

October 21, 2021

I'm so tired of crying myself to sleep.

***

October 23, 2021

I checked myself into mental health today. I met with an officer who will be my therapist for the rest of my time overseas – I felt comfortable with him and didn't have any problem talking to him. I hope he can help me get to where I need to be. I hope this turns out well.

***

October 27, 2021

Today was my first full session of therapy at the mental health clinic. I walked out of that 60-minute session somewhat mind-blown with a lot to think about. He said he wants to start by getting my sleep habits corrected because if my sleep is messed up, I can't really focus on healing anything else. We discussed ways to fix that.

He asked a series of questions and, based on my answers, told me I definitely have a moderate to high level of anxiety and that I overthink and hyperventilate in situations that should not be very stressful. He showed me a stress/performance chart and explained that most people begin with a low stress level accompanied by a low performance level. Both stress and performance go up till they find a sweet spot where the performance level is at its highest, and stress is at an appropriate medium level. But once pushed over the edge, stress levels will continue to rise, and performance will plummet. Most people begin at the low stress level, but he explained that I more than likely start out already at a medium to high level of stress or anxiety, so any added stressors will just push me over the edge more easily than they would other people.

He told me there are generally two ways of dealing with anxiety and high stress. The first method is medication, which would help me calm down, but would not be a permanent fix, and if I were to forget to take a pill, I would be right back where I was, or even worse. The second method is to give me coping skills and ways to deal with my anxiety in the moment and to teach me how to handle myself when I begin to get overwhelmed or my stress level gets too high. I would much rather pursue the second option and actually learn ways to manage my anxiety and stress instead of just covering it up.

He also brought up my mom. I had mentioned last week in our introductory session that I thought my mom was narcissistic and explained how she is very controlling. Today, he mentioned her tendency to be controlling and asked, "But is she good at it?" I didn't understand what he meant, so he explained. He said that she may try to be controlling, but unless she meets her goal, she is not actually good at being controlling. He asked if I am where I want to be in my life, and I said yes. I am pursuing the degree of my choice, I wanted to enlist, and I did, I married the man of my dreams, I have a perfect little home and family, and I am striving to meet my goals. He said that if mom were good at controlling things, she would have the perfect life – her house would be perfect, her kids would always be well-behaved, and all of us would have followed whatever she wanted us to do with our lives. Therefore, despite her trying to control aspects of my life, I am actually succeeding at controlling my own life, whether I realize it or not. Every time I set a boundary with her, I am the one in control of my life.

After he said that, I realized that I've met every goal I've ever set for myself, despite feeling like someone else was always trying to control me. I'm stronger than I think I am.

He told me that all my underlying issues – anxiety, high stress, overthinking, depression – are probably a legitimate reason as to why I am having trouble coping with a recent traumatic incident. I have spent a decade sweeping depression and anxiety under the rug and trying to act "normal" and happy and bottle up my feelings. Now that I am trying to deal with a traumatic issue, all those other issues are coming up and preventing me from healing. Essentially, I have a lot of stuff from the past to fix if I want to fix the current stuff. This is going to be a long process, but I am willing to do whatever it takes to be better mentally. This is draining me.

He talked about Mark for quite a while; he said Mark is like an outrigger on my boat. I can row the boat and move by myself, but if a wave comes along, it will just push me over. With Mark as my outrigger, I can still move by myself, but instead of being pushed over whenever a wave comes along, he will keep me steady and help me to get through it. He is not an anchor because then he would be keeping me in one place, not allowing me to move. As an outrigger, I still have the ability to move my own boat – live my own life, make my own decisions. But whenever I begin to get overwhelmed or I'm in a situation I just can't handle, Mark will be there to calm me down and help me through it. I had been so worried that I was leaning on him too much and that I was using him as a crutch. But today I realized he's always there when I need him and I can rely on him to help me whenever I need it, but there are also times I can do things by myself. I just need to know he'll be there when I can't handle it anymore, and he always is.

15

Epiphanies

2021-2022 | AGE 24

Therapy was helping; I could tell. The more sessions I attended, the more I was able to breathe a little easier and think through situations rationally. I still had all the same emotions swirling around inside my head, but I could keep them at bay. Things were more manageable on regular days. Some days were still hard, though. Holidays were hard. I was away for the entire 2021-2022 holiday season, and it was so difficult not to let my mind go wild. I tried to think of holidays as regular days. It wasn't Thanksgiving; it was just Thursday. It wasn't Christmas; it was just Saturday. Mark wasn't really having a ton of fun at holiday functions back home, either, and I felt guilty for that, too. I felt guilty for meeting him right before I had a bunch of orders and a deployment. I felt guilty that we got married, and I immediately left. Celebrating our first anniversary half a world away from each other was probably the hardest part of the whole thing. And, of course, I felt guilty. I felt like it was my fault we weren't together for it. Irrational, I know, but that seemed to be a theme for me.

I started to have a lot of epiphanies in therapy. I felt like I walked out of the office every single week with another mind-blowing realization. I'd learned I had anxiety and depression; I'd learned my mother was a narcissist; I'd learned I was abused for the entirety of my childhood... I'd never in my life thought of myself as "abused." Other children were abused, not me. I talked to Mark about it, and he agreed, based on stories I'd told him and his knowledge of my parents. I then started to follow that thought a bit further.

I was abused; therefore, my siblings were also abused, right? Were the younger kids also being abused? Mom and Dad treated T like shit - I mean, they actually hated her. But then again, they hated all of us, didn't they? They never actually wanted any of us in the first place. At least, that's how they treated us. Like we were unwanted from the very beginning. They used to joke that they only had kids for child labor, but I wasn't so sure it was actually a joke.

I did a lot of deconstructing over the next several months, trying to understand what was happening in my family and what had happened throughout my childhood. My mind was everywhere all at once, and it was overwhelming. I spent a lot of time on Google, trying to figure out if what my husband and therapist were saying was true.

I learned that children naturally love and trust their parents by default. For children who are isolated, their whole point of reference is what they are permitted to know. I had nothing to compare my experiences to, so I thought my life was normal. Kids don't know their abuse is abuse when it's all they've ever known. For kids, it's safer to think the kids are the problem, rather than thinking the adults are unsafe; you can change yourself and your behavior as a child, but you can't change your parents, so you adapt to survive. It's just normal. Kids aren't naturally going to question their "normal" until they grow up and somehow experience something that shows them their "normal" wasn't normal.

I learned about the concept of "learned helplessness," which is a psychological response that children develop when they've been raised in an environment where they have no power, their reactions don't change anything, and every attempt at autonomy is punished, ignored, or twisted. Eventually, the child's brain just adapts for survival by concluding that nothing they do matters, nothing they feel is valid, they can't change anything, so they shouldn't even try.

They believe their environment is normal because it's the only world they know. Instead of identifying the adults as unsafe, they begin to identify themselves as the problem.

If I can't make them happy, it must be my fault.

If trying makes it worse, I should stop trying.

If speaking up gets me punished, silence must be safer.

If escaping isn't allowed, wanting freedom must be wrong.

As they reach adulthood, that "learned helplessness" psychological response portrays itself as chronic self-blame, decision-making paralysis, remaining in harmful situations because leaving feels impossible, automatically yielding to authority or control, thinking they don't deserve better, struggling to advocate for themselves, believing discomfort is normal, assuming they're the reason things go wrong all the time, mistaking survival skills for personality traits... instead of feeling like a trauma response, however, it feels more like "it's just who I am." Was that me? Had I been conditioned to respond this way? Did I have learned helplessness? Everything I was reading sounded like it was hitting the nail on the head when I reflected back on my childhood and how I had been operating as an adult.

I also learned about the concept of "cognitive dissonance" and realized it perfectly described my childhood. For years, I held two conflicting truths in my mind: that my family was loving and that I'd been hurt. My brain had bent reality to survive, twisting the abuse into normalcy, until I was forced to face the painful truth I'd been avoiding. I never realized that's what I'd been doing. Somewhere in my brain, my subconscious knew I'd been hurt, but I'd been wired to ignore it, rename it, or minimize it.

I learned about indoctrination and how it rewrites your internal operating system. It replaces your own values with the ones you were handed and punishes you - psychologically, spiritually, etc - any time you try to deviate. Had I been indoctrinated? Even as an adult, thousands of miles from home, I was still so steeped in my parents' religion - which I also thought was my own - that their voice sounded like God's voice. I genuinely believed that calling CPS would be the ultimate sin, the final betrayal of the family that God supposedly gave me. The ideology they planted in me demanded loyalty at the expense of reason, morality, and my own instincts, but I'd never recognized that before. I was convinced that protecting my siblings from harm was more sinful than protecting the people who were harming them. I couldn't call CPS. God would never forgive me. Mom would never forgive me. I had to just leave things alone. God knows what's going on, and if He had a problem with it, He'd stop it. Right?

One of the hardest truths I had to face was how thoroughly I'd been conditioned to minimize what happened to us. I had buried my own trauma so deeply that I couldn't recognize the severity of my younger siblings' abuse either. What happened to me had apparently numbed me; therefore, what happened to them seemed "not that bad" because my baseline for harm had been set so catastrophically low. I was so desensitized, so accustomed to cruelty that was disguised as godly and Biblical discipline, that nothing shocked me anymore. Since I trusted my parents - because children are built to believe the people who raise them - I accepted their justifications without question. They said T deserved harsh treatment, and I believed them. I didn't see abuse; I just saw a narrative I'd been trained to repeat. Until deployment, when I started to see the real truth begin to surface. That truth was that we had all been hurt, and none of us had deserved any of it. But why did I have to be the one to realize everything and take action? Why couldn't somebody else have realized a long time ago and saved all of us?

As I was unraveling everything, guilt hit me like a truck. One thought kept circling in my head: I practically raised my siblings, so wasn't I the one responsible for everything that happened to them? My older sister and I had been the ones changing diapers, calming them down from bad dreams, helping them with homework, making them meals, shielding them from Mom, and teaching them how to navigate her moods. We were the buffers, the babysitters, the caretakers who stepped in long before we knew what we were doing.

Once I was finally able to admit to myself that my siblings and I were abused, the blame infiltrated my mind. I felt like I'd failed them, like I should have protected them better, like their pain was somehow proof that I hadn't done enough or been enough for them. It didn't matter that I'd been a child myself; I'd been trained to be responsible, so when I finally found out the truth, I instinctively believed it was my fault.

When I was younger, I remember feeling disconnected from the chaos around me a lot, as if I were watching my own life, but

I was just out of reach. I learned that this is called "dissociation," which was my mind protecting itself from pain. I didn't know it had a name; I just thought it was "spacing out" or "feeling numb," not realizing my brain was quietly shielding me from the reality of abuse I couldn't yet face.

Thinking about that, I realized I'd carried the same coping mechanism into adulthood, especially during deployment. In the chaos of deployment duties, post-court emotions from my sexual assault trial, realizations of my abusive childhood, guilt, and everything else that was going on, I realized I was detaching myself from my surroundings, watching myself act, feel, and survive as if I were in someone else's body. I know now that it was dissociation, but I just knew it kept me sort of sane, and created a necessary distance between myself and fear or danger, the same way it had protected me as a child from a home that should have been safe.

Toward the beginning of deployment, I think I tried to distance myself from the world so completely that my brain blocked out much of my family trauma, my siblings' abuse, my sexual assault case, just so I could focus on surviving deployment. I hadn't realized I'd been in survival mode, but I couldn't go back to it. Once I began putting things together and learning about the reality of the abuse happening in my family, I could no longer ignore everything and live in my own little bubble, disconnected from the world. I had to face the facts and make a choice: leave things alone, or blow everything up.

I started messaging Mom and my sisters a lot more toward the end of deployment; I wanted to learn as much as I could about what was going on at home since I had unlocked a totally different perspective on my family. I knew how I grew up, and I knew how Mom and Dad treated the rest of the kids, but I'd never thought of it as abuse before. My therapist had been opening my eyes to a lot of things, so I started seeing everything in a whole new light.

Mom was constantly texting me about T and how annoying she was, what she was doing each day, and how much of a burden she was. I had asked what the kids wanted for Christmas so I could order things on Amazon and have them sent to the house, and Mom sent me a link for a waterproof dog blanket. She said it was the only thing T would actually use since she just wet herself all the time. She sent toy ideas for the younger kids, but not for T. I didn't buy her the waterproof dog blanket. I couldn't justify buying a doggy pee pad for a child once I started recognizing Mom's reasoning as hostile and hateful. I remember thinking it was crazy that I'd thought her treatment of us was "normal" before.

I saved all my messages from Mom; she didn't hold back whenever she talked about the kids, especially T and the sister we'd adopted as a teenager. She hated them, and I was beginning to see that more clearly. My other sisters were texting me T's daily routines, things Mom did to her, and how Mom ran the house in general. Things had definitely changed since I'd moved out. I think when I was there, I took care of most things, so Mom was pretty hands-off when it came to the kids. Once I left, she didn't have as much help, so she took a more hands-on role, which meant more abuse and hatred.

Mom also filled me in on all the diagnoses she'd been able to get for the kids. The baby had been diagnosed with autism, I think there were a few ADHD's, some Fetal Alcohol Syndromes, anxiety, behavioral issues, and some more stuff. I thought that was odd, since she had been so adamant about never getting any of us biological kids tested for anything. She always said she didn't want us to be "labeled" or diagnosed with stuff. She said my older sister was diagnosed with dyslexia when she was little, but that Mom had cured it. I've spoken with my sister about that, she's done some research, and we're pretty sure she never actually had dyslexia. Apparently, dyslexia cannot be cured, either. I guess Mom's just a miracle worker.

Anyway, she got the adopted kids diagnosed with endless lists of ailments and disorders. I knew there was some way to raise the adoption stipend amount due to various things or that special needs kids got a higher amount, and I wondered if that was her motivation for seeking so many diagnoses. I thought that might explain why she did that for the adopted kids but not for her biological kids. She probably couldn't get money from her own kids. She also got a lot of attention for having children with special needs. I wasn't sure if they actually qualified as "special needs" because they seemed pretty normal to me, but then again, I didn't actually know what fell under the "special needs" category, and I was also pretty sure they were being abused.

I learned a LOT from two of my sisters about how T was living, and how Mom and Dad were treating her. I learned that T lived in a closet-sized room behind a dead-bolted door on the opposite end of the house from all the other bedrooms. I'd never been to that house since they moved while I was deployed. Oh yeah - Mom contacted Mark and had him come help them move since he had a truck. Mark obviously told me immediately that she had reached out to him, and I said she hadn't reached out to me first, which really frustrated me. Mom called me later and talked about Mark helping them move, as if I wasn't aware. She was like, "Oh, oops, I think I forgot to tell you about that!" I told her I already knew because Mark had told me as soon as she'd messaged him, and she seemed surprised. Did she really think I didn't talk to my own husband? She tried to make it sound like she and Mark talked all the time, like she wanted me to think she talked to him more than I did. I didn't understand her reasoning behind that because I knew she didn't like him. He had tattoos, wasn't a Christian, and lived with me before we were married. Sinner. Unforgivable. And yet, she bragged that she talked to him all the time, acting like she was closer to him than I was. Whatever. Anyway...

From what my sisters were telling me, I began to think T's abuse was worse than what the rest of us kids had been through. I saw Mom's behavior toward her from a different perspective once I was thinking a bit more clearly, and I began to realize it was really wrong. I also began to realize that I need to do something about it. I didn't know if I should talk to my parents - that had never worked before - or if I should get someone else involved. I talked with Mark about it a lot, and we both came to the conclusion that a call to Child Protective Services was probably the best idea. I was petrified. I couldn't do that.

16

Decisions

2022 | AGE 24

I knew that calling CPS on my parents would effectively destroy my family as I knew it. I knew Mom and Dad would never speak to me again; I didn't know if any of my siblings would agree with that decision, and they might never speak to me again either, and I probably would never see my youngest siblings again. I also figured nobody would believe me. Mom was well-known back in Idaho. She taught foster parent classes, and she spoke at conferences. She was a leading authority on foster parenting, adoption, trauma-informed parenting, and everything else. She was able to manipulate people and make them believe her so easily, and I knew I wouldn't be believed.

I also thought that if I called CPS and they did listen, they'd go to the house, see that everything was fine, and they'd leave. If that happened, Mom would take it out on T, and I knew she could very easily kill her if she took things too far. I was so afraid that Mom could destroy my adult siblings and me, and she could make life hell for the kids who still lived with her. Then I thought about what might happen if CPS did take the kids: they'd take them and put them in foster care for a minute, Mom and Dad would get them right back after a few days because Mom is so good at manipulation, and then the same thing would happen anyway. Mom would take her anger out on T; I'd never see the kids or any of my family again, and I was completely convinced Mom could destroy me. I didn't know how, but she'd spread rumors about me being pregnant at 16, so I was pretty sure she was capable of far more than that.

Wasn't it better to just leave things alone and not disrupt the status quo rather than destroy the entire family? Also, why did it have to be me? Why could nobody else have called CPS while we were growing up? Why was it my job to be responsible for saving my siblings? Would I even be saving them, or would I be messing things up forever?

I wrestled with those questions for the rest of the deployment and struggled to make a huge decision - call CPS, or leave things alone. I was absolutely terrified of what would happen if I called. I think my deployment ended up getting extended once or twice, but I was finally on my way back in April of 2022. T turned 14 that month, and again, Mom said she didn't deserve anything for her birthday, and she didn't even want a cake. I found that hard to believe; what kid doesn't want a birthday cake? I was pretty sure Mom just didn't care about her birthday and kept her in her closet behind that locked door.

As I completed my post-deployment tasks and prepared to come home, I began to feel a lot of things toward Mom. I felt resentment and hatred - a lot of negative emotions. Partly because of what she'd done to my biological siblings and me while we were growing up, but also because of what she was currently doing to

T, I hated myself for not seeing it before. I hated that I had never seen her for who and what she was, and I never saw the abuse for what it was. I thought everything in my life was so normal, and I thought I'd had pretty normal parents. I hated Dad for not standing up for us, for not loving us enough to save us from her, and for not defending T from what was currently happening to her. He was just as bad as Mom was. He didn't care anymore. He didn't even try anymore. He just went along with whatever Mom said, and that was just as bad in my mind.

I had planned with Mom to come to the house to surprise everyone that I was home. She made me wait two weeks after I got back to schedule an appointment to come by, though; she said since I didn't give her a heads-up that I was coming home, she didn't have any availability. Mark and I pulled in, and Dad was on the lawnmower. He stopped as soon as he saw me, turned it off, and came running to me without saying a word. He didn't speak for several minutes, and he was just hugging me. I'd never been hugged by Dad like that before; it was like he actually loved me. It was so weird. He just didn't let go. I let myself think that maybe he really did love me, maybe he really did care. Maybe he would listen to me if I brought up my concerns about their treatment of T. Maybe I wouldn't have to call CPS if he really did care.

The youngest two kids came running out and gave me bear hugs. Mom was still making all of us wear masks, so that part sucked, but I was so happy to see them. Something in the back of my head was telling me I didn't have much time left with them. I had a strange feeling that I can only describe as ominous. Like impending doom.

I asked to see T. For some reason, I thought that maybe if I saw her and she was okay, I could dismiss everything my sisters had texted me about how Mom had been treating her. I think I was hoping my sisters were wrong. But they wouldn't let me see her. I was sort of taken aback, honestly. I had brought back some shirts and toys from Kuwait for the three kids, and I asked if I could give T what I'd brought for her. Mom said she didn't deserve any gifts or clothes, so I needed to give her things to the younger two kids. I wasn't thrilled with that response, and I pushed a little harder. Mom and Dad said T wouldn't even remember me; she was too stupid to remember who people were, and if she did remember me, she probably didn't even realize I'd been gone.

They talked so negatively about her and absolutely refused to let me see her. I didn't want to push too hard because I hadn't even decided what I wanted to do yet. I was still hoping I wouldn't have to call CPS and that maybe it wasn't as bad as my sisters had made it seem. I was hoping Dad might have some sense, but it wasn't looking like that was going to happen. Mom seemed to be getting pretty agitated about me pushing to see T, so I decided to leave it alone for the moment and come back later. I had barely been home after being gone for a year and having a million epiphanies, and I needed to get my head on straight. So many thoughts were swirling around in my brain, and I couldn't figure out what I was supposed to do.

Over the next month or so, I talked to both of my sisters a lot. I learned a lot more about T, how she was being treated, what Mom and Dad had said about her, what my sisters had seen themselves, and what Mom had told them. I learned as much as I could and started writing it down in a Word document, mixed in with things I'd seen during my time living at home. For some reason, I was under the impression that I had to have evidence in order to make a call to CPS. I don't think that's true, but I didn't know that at the time. I also thought I needed evidence of T's living conditions in order to make a report. I started brainstorming ways to get inside T's closet to see the situation for myself.

Throughout the deployment, I had been working on a photo book for Dad's 50th birthday. I hadn't finished it by his 50th, so I had decided to give it to him for Father's Day instead. I had contacted his parents and gotten baby photos and school portraits from his childhood, and organized the book from birth to 50, documenting his younger years, marriage, each of us kids, adoptions, and all the memories I could find in my photos. It took me a long time, and I really thought it would make him realize that he did love us and care about us. I thought he would look through it and realize how badly he'd been treating T, at the very least. I left a page blank at the end of the book for each of us kids to sign. That was how I was going to see T.

Throughout the week leading up to Father's Day, I met up with each of my siblings to have them sign the book. When I met with my sisters, I asked for their opinion on whether to call CPS. Neither of them thought it was a good idea. They both agreed it needed to be done, but they didn't want to be involved; they were both as scared as I was. We all assumed Mom would destroy us, and we were all terrified. They said they did think their treatment of T warranted a CPS call, but they didn't want the call to come from any of us.

I met up with both of my brothers, too, and saw where they were living. They shared an apartment - or a townhouse, maybe - and there were posters all over the walls that had been made by Mom. The boys were 22 and 21 at that point, but Mom checked in on them every week to make sure they were following her rules. She had checklists on the walls for what they were to clean each day, and she checked to make sure they were doing it. She had a poster above the trash to remind them when trash day was. It was beyond just being a helpful and concerned mother. It was very micromanaging. In my opinion. I didn't need my mom to make a cleaning schedule in Excel, print it off, and post it all over my house and then check in on me once each week to make sure I was following it. Weird.

Once I'd gotten signatures from all my adult siblings, I just had to go to the house. I believe it was the day before Father's Day - Saturday - that Mark and I went over. His job was to distract Mom while I went to see T. I asked Dad if I could see her since I needed her to sign something for his gift, and he said no. He said she was so dumb that she didn't even know how to write her name. He said he didn't care if her signature was on it, anyway. I said I hadn't even gotten to see her yet since coming home from deployment, and after refusing a few more times, I think he just gave up. He said "fine," but that she probably wouldn't even know who I was, since she was so stupid.

We went into the kitchen, and he unbolted a door. He opened the door, let it swing open, and said, "T, you have a visitor." I remember thinking it felt like I was at a prison visiting a prisoner. I heard a door open, and I peeked through the kitchen door. Her closet door was open a few inches, and I could see her face peering through. I asked Dad if she could come out, and he said absolutely not. I asked if I could go in, and he said I could if I wanted to, but that it probably smelled like sewer. I went in, and Dad went back outside.

I walked toward her door and asked if I could come in; she opened it a little wider and just stared at me as I walked into her closet. It was exactly like my sisters had described. There was the mattress on the floor with a fitted sheet and a blanket, a pile of clean diapers, a roll of doggy bags, and a pile of bagged dirty diapers. Nothing else. I asked if she wanted a hug, and she warily gave me one. I had her sign the photo book for Dad, and she wrote her name just fine. I took some selfies with her - with my mask on, of course - and also some pictures of her room. Again, I was under the impression that I needed evidence to make a CPS call, so I figured I needed to take pictures of her room.

She seemed so happy to see me. Actually, she was probably just happy to see anyone who wasn't Mom or Dad. She was fourteen, but she seemed so small and so timid. I knew she wasn't allowed to speak, but she did whisper a few words to me, most likely afraid Mom or Dad would hear her and punish her for speaking. I told her I'd see her soon, gave her another hug, and went to find Mark. I was so angry. I was finally convinced that I had to call CPS. I had been hoping for so long that my sisters were wrong, that my own memories were wrong. I had been hoping it wasn't abuse, but I knew better than that. I think I didn't want to accept the fact that it was abuse, because if I did that, I'd also have to accept the fact that I was abused as well. I didn't want that to be true. I had thought everything in my life was normal for so long; I didn't want to have to deal with the aftermath of realizing I'd been abused.

As Mark and I said our goodbyes, I hugged the younger two kids extra long. I had that ominous feeling again, but this time I knew why. I was about to do something that would cause this "family" to never be the same again, and I knew that. I had to. I didn't really have a choice. I was still scared out of my mind, but I was also incredibly angry. I had hatred boiling in my veins. I hated Mom and Dad not only for what they'd done, but for what they were about to make me do. I wouldn't have to do it if they'd been halfway decent parents. I wouldn't have to do it if they'd just loved us. But no, that was too hard for them. Love was out of the question, apparently. Mark got me out of there, and I don't think I spoke a single word that entire drive home.

I added to my Word document I'd created about T and called my mother-in-law. She was a social worker - for adults, not for kids - but she was still a mandatory reporter. I told her everything, and she said I absolutely had to make the call. She said since she was also aware of the situation, she had to call. She said she'd let me call first and make another call as soon as I was done. I think she knew it was important for me to take that step and make the first call. She knew it was the biggest decision I'd ever had to make, and she knew it was going to destroy me, in all likelihood.

I spent Sunday pacing, crying, crashing out, and finalizing my Word document. I knew that I'd possibly freeze up as soon as I made the call and forget everything I'd wanted to say, so I figured if I had it all written down, I'd be able to follow it like a script and not leave anything out. Since that day, I've added to that document as my sisters and I have remembered more things; I think I'm documenting every little thing I remember so that I can hopefully submit it as evidence in a criminal case against Mom and Dad someday. Anyway, here's what I have so far about T:

1. T was five years old and potty trained when we got her in 2013. She had visits with her biological mom and wasn't treated very lovingly in our home, so she started wetting herself and having accidents as a trauma response. Over time, Mom eventually put her in pull-ups at night, then all day, then just switched to diapers full-time.
2. Mom would walk right through T if she passed her in a doorway, hallway, or anywhere. She wouldn't even shove her aside; she'd just walk straight through her. T would try to get out of the way, but Mom would follow wherever T swerved so she could walk through her. T often got knocked down, and Mom would just step on her and continue walk-

ing. That happened a lot. If T was standing somewhere fidgeting with her hands, picking at her face or clothes, or just literally doing anything with her hands, Mom would go over to her and slap her hands down. There were times when Mom's nails would scratch T's face, neck, or arms on their way down, and T would be bleeding but not allowed to wash off the blood.

3. If T ever "sassed" Mom, basically, if she ever spoke at all, Mom would slap her across the face. There were a lot of times when T would be standing by a wall or doorway, so when Mom slapped her, T's head would get smacked against the wall or doorway. Mom and Dad both frequently dragged T across the house, up or down the stairs, around the deck or yard by her hair, clothes, arms, legs, etc. The last time Mom did that, T "fought back," meaning she tried to get away, and Mom said T tried to break her wrist, resulting in a sprain or something. To this day, I'm not sure if Mom was ever actually injured, but ever since then, Mom has refused to touch T in any way, claiming she was traumatized by T. After that, Mom has used props to shove or prod T to where she wanted her to be.
4. Whenever she was "naughty" or "bad," she had to walk laps around the backyard, regardless of the weather. Mom called it "Big Body Movement." Mom had said the doctor told her T needed more cardio because she was getting too fat, so Mom made her walk around the yard outside for hours. I thought that was weird because T was extremely short and underweight for her age. When I was living there, I'd frequently see her walking or running laps with no socks or shoes on, no pants on, no coat on in freezing temperatures, no jacket or umbrella in the rain... it didn't really mat-

ter; Mom made her do her laps anyway. She also added laps if she felt T wasn't doing them fast enough or if she decided T was being naughty again, or really if she just got a whim. T usually started out with 50 or 100 laps to complete, but it always ended up being around 200-300 by the end of the day. She did laps late into the night some days; if it got late enough for Mom to be going to bed, she brought T inside and just tacked her unfinished laps onto the next day's lap count. Mom never counted her laps; she said it was T's responsibility. However, when T would come in saying she was finished, Mom would say, "I only counted ###," and make her go back out. She also wasn't allowed to touch the back door, so when she wanted to come inside, she had to knock and wait for Mom to decide to open the door for her. Sometimes, Mom would make T stand at the back door for hours in all kinds of weather and temperatures before deciding to open it for her and let her come inside.

5. One time, I saw T just stop and collapse onto her knees in the middle of a lap; Mom got so angry that she'd stopped, so she went outside and yelled at her to get up. I was watching from inside, so I couldn't hear what T was saying, but I could tell she was crying. Mom marched over to her, grabbed her by the shirt, and started dragging her around the yard. Eventually, T got up and started walking on her own again; Mom, of course, added laps since T had been "belligerent." Knowing what I know now, and being able to see things for what they were, I think T most likely collapsed from fatigue, and I'm not sure how she didn't die because she was doing so much exercise and not eating enough to balance it out. I thought it was fine at the time. I'd had to do things like that when I was younger, so I thought it was

okay. I thought it was just regular discipline. I thought it was normal.

6. She had a bed on the floor, similar to every previous house we'd lived in, and she wasn't allowed to leave her closet except to eat on the porch, walk laps around the yard as punishment, and clean herself up in the bathroom. She had a stack of clean diapers in her closet, along with doggie bags for the dirty ones, but no toys or books or anything like that. T's mattress was covered with thick, noisy plastic, and she had one fitted sheet and one scratchy wool blanket and no pillow. She had to strip her bed each morning and only got her bedding back each night if she did her laundry and completed her Big Body Movement. If she didn't finish her laps or do laundry, she had to sleep on a waterproof pad on the hardwood floor. Apparently, Mom said that she had to sleep on the floor because if the bed didn't have sheets on it, T would suffocate due to how loose the thick plastic was. If she did earn her sheet and blanket back, she could only make her bed if she had direct supervision. Mom was pretty good at making sure nobody was available to supervise.
7. She had to change her diapers herself; she bagged the dirty diapers and put them in a pile in her closet near her bed. Every once in a while, whenever someone was available, she would be escorted to the outside garbage dumpster to throw away her dirty diapers, but she was only allowed to take one trip. Whatever she couldn't carry stayed in her closet until the next time she was escorted outside to the dumpster. At the previous house, T had to carry her bagged dirty diapers with her while she walked laps around the yard as punishment.

8. T used to eat somewhat normal food in somewhat regular portions, but over time, Mom started saying the doctor said they were starving T, so she started the "free-for-all" phase and gave T containers overflowing with bland foods like yogurt, plain oatmeal, and greens. The containers were so full they would often spill on the way to the table, and once she was a few feet away, Mom would toss the containers to T, and more would spill as she tried to catch them. T got in trouble - slapped, flicked, laps, etc - for spilling, and she also had to clean it up, which cut into her meal time.
9. At the new house, T was fed a mound of food from a mixing bowl on the back porch. Mom, again, said it was "doctor's orders," and it would usually be a can of "greens" like canned peas, turnip greens, or collards, a cup of dry oats, a protein like a can of beans, cold hot dogs, or fried eggs, a fruit like a whole grapefruit or a lemon, and a powdered formula. All just dumped into the bowl. It smelled so bad that Mom would gag and have to leave the room while T was eating it, so that's why she started sending T outside to eat it on the back porch. Whatever she didn't finish in her time limit stayed on the back porch until the next meal, even if it was overnight. Anything that blew into the bowl - pollen, bugs, twigs - was just part of her next meal.
10. At the new house, Mom stopped caring about having T on any sort of schedule. She slept in her closet a lot, sometimes waking up at 4 pm, and then cleaned herself up in the bathroom. She had to knock on the locked kitchen door to ask for toilet paper and her toothbrush and toothpaste, since she wasn't allowed to have any of that without permission. Then, someone had to spray Lysol on the floor, and she had to clean it up; if nobody was available for any of that or no-

body wanted to help, she just waited till she heard someone in the kitchen again so she could knock again. When all the cleaning was done, she could eat her bowl of "food" on the deck. Basically, Mom stopped caring about what T did; she never came to get her; she just made her live in her little closet and ignored her. That included her birthday and any holidays - Mom told me T "missed" Christmas because she didn't care enough to come out of her room. But she was locked back there, and nobody would let her out, and she wasn't permitted into the rest of the house.

11. Her clothing was kept outside on the back porch in a laundry basket; when she had dirty clothing, she had to do her own laundry but only under direct supervision, and Mom conveniently made sure nobody was ever available to supervise her, so she wouldn't have any clean clothes to wear. T had to soak the clothes in bleach with no gloves on, and they would get eaten by bugs and things if they sat outside long enough. Mom only bought her basic boys' clothing - black, grey, blue tees and sweats - nothing with prints, words, or designs because Mom claimed T would just ruin them, so why waste the money. Mom used T's birthday or Christmas money from grandparents to buy the clothes, but T didn't even know people were sending her money.
12. Mom also randomly decided sometimes that T didn't deserve clothes. She usually just wore black garbage bags or pillowcases with holes cut in them as clothes. Most times, T would wear the same garbage bag for days, maybe up to a week, and if the head hole got too stretched out, Mom would duct tape the bag to T's neck, shoulders, head, or hair to keep it on. When Mom decided it was time to take the bag off, she would rip the tape and the bag off, usually

pulling out hair and leaving awful red marks on T from the tape. Again, some of that was normal to me; I'd been made to wear a trash bag as a child. I thought it was fine; I didn't know other families didn't make their kids wear trash bags as clothes when they were bad.

13. T was on a lot of medications: Vitamin D, something Mom called "anti-pee pill," a few others, and then birth control pills. Mom put T on birth control before she got her first period so she could avoid having "the talk" with her and avoid dealing with her period. T skipped the placebo weeks and went straight to the next set of pills so she would never have a period.
14. We would go camping as a family in the RV/travel trailer, and I remember multiple occasions when Mom kicked or shoved T out of the trailer onto the ground. Our RV had a few steps that folded down; without the steps, it was probably about a 3ft drop. Mom would just shove or kick T out the door, and a few times she hit her head on the picnic table or fire pit if it was too close to the RV when she fell.
15. There were at least two occasions when the family was camping, and the police got called to our campsite. Both times, nearby campers had heard yelling and screaming, and both times Mom and Dad told the officers that T was just being naughty. The officer looked at T and told her she needed to obey her parents, and then they left.

17

The Call

2022 | AGE 24-25

I'm pretty sure you can call CPS to make a report on a weekend, but I didn't know that at the time. I thought it was a Monday-Friday, 8-5 type of thing. Monday morning, June 21, 2022, I was up at the crack of dawn, terrified. I was about to make a phone call that would change everything, but I knew I had to do it. I couldn't back out - I didn't want to back out. I was mostly angry that I was the one who had to do it. It shouldn't have been me. It should've been done years earlier by a concerned adult in our lives, but that never happened. It was my responsibility, and it shouldn't have been.

At 8:01 am, I called the number I'd found online. I said I wanted to make a report, and I basically word vomited on the poor lady for the next five or ten minutes. I felt like I'd speed-read everything in my Word document and hadn't even taken a single breath until I was done. She said thank you and that they'd look into it. I hung up. I was shaking. I let my mother-in-law know that I'd called, and she said she was about to make her own report as well. I'd sent her all the pertinent information - names, addresses, etc.- so she already had everything she needed to make her report. I'd prepared for this as much as possible, but how does one properly prepare to destroy their own family?

I couldn't sit still that day. I was pacing; I couldn't eat; I couldn't think, but I was also overthinking. Mark came home from work at lunch; I think he could tell I wasn't okay. I didn't know what to do; it was like I was waiting for something to happen, but, at the same time, I didn't really expect anything to happen. I didn't know what I was waiting for, but I couldn't calm down or sit still or distract myself with anything.

Around 2 pm, one of my sisters called me; she was hysterical. She asked if I'd called CPS. I asked why. She said social workers and police were currently at the house removing the kids. I broke down in tears, and I didn't know why. I was devastated - I'd just ruined a family - but I thought I was supposed to be happy. That's what I wanted, right?

Mark and my mother-in-law were telling me I'd done the right thing, but it sure didn't feel like it. My mom was calling, my brothers were calling, and I ignored every call. They wanted to know if I was the one who'd called CPS, if I'd take the kids, if I could put in a good word for Mom and Dad... Mom convinced one of my sisters to take the kids until the social workers could find somewhere else to place them. My brother left me a threatening voicemail - I could tell he wasn't going to hear me out or take my side in the whole thing. My brothers were very loyal to Mom. They didn't see what I saw, but I couldn't blame them for that because I'd shielded and protected them from everything growing up. How were they supposed to see it if I hid it from them?

I tried so hard, but I couldn't convince myself that I'd done something good. I was convinced I'd just ruined the only family

I'd known, and nothing would ever be the same. Mark kept telling me I had done the right thing; I'd saved my siblings; my mother-in-law said I was strong, that I'd finally seen who Mom and Dad really were and I'd done something about it. I hated myself for not seeing it before, but I also hated myself for putting my little siblings through such upheaval and confusion and pain. Mark told me the confusion they experienced being removed from the home that day was much better than the continued abuse they would've gotten if I'd done nothing. I really wanted to believe that.

My emotions were everywhere all at once, and I couldn't even think straight. What had I just done? Who calls Child Protective Services on their own parents?

In the next weeks, the kids were moved to Mom's parents' house, and she was allowed to see them from sunup to sundown. She was still parenting them; they were just living with Nana. Nana, who did whatever Mom said to do. Nana, who never blew the whistle on our abuse but instead just joined in for as long as I could remember. I felt like the foster system had failed. You removed them from the house - cool! But you put them in Nana's house where Mom can still be in control 24/7 - what the fuck? More than ever, I thought I'd fucked up. Why did I ever make that phone call - I should've known they'd do some shit like this. It was all for nothing, wasn't it? Now the kids are going to go back home and get treated even worse because Mom has to take it out on someone. And I'll never see them again because Mom pretty much knows who called.

After five months, the kids were moved to actual foster homes. T went to one home, and the younger two kids went to another. Mark and I attended every single court hearing and listened to Mom bullshit her way through the process. My sisters took my side, and my brothers sided with Mom and Dad. They didn't see our parents for who they really were; they didn't see their childhood as negative in any way. Again, I couldn't completely blame them - my older sister and I had shielded them from so much over the years, hiding them in a bedroom when Mom and Dad were fighting, taking the blame for something when we knew one of them had done it... We thought we were protecting them, but it ended up turning them against us because they didn't see what we saw. I felt guilty for protecting them. Maybe if I hadn't, they'd understand that our childhood wasn't as great as they remembered. Maybe they'd believe me. Maybe they could get out.

Mom and Dad played their roles as the perfect parents flawlessly in court, but they weren't convincing. The judges, caseworkers, the guardian ad litem, and even their own appointed attorneys began to recognize that they were a bit off. They brought a Bible with them to each court hearing, as well as a framed photo of the kids. They held hands and leaned on each other throughout the proceedings, which was something I'd never seen before and made me cringe. I'd never seen them touch each other, let alone hug each other or portray any affection. It seemed disgusting to me, but I was the only one in the courtroom who knew it was fake. I hated how confident they seemed. I hated how sure they were that they would get their kids back. I hated how easily they could lie.

I already knew Mom's parents had taken her side in the whole thing; not only had the kids gone to live with them before being moved to actual foster homes, but Nana and Mom had always been two peas in a pod. Nana was always narcissistic, but her student had far surpassed her. Mom became the master. Mom's word was law; Nana could see no wrong in her daughter, so she obeyed every word Mom breathed. They were joined at the hip, operating in unison for my entire life.

Growing up, whenever the landline rang, we knew it was probably Nana. When Mom started using her cell phone more, nine times out of ten, an incoming call was from Nana. Back when we had to memorize phone numbers rather than programming them into our phones, I had my parents' and Nana's numbers seared into my brain. Mom and Nana think the same, abuse the same, act the same, and treat their husbands the same. Dad and Grandpa had no say in their marriages or families. They simply followed their wives.

Nana had stopped speaking to me not long after she got the kids. She attended a few court hearings and always tried to hug me, but I always walked away without even looking at her. I could hear her crying behind me, but I didn't care. She was exactly like Mom. The tears were fake. The emotion was fake. It was manipulation and control. It wasn't genuine.

I knew where Mom's parents stood - with Mom - but I didn't know about Dad's folks. I barely knew them, so I wasn't sure if they were the type of people to agree with Dad and take his side, or if they would hear me out and listen to my side of the story. I didn't even know if I should bother calling them. Did they have any idea what went on in our family? Did they know how Mom and Dad were, or were they too far removed? Would they believe me? Had Dad gotten to them first?

It took me a while to think things through, but a few weeks after calling CPS, I decided to call them. I figured a phone call was good because if they didn't believe me, I could just hang up. I just wanted them to know what was going on, but I'd find out pretty quickly if Dad had already told them his side and where they stood. A phone call couldn't hurt, right?

I called, they answered, and it was awkward for the first several minutes. Neither of us knew what to say - honestly, we didn't really know each other. I asked if they knew what was going on with our family, and they said they had received a cryptic text from Dad but had no context or idea of what was happening. Apparently, the text from Dad said something like, "We have been viciously attacked. Please pray." Or something to that effect. No information, no context, no follow-up.

I explained what happened in the most matter-of-fact way I could; I didn't want to sound like I was trying to sway them to my side; I just wanted them to know what happened. I explained about realizing we were abused, gave them a few examples, told them what was happening with T, told them about calling CPS, explained Mom and Dad's position, and told them where the kids were.

I tried to say it all really fast so I could get it all out; I wanted them to have the information, and I wanted to know where they stood. I didn't want to waste my time or theirs. I think I was just trying to be as unemotional about it as possible, like it was a business meeting. Just an exchange of information - I tell them my piece, they tell me their stance.

I'm not sure what I expected from that phone call, but I think I half expected them to side with Dad. He was their son, after all. Why wouldn't they side with him? I was the wayward and rebellious child who'd just destroyed their family. I don't know if I actually thought they would believe me, so I was really taken aback when I heard them both sobbing. They were crying.

They said they knew in their hearts that something was going on and that our upbringing was shady, but they never got to see us enough to actually have any proof. They just had suspicions but hoped they were wrong. They also said they knew I'd be the one to blow the whistle if anyone ever did. They said I'd always been strong-willed, a little bit rebellious in a good way, and that if anyone was going to stand up to Mom and Dad or leave, it would be me. I didn't see those traits in myself. They only saw me a handful of times throughout my life, but they formed that impression of me? Maybe they were right. In the end, I did end up being the one to blow the whistle.

Once I knew they were listening and that they believed me, I spent the next hour on the phone with them, telling them anything they wanted to know. I answered all their questions, and I left nothing out. I had always known that what happens in the home stays in the home, and we were never to talk about our lives with outsiders. But I felt like that era was over, somehow. I felt like those rules didn't apply anymore. I felt free to say anything and everything, and I had people who actually wanted to listen. I left certain things out that Dad had done to us, like some of the more severe abuse, because a part of me still wanted to preserve their idea of him in their minds. He was their son, and I knew it was breaking their hearts to hear what he'd been doing to his children all those years. I wanted to tell them everything, but I held back the worst of it at that point.

They told my aunt - dad's sister - and her husband everything. My aunt and uncle ended up calling me and talking to me for hours, either that day or the next day. It was the same thing - they felt like something was wrong within our family, but they didn't see us enough to have any kind of proof. Just suspicions. They told me I'd done the right thing, even though it still felt like I'd just destroyed the only family I'd ever had. They told me they had my back; they'd give statements to social workers if needed; they'd fly out and support me if I wanted them to; they'd do anything to help me. They said they were proud of me. Mom and Dad had never said they were proud of me for anything.

Over the next several weeks, I spent a lot of time on the phone with Dad's side of the family, telling them stories from my side, hearing stories from their side, and getting to know the family I knew I had but was never allowed to really *know.* Papa and Mimi told me stories about the few times they got to see us when we were little kids. One of those stories is how I know for sure the abusive nature of my mother was there from the very beginning. This is the story they relayed to me:

They said they came to Idaho to visit, probably only a week or two after my older sister was born. She was my parents' first child and the first grandchild on both sides of the family. This would have been late 1995 or early 1996, as she was born toward the end of the year.

Papa and Mimi went to the trailer home my parents were living in and sat in the living room for hours, listening to my sister scream from her crib in the bedroom. They kept asking if she was hungry, if she needed her diaper changed, if they could hold her; each time, they were met with "she needs to learn she can't just be picked up every time she cries" or "she's fine, she's just being needy - I've already fed and changed her" or "she'll cry herself to sleep eventually."

They felt awkward going against their daughter-in-law (my mother) and didn't want to seem like they were telling her how to parent, but they were also very concerned since the baby had been crying for hours and she was only a few weeks old. They pushed hard enough that Mom got angry, stormed off to the bedroom, and slammed the door behind her. They apologized to Dad; he said he'd go check on her, and he went to the bedroom.

A little while later, Dad came out with my sister and handed her to Papa - apparently, he said Mom didn't want Mimi holding her, presumably since Mimi had been the main one pushing and questioning why they were just letting their newborn scream for hours. Papa said he held my sister for several hours; he said it took her a while to calm down as she had worked herself up so badly from screaming.

Eventually, she quieted and melted into his arms, and he sat there holding her until they left later that evening. I don't know if Mimi ever did get to hold her. After that day, Mimi said it was like pulling teeth to see us kids or to arrange a visit. They told me several other stories similar to this one that I'd never heard before, and they said Mom's behavior toward us always seemed concerning to them.

In November of 2022, Mark and I had a "real" wedding - a family, white dress, traditional wedding. My Dad's parents came; my aunt and uncle and my cousins came, and my parents did not. They were not invited; they had no idea it was even happening. They didn't even know Dad's family was in town. The night before the wedding, I asked Papa to walk me down the aisle. He said yes, but he was crying when he said it. I know he was honored to do it, but I also know he recognized it should have been his son. I know that the weekend was heavy for both him and Mimi, as well as my aunt.

We talked the entire weekend about my family, about how Dad grew up, about what my grandparents' perspective was, about what my cousins were told, about everything. Mimi told me she wanted to know everything. She didn't want me to hold things back for her sake. She said it would break her even more to learn what her son had done to us, but she wanted to know. So, I told her. There were a lot of tears that weekend, but also a lot of hugs. I reconnected with an entire side of the family I really never knew before. All the secrets were out in the open. I didn't have to hide anything anymore.

About a month or so after the wedding, Mom and Dad found out about it. I'm guessing they saw pictures on social media or something. I didn't care about them finding out after the fact; I just didn't want them to know about it beforehand and come crash it or find some other way to ruin the weekend. Once they found out, Dad sent a nasty text to Mimi that said,

> "Hope you enjoyed your time in NC. Would have been nice to see you..."

Papa and Mimi wanted to have some time to think about how to reply, so they didn't text back right away. A few hours later, Dad sent them another text:

> "But it is a reasonable assumption that my entire family has a skewed version of what has transpired, especially since we were not invited to the wedding, and my own parents weren't willing to see us while you were here. We are saddened but not surprised, given our daughter's skill at deception. I pray that someday you will be interested to hear the whole truth, not just her twisted version. We will no longer be providing updates on our family situation since it is not being believed anyway. We love you and pray for you, but we now know that there is literally no one in my family we can trust or depend on. But we have accepted that. We have God and He is enough."

Papa and Mimi thought and prayed about how to respond to those messages from Dad, and this was their reply:

> "We did enjoy our time in NC, and it would have been nice to see you too. As for your 2nd text it seems you are assuming the worst, which couldn't be further from the truth. In fact we are deeply hurt by your accusations and are heartbroken that you have written all of us off so readily. You are wrong to think you can't trust or depend on us. As for the wedding, Dad was honored to give her away, but it could have been you. It should have been you! Don't blame us for being included. We've always stayed in touch with any of our grandkids who desired to have a relationship with us. We need to talk at some point... In the meantime, if you truly do trust God as you say you do, ask Him what you need to do to restore your family. Love you lots! Mom and Dad. (We've spent hours talking and praying about our response. This message is from both of us.)"

That last bit in parentheses was essential because Mom has always told Dad that his mom is the problem, she's evil, she hates our family, etc. Mom was so manipulative that she convinced Dad that his own mom didn't love him, only his dad did. So, when the text message came from his mother's phone, she had to add a caveat that it was from both of them. Usually, Dad only texted his dad; when health issues got too bad later on, Mimi would text back on Papa's behalf, and Dad refused to entertain any messages that came from her phone.

18

Final Farewell

2022-2025 | AGE 25-28

The first Christmas the kids were in care, in 2022, I got permission from the social workers to have the three kids over to my house for an early Christmas. We'd never celebrated Christmas without religion, so that was a first for me. I got my other sisters and their families to come as well, and we had a blast. The three kids didn't want to come at first. Apparently, Mom had told them they had to wear their COVID masks the entire time, and that it was okay for them not to have any fun. She had argued against them even coming, but the judge ordered that they had a right to see their older siblings. She also warned the kids that I was the one who had destroyed their family, so they were all angry at me and afraid of coming to my house. I found out all of that after the fact.

When they arrived, they were all so hesitant to come inside. Once they came in, however, they saw the decorated tree with tons of presents with their names on them, sparkling cider, gingerbread houses and sugar cookie decorating supplies on the table, finger foods and desserts, decorations everywhere, Nat King Cole playing on Alexa, all of us dressed up in Christmas outfits... it was nothing like their normal Christmases with Mom and Dad. You know, in books, when the author says someone's eyes were "full of wonder?" That's the only way I can describe their faces. It took about five seconds for their anger and hesitation to disappear.

The social workers stayed the whole time to supervise, so they could ensure nothing negative was said about our parents, that no inappropriate conversations came up, and that nothing went wrong, etc. The girls got makeup and nail polish for Christmas, and all the sisters took turns getting makeovers, sitting on the bathroom floor. Hair got braided, nails got painted, and the smiles never left their faces. They stayed all afternoon, and then they didn't want to leave.

On their way out the door, my baby brother said, "I want to have a sleepover here," and I broke a little inside. As soon as everyone left and we cleaned up the aftermath, I just cried. I'd never seen them that happy, and I hated that they had to leave. I hated that I had to schedule times to see them and get visits approved through the social workers. I hated that my call to CPS to save them somehow started to feel like I was losing them.

Mom complained about everything after the Christmas party - makeup and nail polish were sinful, she said we were not allowed to give the kids any more toys of any kind, she said the kids had eaten too much sugar, and came home with too many gifts. The social workers passed all that back to me but said not to worry about it because they'd literally been there the entire time and hadn't seen any behavior that was a cause for concern. They said the kids all had a blast and gave us the go-ahead to do it again for Easter, this time unsupervised.

We made Easter baskets for each kid, which is something we'd never had before. Mom and Dad said Easter baskets were part of the secular celebrations and took away from the reason for the holiday. Easter was about Jesus being raised from the dead, and that was it. No candy, no bunnies, no eggs, no baskets. But we had all those things - baskets, decorations, colored eggs, Cadbury eggs, themed food, Easter egg hunt in the backyard... all of it.

After the success of the Christmas party, the kids were over the moon about coming back for Easter. Since it was unsupervised, I was allowed to go to their school and pick them up. Mom had demanded they be homeschooled, but that's not allowed in foster care, so the social workers found a super tiny school inside a church for them to attend. When I got there, all the kids were in the chapel listening to the Easter message. They all wore identical Catholic-style uniforms that felt super itchy. I sat in the back so I wouldn't disrupt the service, but the kids saw me and ran back to sit with me. My little brother sat on my lap and held my hand for the rest of the service, which was probably about another half hour. The girls sat on either side of me, so close we were all three practically sharing a chair. I had a lifted truck with a pretty loud exhaust, and riding home in that was probably the highlight of the day for my brother.

The kids had a blast again, smiled and laughed the whole time, and balked when it came time to leave. Something in my head told me to relish the time I had with them on the drive back to meet their foster parents. Something inside me knew an end was coming. It was like that impending doom feeling again, but this time with way more sadness attached. I hugged the kids so tight, told them I loved them, packed them into the car with all their Easter goodies, and waved goodbye as they rode away with their foster parents. Alone in my truck, I cried the whole way home.

That was the last time I ever saw my two youngest siblings.

After about a year, the judge allowed the youngest two to go back to Mom and Dad. Their cases were officially closed by the end of 2023. All they'd had to do was take an online parenting course, clean their house, and get a psychological evaluation. The judge mandated that they use the psychologist provided by the court, but Mom decided to pay for their own evaluation. They both, of course, passed with flying colors, with a suggestion that they go to therapy as a family. Apparently, that's all it takes for two pathological abusers to get their victims back - I mean, their children. Take an online class and clean up the house. That bar seemed pretty low to me.

I felt like I'd failed. I'd called CPS and gotten the kids out of the house, but for what? For them to go right back a year later? Would it have been better if I'd just done nothing? Everybody was telling me I'd done the right thing, but why did it feel like I'd just fucked everything up?

During the court hearing where the judge returned the two youngest kids and closed their cases, Mom stared at me with a smirk on her face the entire time. It was that look I'd seen a million times before; the look that said, "Nice try, but I always win." Her eyes looked like they belonged to a demon, not a human. They were so empty and lifeless, yet so full of hatred at the same time.

I tried not to let it bother me, but it did, and I think she knew it did. She and Dad were so happy leaving the courtroom that day. They'd gotten their kids back. They'd proved to the court they were fit parents. They'd shown that they were right, and I was wrong. They were the victims; I was the villain. They were smiling, thanking their attorneys, and joking with the bailiffs. They practically skipped out of the courtroom like little kids on their way to a candy shop.

Did they forget about something? Or someone? T? They got the youngest two back... What about T? They were so happy about getting their kids back, but it was honestly like they'd gotten all they came for. They didn't want T back. They never wanted her in the first place ten years ago, so of course they didn't want her back once they finally got rid of her. They seemed perfectly content to get the little two back and have T stay with her foster family. They weren't fighting for her like they fought for the younger two. They weren't sad they were leaving her behind. They didn't even look back. Not even a glance.

Over the course of all the court hearings, Mom and Dad never once sat by T, never hugged her, never looked back at her when they left, not even so much as a wave. The first few court hearings - when they were trying to establish themselves as perfect, loving Christian parents who were wrongly accused - Dad would say "I love you" to T in the hallway as they were leaving. A few times, T responded with "I love you, too." She asked me once if she had to say that, and I said no. I told her she gets to decide who she says "I love you" to, and if she doesn't want to say it to Mom and Dad, she doesn't have to. She never said it again after that. Eventually, Dad stopped saying it, too. Mom never said it to begin with... actually, I don't remember Mom ever saying those words. To any of us. Or to Dad. I just don't remember those words ever coming out of her mouth.

***

Throughout the years, I always texted or called my Dad's side of the family to let them know what had happened at court, what the judge ruled, what the new plans were, etc. I don't have a written update from every court hearing simply because some of them were phone calls, but here are a few of my messages from various hearings throughout the process:

6/7/2023

The youngest two are to start overnight visits with Mom and Dad, and work toward being placed at home. Mom wants them back in her care quickly because she wants the adoption assistance monthly paycheck. If the kids are out of her house for too long, she could lose the check. Mom and Dad also had to do psychological exams and refused to use the psychologist on retainer with the state, so they paid for their own. They also want more visits with T because they "can't form a bond" with the little they get. They want one on one with T, and the guardian ad litem said no.

**For context, the youngest two went back to Mom and Dad full-time around July 2023, but were still being monitored by the caseworkers, and their cases weren't closed till the end of the year.*

8/2/2023

T is likely never going home, it's her decision where she wants to live and she wants either her foster parents or Mark and I... she was told that if she doesn't want to go home she had to actually say that in front of Mom and Dad as well as give reasons and boy did she!

Court is continued to August 30th to allow time to get a witness - Mom and Dad are now fighting to homeschool the youngest two but the state wants to order they remain permanently at an actual school.

Some of T's doctor appointments somehow don't take insurance all of a sudden so Mom got the court to approve dropping her from their insurance and she's now just under Medicaid. (Mark says that's convenient timing now that they've realized she's probably not coming home they probably don't want to pay for her anymore.)

8/30/2023

They're fighting now to homeschool the younger two and Mom took the stand and showed how qualified she is to be a teacher because of her college degree and foster care experience and training she's done and all that which pisses me off but they were both ALL SMILES when the judge ruled T would be permanently placed elsewhere and he reduced the visits from weekly to monthly. They were so freaking happy and kept smugly smiling at us like they won. As if they were trying to get rid of her and they feel like now they freaking won because she's gone and they don't have to deal with her. Makes me absolutely furious.

***I can't find any messages from this timeframe, so those updates must have been phone calls. The cases for the youngest two were closed at the end of the year, and all future court dates were only for T.**

5/15/2024

Great day in court this morning!

The judge approved the APPLA (Another Planned Permanent Living Arrangement) program for T which basically means now that she's 16 she can choose to stay with her foster family (permanent foster care placement) until she's 18. At 18 she can then enter another program that is the same thing but from 18-21 and she'll continue to get assistance from the state.

T is so happy and excited and did NOT want to go back to school after court! If anyone does not already have her phone number let me know and I'll get it to you so you can message her if you want!

The other thing - the state and guardian ad litem asked for child support to be paid by both parents to the foster family but Mom and Dad (through their lawyers) argued for quite a while about that. Apparently the state of Idaho ceased their adoption assistance for T several months ago because she was out of their home for too long so they argued that they already lost that money they relied on and are now being asked to lose even more. They stated repeatedly that they shouldn't have to pay money since they really want T home but it's her fault they don't have her. They kept saying over and over that the reason T is not back is because she doesn't want to come back and they shouldn't have to pay for that. The judge didn't buy that at all.

Judge continuously corrected them saying it was not T's fault but a court order, and reminded them that she is a child. The guardian ad litem also very loudly reprimanded Mom and Dad to the judge saying it is unbelievable that they would say it's T's fault when it's their actions that got them here, and also they are unwilling to support a child they literally swore to support when they adopted her.

Judge was visibly getting annoyed and frustrated with them and ended up ordering full child support - Dad in an amount based on his salary as required by the child support worksheet, Mom $50 since she does not bring in income.

We are absolutely overjoyed that T will be safe and happy in a home with very loving parents who would do anything for her - she is doing SO WELL getting As and Bs in school and loving life!

11/13/2024

Court today! T is doing amazing, loves school, enjoys her friends... she's loving life!!

T wanted to have a visit with the younger two siblings only without Mom and Dad, and the state requested a visit at the dept in the visitation room but on the other side of one way glass.

They agreed to this at the last team meeting but in court said they never did, and that it's both of them IN the room or no visit at all. They claimed they're concerned because T always says negative things to the kids, talks about stuff that does not align with their beliefs, and influences them to pursue a negative way of life (she's actually never done that)

Judge called counsel back to chambers and they argued for quite a while, finally judge came out and ordered exactly what was agreed to in the beginning so just Dad and behind the glass. Mom is not allowed at the visit.

**Mark was unable to attend this court hearing with me, so these are my texts to him throughout the session:*

2/5/2025

Mom is complaining about visits because she had to take [youngest sister] to the hospital after one for anxiety... they were yelling at the case worker in the hall for about 30 minutes

Mom is purposely staring straight at me and won't look away so I was staring back and smiled but I got bored

When Dad showed up for the visits he brought a "resource" family friend and wouldn't do the visit till that person was allowed to be in the room

Mom keeps speaking out of turn

According to Mom... the two youngest are not understanding why they have to have visits with T, they are exhibiting anxiety after visits

The caseworker said both visits went well. Second visit was amazing, they didn't want to leave, went late because they were having too much fun but then later Mom said the stuff about anxiety and the kids not wanting to visit

The judge says why did the kids all of a sudden have issues with the visits when they were fine before and Mom's lawyer said it's not sudden then the state said actually it is.

19

Bruce Banner

2022-2025 | AGE 25-28

After calling CPS in June of 2022, my mental health absolutely tanked. I was spiraling just about every single day. I would go from "normal" one minute to hysterical the next, sobbing, convincing myself that my husband was going to leave me, thinking he and his family would be better off never having met me, thinking I should just disappear and everybody's lives would be better for it. I *spiraled.* Constantly.

You know how the Hulk goes crazy and mental and destroys everything, then when he's back to being human, Bruce Banner doesn't remember what "the big guy" was doing? That's how I explained it to people. I felt like I had two sides. I had what I called the "rational" side, where I was normal, level-headed, and could mostly think straight. Then I had the "spiral" side where I was completely mental. I'd burst into tears at absolutely nothing; I'd convince myself Mark hated me or wanted to divorce me, and I found out later that I'd say pretty rude and harmful things to people. But then, when I flipped back to rational me, I had no recollection of anything I'd said or done. I noticed people were mad at me, didn't want to talk to me, whispered in corners while glancing at me, and I had no clue why. I legitimately had no memory of saying anything mean, but I had.

Mark tried to play both sides - he protected me and tried to keep me on an even keel, but then he'd have to go apologize to people because of what I'd said. I had no clue that was happening. Finally, I realized that I was hurting Mark. That's when I knew I had to do something.

I hadn't wanted to go back to therapy after deployment because I thought I'd figured everything out already. I'd realized my parents were abusive; I'd called CPS; we were navigating that process; I had nothing left to discover. Or so I thought. I also didn't want to be on medication. I didn't want to take a pill every day for the rest of my life. I thought that taking a pill was confirmation that I was psychotic. That I was insane. I thought I could deal with a little anxiety on my own - tons of people deal with their own shit. I drank calming tea and took ashwagandha gummies because Google said that would help with anxiety. I thought I could do it on my own. After all, I'm only hurting myself.

But, of course, I wasn't only hurting myself. I was hurting everyone around me, and I didn't even know it. When I finally recognized that, I made an appointment the next day. The first therapy appointment I could find was three months away. I tried so hard to pay attention to what I was saying and doing, but it felt so hopeless because when I was in spiral brain, I couldn't access rational brain. I couldn't police myself, and it was destroying me.

When the appointment day came, I drove an hour to the office, waited two hours in the waiting room because they forgot about me, and then I finally got called back. I told the lady everything and ended up sobbing, of course, and she said, "Yeah, I would definitely recommend therapy."

What? Wasn't that what I was doing there? I told her I thought I was there for therapy, and she said, "Oh, no, this is just triage. I recommend you go to therapy, but I don't have any openings for another three months." Okay, so I'd waited three months for a therapy appointment only to have some lady say oh yeah, you should probably go to therapy?! Obviously, I left in tears, called Mark in the car, and he calmed me down enough that I could drive home.

When I got home, all I did was search for both therapists and psychiatrists. I had come to the conclusion that if therapy was going to be a three-month wait, maybe medication would be a good idea in the meantime. I needed something. Anything. Literally anything.

I found a therapist within walking distance of my job and had a start date lined up. And when she emailed me, I made sure to confirm that the first appointment was, indeed, for therapy. It was. Next, I found a psychiatrist who had a cancellation and got me in the next day. She listened to basically none of what I told her and prescribed Zoloft, available for pickup in an hour. I drove straight to the pharmacy, got the meds, and took one immediately. She said to take them for three weeks, then come back.

I went back every three weeks for about five months. I kept telling her I felt worse, and she kept upping the dosage. When I say I felt worse, I mean like ten times worse than before. The hulk/human spiral/rational thing was out of control, and I cried about twenty times throughout the day. About nothing and everything. Mark would walk in the door, ask what I wanted to do for dinner, and within seconds I'd be crying hysterically, asking if he just wanted me to sleep on the couch tonight and pack my shit in the morning. He'd still be standing there in the doorway like wtf just happened. I was getting way worse, and I internalized the possible reasons.

I figured it was my fault somehow. Maybe I'd forgotten to take a pill, or maybe I wasn't trying hard enough in therapy. Maybe - and this is the one I usually landed on - I was actually, like, legitimately insane, and getting better wasn't possible for me. Maybe I was minutes away from being involuntarily admitted to a psych ward for the rest of my life. Maybe I actually was crazy.

After five months on Zoloft, in the late summer of 2023, I went back to my psychiatrist, and she upped my dosage again. I stopped her and basically said, "You don't understand, I'm getting worse." She looked at me and said, "I don't know why you're not getting better, because if you're actually taking the pills correctly, you should be improving. The only reason you're not getting better is because you don't want to. You're fighting against the medication in your brain and not allowing yourself to improve. You're the reason you're not getting better."

You guessed it - I was crying in the car again, on the phone with Mark. He begged me to ditch that psychiatrist and find a new one who would actually listen. He'd never been to one, but he figured they weren't supposed to tell patients that they're the reason they aren't getting better. I decided to call my primary care provider and ask if he had any psychiatrists to recommend, but he said to just come in and see him. I'm not sure why I didn't know this, but apparently he's able to prescribe SSRI's and other mental health medications. If I'd known that, I would've just started with him.

He explained to me that many people need to try multiple meds before they find the one that works best. He agreed that I should not have been kept on Zoloft for that long if it was continuously making me worse. He gave me some other options, and we landed on Lexapro. He told me to give it a few weeks for one to wear off and the other to take hold, and then come back.

It was about three weeks later when I had my first "good day." I realized it as I was getting into bed that night. I had woken up with a clear mind, gone all day happy and not shed a single tear, and I went to bed never having a single thought that Mark wanted to leave me or that maybe the world would be better off without me. I had a good day. I was so excited - I had really started to believe that it would never happen. I thought good days just weren't in the cards for me.

Now, not every day after that was a good day. I had a good day once a week, then I'd have a few good days in a row, then I'd have a good week. Eventually, I got to the point where good days were the norm, and I'd have a bad day here and there. Maybe I wasn't too far gone, after all.

Throughout this time, I'd been attending every single therapy session. I never missed one. I never wanted to miss one. I thought that if I missed one, it meant I wasn't trying to get better as hard as I should be. I wanted results fast, but my therapist reminded me that progress takes time, and I slowly began to accept that, but only after switching meds. Once I was fully on the new med and started having good days, it felt like the fog had lifted, or someone had given me glasses with a perfect prescription or something. My mind was so much clearer, I could actually think, I could remember things, and the spiral times became less and less frequent. It was like the world was in pastels and grey tones before, and now it was all vibrant colors and sunshine.

I don't know if I'm describing it well, but it was like a night-and-day difference. Once I was on the right medication, therapy started making sense. The tools she gave me made sense. Once I had a clear mind due to the meds, I was actually able to apply what I learned in therapy. I still wanted to get off the meds, though.

I constantly asked my therapist how long it might be until I could go off the meds and just be better on my own. She gave me a reality check and explained that I may be able to ditch the meds soon, but I may also never be able to be off them. But either way, it doesn't make me insane or crazy or psychotic. It just means I need a little more help balancing the chemicals in my brain, and that's okay. It took me a long time to accept that.

Oh - how could I forget?! On my birthday in June of 2023, one year into the CPS case, Dad texted me. I had gone no-contact beginning the day I called CPS; I'd seen my parents in court, but I hadn't reached out to them, nor had they reached out to me. His text said:

> "I love you. For your birthday, I am praying that you discover who Jesus really is and the life he wants for you."

I never responded. Thanks, but no thanks, Dad. I'll pass.

20

Deconstructing

2022-2025 | AGE 25-28

While I was desperately trying to get my mental health under control, something else was quickly unraveling at the same time: the religion I had been raised to believe was the absolute truth. Not just *a* truth. *The* truth. The only religion that was correct. God's Christianity. Or that's what I was told it was by Mom and Dad.

I had never been taught Christianity as something to explore or question. In fact, I was taught never to question it. It was handed to me as fact, complete and true, not to be examined. It was to simply be accepted, not understood. So, when I finally tried to define it for myself, I realized I had no idea what it was, and that none of it made any sense.

I started asking questions. I had constant conversations with Mark, with my in-laws, with my older sister, with Google, trying to understand, desperate for clarity. I wasn't trying to dismantle my "faith" or my religion; I was trying to save it. I wanted it to make sense. Instead of understanding and making sense of things, however, everything just became more muddled. The more I searched for answers, the more confused I became.

It wasn't just one or two things here and there; it was everything. The Bible stories I'd been taught to accept as literal truth suddenly felt impossible to reconcile with reality. Virgins can't get pregnant, and that single biological fact seemed to destabilize the entire foundation of the whole religion. Adam and Eve were supposedly the first and only humans on earth, so their children must have had sex with each other to populate the planet. And yet, Christians say incest is condemned, immoral, and sinful. Samson was strong until someone cut his hair? Yeah, okay, because that totally makes sense. The Grand Canyon was formed rapidly by one catastrophic flood? Not buying it. And somehow, eight people were able to gather two of every single living thing and put them on a boat.

Here are a few more things that I became even more confused about while searching for answers:

- If God is all-loving and all-powerful, why do children die from starvation, malaria, or preventable diseases every day?
- If God is omnipresent, why would missionaries need to "bring God" or "bring the gospel" to people in remote villages? Wasn't He already there?
- If salvation depends on hearing the gospel, what happens to people who are born, live, and die without ever hearing it?
- If God answers prayer, why do faithful people pray equally hard for opposite outcomes, and why do both unanswered prayers and answered prayers seem indistinguishable from chance?

- If suffering always has a divine purpose, why were children born into abuse or extreme poverty given such vastly different starting points than others?
- If God created every person, why create someone He already knows will spend eternity in hell?
- If free will explains evil, how does that account for earthquakes, childhood cancer, genetic disorders, or natural disasters?
- If every life is part of God's perfect plan, why pray for Him to change it?
- If God never changes, why do Christians disagree so profoundly about what He wants?
- If the Holy Spirit guides believers into truth, why do sincere, prayerful Christians reach completely opposite conclusions on major issues?
- If morality comes only from God, why have Christians changed their views over time on issues like slavery, segregation, homosexuality, and women's roles?
- If God is everywhere and knows every thought before it's spoken, why is prayer necessary to tell Him our needs?
- If faith is freely chosen, why was I told that questioning it was sinful or dangerous?

I had nodded along to these stories and concepts my entire life, reciting them and accepting them without hesitation. But once I paused long enough to actually think about them, I couldn't erase all the questions in my mind. I began to notice how often explanations ended whenever curiosity began.

When I'd ask people how they knew the Bible was true, they said, "Because God said so." But then, when I'd ask how they knew God was real, they said, "Because the Bible says so." I'd listened to that since I was born, and I'd always believed it, no questions asked. And it made total sense until I started asking questions. I realized that as soon as I took a step back and tried to actually understand Christianity, the entire thing completely fell to pieces. It had no structure, nothing coincided, nothing made any sense. The logic was just going around in circles, using God, then the Bible, then God, then the Bible over and over again, with no real explanations for anything. It was a never-ending loop, perfectly engineered to stop thought.

I had believed that loop my entire life. I'd never been encouraged to test it, examine it, or step outside of it. Doubt or curiosity wasn't framed as a normal human response; it was framed as dangerous and sinful. Being curious was being rebellious. Questioning was calling God a liar. I didn't realize until after the CPS call how deeply I had been conditioned.

I wasn't just taught Christianity; I was taught one specific version of it, filtered entirely through my parents' worldview. Catholic, Mormon, Lutheran, Methodist, Protestant, Presbyterian... These were different religions altogether, not variations of the same belief system. But didn't they all focus on the same exact God? Yes, technically, but they were false. Only ours was right. Everyone else outside our family was confused, deceived, or doomed. There was no room for different interpretations. No room for nuance. No room for curiosity. No room for me.

As my anxiety intensified, my mind felt like it was spinning out of control, racing to reconcile belief with reality. I was going crazy. I was doing so much reading and searching, almost begging for answers, not finding a single one that actually explained anything I'd grown up with. I wanted so badly to understand everything and put the pieces back together, but nothing seemed to fit. The more Christian explanations I encountered, the more hollow and empty they felt. "This happened because the Bible says so." End of discussion.

Then, almost accidentally, I began reading non-Christian, non-Creationist science articles, and - by golly - they actually made sense. They didn't demand belief before explanation. They didn't punish questions. They didn't rely on circular logic or fear of eternal consequences. They offered evidence, theories, uncertainty, and room to be wrong. For the first time, a puzzle piece finally clicked into place. The spinning in my brain slowed, just a little.

That realization was both liberating and devastating. If the world could be explained without God, then what else had I been wrong about? Admitting that possibility felt like betrayal. Possible betrayal of my parents, my upbringing, my religion, my entire identity. Christianity wasn't just something I'd believed; it was the framework through which I understood everything - morality, worth, purpose... Letting go of it felt like free-falling, and I couldn't see the ground.

I grieved the certainty I'd lost. I grieved the version of myself who believed she had all the answers. I grieved the comfort of thinking suffering had a divine reason, and justice would eventually be served. But underneath that grief was something quieter and truer: relief. I didn't have to twist myself into mental knots to justify cruelty, shame, or control anymore. I didn't have to believe that love came with conditions or that goodness required obedience. I didn't have to fear hell to choose kindness.

The hardest part wasn't losing God, Christianity, or a religion. It was realizing how thoroughly I had been taught not to think for myself. Deconstruction wasn't a single moment or a dramatic rejection. It was slow, painful, and deeply confusing. It meant untangling my own thoughts from my parents' voices. It meant learning that morality could exist without punishment, and meaning could exist without a divine overseer. It meant accepting that I could be a good person, not because I was told to be, and not because I was afraid not to be. But because I chose to be.

For the first time in my life, that choice felt like freedom.

Once the belief itself started to crack, a much more frightening question rushed to fill the silence: Who am I without God?

Christianity hadn't just shaped what I'd believed; it had shaped who I was allowed to be. It dictated my values, my fears, my definition of goodness, even my thoughts. Without it, I felt like something was missing. Like someone had stripped away my internal compass, leaving me standing in the dark. If I wasn't a Christian, what was I? What stopped me from becoming selfish, cruel, lost... If heaven and hell weren't waiting on the other side of my choices, what reason did I have to be good at all? What was my purpose?

Those questions terrified me because they revealed how little I trusted myself. I had been taught that humans are inherently broken, sinful, incapable of goodness without divine supervision. That without God, we would descend into chaos and immorality. I had absorbed that message so deeply that I didn't realize how insulting it was, not just to humanity, but to me. I was afraid that letting go of religion meant letting go of structure, purpose, and morality all at once. I imagined myself drifting, unanchored, no longer recognizable even to myself.

But then there was my husband. Mark had grown up without religion. No church every Sunday. No Bible stories memorized as fact. No VeggieTales. No AWANA. No fear-based morality drilled into him from childhood. And yet, he was - and is - one of the kindest, most considerate people I've ever met. He is patient when no one is watching. He is generous without expecting credit. He listens. He apologizes. He chooses empathy instinctively, not because he's afraid of punishment or hoping for a reward.

That reality quietly dismantled one of the biggest lies I'd been taught. If God was required to make someone good, then Mark shouldn't exist. But he did, and not as an exception or anomaly, just as a decent human being. Watching him move through the world forced me to confront an uncomfortable truth: morality clearly did not belong exclusively to religion. Kindness didn't need a Bible verse to justify it. Compassion didn't require divine instruction. Love wasn't something God loaned out to believers only.

For the first time, I allowed myself to consider that goodness might be intrinsic. That people might care about one another simply because we are social, empathetic beings who understand suffering. That we might choose kindness not out of fear, but out of connection. That morality could come from shared humanity rather than divine command. Basically, people can be decent fucking humans regardless of whether there's an invisible man in the sky telling them to be decent.

This realization was both destabilizing and freeing. If goodness didn't come from God, then it had to come from somewhere else. From us. I began to notice how often religion had taken credit for qualities it didn't invent. Love, patience, generosity, forgiveness - these existed long before Christianity claimed ownership of them. Religion hadn't created morality; it had branded it. Once I saw that, I couldn't unsee it.

The fear that had once kept me obedient started to lose its grip. I didn't suddenly become reckless or cruel. I didn't wake up one day wanting to harm others or cause chaos. In fact, I felt more intentional than ever. Every kind choice mattered more because it was chosen, not commanded. I wasn't being good because I was told to be; I was being good because I wanted to be. That distinction changed everything.

Without religion, my actions belonged to me. My values were no longer outsourced. I had to decide on my own what kind of person I wanted to be, what I stood for, what I would tolerate, and what I would refuse. It was a terrifying responsibility, but it was also honest. I realized that a morality built on fear is fragile. Take away the threat of hell, and it collapses. But a morality built on empathy, responsibility, and mutual care is stronger; it doesn't require holy surveillance to survive. Loving people because they are people felt more authentic than loving them because I was told to by God.

I stopped asking who I would become without a God. I started noticing who I already was. I was still compassionate, still thoughtful, still capable of love and restraint and generosity. If anything, I felt more present, more accountable, more human. Letting go of religion didn't make me worse; it made me honest. I wasn't losing myself; I was finally meeting her.

After everything fell apart, I was left with a question that felt both simple and enormous: If I wasn't living by God's rules anymore, what did I believe in? I expected the answer to feel complicated, philosophical, and overwhelming. Instead, it came quietly, almost gently, through instinct and relief. When the fear loosened its grip, what remained was surprisingly clear.

I kept the values that had always felt human. The most important one was simple: treat others the way you want to be treated. Not because a verse commanded it, not because I was promised heaven for compliance, but because I knew what it felt like to be hurt, dismissed, controlled, and shamed. I didn't need divine instruction to know I didn't want to pass that pain on.

But I also changed something crucial. I learned that kindness does not require self-sacrifice to the point of destruction. Christianity had taught me endurance masquerading as virtue. Forgive endlessly. Turn the other cheek. Stay. Submit. Love harder. Pray more. If someone hurt you, the solution was always internal: examine your heart, your faith, your obedience. Maybe you weren't praying hard enough, or maybe you had sinned in your mind or had impure thoughts.

What it never taught me was that I was allowed to walk away. Rebuilding my values meant accepting that I could be compassionate and have boundaries. That I could care about people without allowing them continued access to harm me. That cutting toxic people out of my life wasn't cruelty; it was self-respect. I didn't owe proximity to anyone simply because I had been taught that suffering was holy.

That realization alone changed the trajectory of my life. I rejected the idea that my existence was meant to revolve around pleasing an invisible man in the sky, guided by a book written, translated, edited, and weaponized by humans. I rejected the constant surveillance, the guilt, the pressure to live as if every thought and action were being graded. I no longer wanted a life built on fear of punishment or longing for a reward in the afterlife.

I chose a life built on presence. I chose peace. For the first time, my life felt like it belonged to me. The decision not to subscribe to any religion didn't come with chaos or emptiness like I had been warned. It came with stillness, clarity, and an immediate, physical sense of relief. I felt like someone had finally removed a weight I didn't realize I'd been carrying on my shoulders my entire life. I could breathe.

There was no guilt in chasing my happiness anymore. No voice telling me that joy was suspicious or that contentment meant complacency. I didn't have to justify my choices to God. I didn't have to spiritualize my suffering or explain it away as a lesson from God. I could simply live.

The most surprising part was that once I made that decision, I never looked back. Not once. There has never been a moment when I've wished to return to Christianity. No longing for church. No desire to be "saved." No temptation to replace one religion with another. The freedom I felt wasn't fleeting; it was permanent. I didn't feel lost without religion; I felt found.

My values now are chosen, not inherited. They are flexible enough to grow and strong enough to stand without threats holding them upright. I try to be kind, I try to be honest, and I protect my own peace. That is the life I chose. Not one dictated by doctrine, fear, or obligation, but one rooted in autonomy, empathy, and joy.

I do not label it. I am not an atheist; I am not an agnostic. I am not anything. I do not believe people should be required to choose a religion or non-religion; I don't think we should have to fit ourselves in a box. I'm just living. I'm just me. And I'm happy.

21

The Aftermath

2025 | AGE 28

People often ask if I hate my parents for what they did to my siblings and me. It's a reasonable question, but it's also a complicated one. When it comes to Mom, the answer surprises people the most. I don't hate her.

Now, that doesn't mean I forgive her - I'm not even sure I believe in forgiveness. It also doesn't mean that what she did wasn't horrific. It doesn't mean it didn't permanently alter the course of my life.

I hate what she did. I hate the abuse. I hate the control. I hate the way she psychologically manipulated me so deeply that I couldn't even see what was happening to my siblings until it was almost too late. I hate that she trained me to look away. I hate that she shaped my reality so thoroughly that I couldn't recognize cruelty as cruelty, harm as harm, evil as evil. I hate that I was made complicit through conditioning, not choice.

But when I search for feelings toward *her*, toward my mother as a person, there's nothing there. No rage, no sadness, no longing, no love. Just nothing. Absence. It's a strange thing to realize you feel nothing toward someone who once occupied every corner of your life. She isn't a source of pain anymore; she isn't a source of fear; she isn't even a source of anger. She's just a person.

Not only do I not hate her, but I also don't love her. That realization came later, as an adult, after the CPS call and the family's destruction. I finally understood that she never loved me - not in the way love is supposed to exist. Not freely, not protectively, not without strings. It wasn't love. Once I accepted that truth, something in me stopped reaching for her entirely. I don't love her, I don't hate her, I don't miss her... I don't feel anything.

Dad is different. For him, I feel anger. Hatred, even. That distinction took me a long time to understand as well, because on the surface it doesn't make sense. Mom was the abuser. She was the architect, the mastermind, the one who orchestrated fear, punishment, and control. For a long time, Dad was simply following her lead.

At first, his abuse felt secondary - something he did because she told him to. An extension of her will rather than his own. But over time, that changed. He became an extension of her. There are memories of him from when I was really young that complicate everything in my brain. Moments when he tried, when he defended us, or at least attempted to. Moments when he seemed to recognize that what was happening was wrong.

But then he reaped the consequences. Every time he stood up to her, he paid for it. He was punished, controlled, and put back in his place. I think, eventually, he just gave up. I think something in him simply surrendered. Instead of leaving, instead of protecting us, instead of choosing us, he joined her.

That is why I hate him. Not because he was worse than her, but because he was the one who could have done something. He could have taken us away. He could have left her. He could have chosen divorce. Separation. Resistance. *Anything.*

But he didn't. He chose inaction. He chose compliance. And eventually, he chose cruelty. He became like her. That choice feels heavier than Mom's abuse ever did, because I expect evil to behave like evil. What I can't forgive is the person who saw it clearly and decided it was easier to become part of it than to stop it.

People sometimes ask if I think Dad was stuck, if he felt trapped, if he believed he couldn't leave. I think that might be true to a degree. Their religion did not allow divorce under any circumstances. No exceptions. No grace. Leaving wasn't an option; it was a sin. One of my aunts divorced her husband because he beat her to a pulp, and the family all but shunned her. Maybe Dad knew Mom was toxic, maybe he knew what she was doing was wrong, and maybe he stayed because he thought staying was what a good Christian man was supposed to do.

Or maybe he told himself he was staying for us kids. I don't know. What I do know is that whatever he believed, the outcome was the same. He stayed, he gave up, he became evil, too. And we paid for it.

Understanding the "why" doesn't soften the impact. It doesn't absolve him or justify his actions. It doesn't turn harm into something noble or necessary. At best, it explains how a man can slowly abandon his children without ever physically leaving them.

My feelings toward my parents are not symmetrical. They aren't neat and tidy, and they aren't easily explained. One is nothing; the other is anger. But both are honest, and I've learned that honesty matters more than forcing myself into emotions that make other people more comfortable.

And for all the people who are going to say, "But she's your mom, but he's your dad, you only get one mom, you only get one dad..." Disrespectfully, fuck off. I don't care. "But I'm their daughter." "They only got one of me." Does that not matter?

The version of me who started this story would not recognize the life I'm living now. For a long time, I believed that needing help meant I was broken. That if I ever had to take medication every day, if I ever depended on pills to function, it meant I was crazy, weak, or beyond repair. I was terrified of that label. Terrified that accepting help would confirm everything I'd been taught to fear.

But here I am. I take medication every day. Multiple medications, actually. I am not crazy. I am stable. I am present. I am alive in my own life. It has taken years to unlearn the shame surrounding mental health, and I'm still working on it. It's taken years to understand that medication isn't a moral failure or a shortcut, but rather a tool. The same way glasses help you to see and insulin helps regulate blood sugar, these pills help my brain do what it struggles to do on its own. And that's okay.

Going to therapy didn't mean I was weak, either. It meant I was finally honest. I learned how to cope with the chemical imbalances in my brain that caused anxiety, depression, insomnia, suicidal ideations... I learned why I respond to situations the way I do. I learned how my childhood experiences affected - and will always affect to some degree - my adulthood. I learned that cutting out toxic people is okay, saying "no" is okay, and setting boundaries is okay.

I no longer see my parents. I am "no-contact," and I have no intentions of changing that. That sentence used to feel heavy and unfinished, like something I needed to explain or justify to other people. Now it just feels factual. Neutral. True. I am no contact, and I have no desire to reconnect. Not someday. Not after more healing. Not for appearances or obligation or guilt. I spent years chasing their approval, their affection, and their love. I convinced myself that if I could just be better, quieter, more obedient, more forgiving, they would finally choose me.

Eventually, I had to face the truth: we were never loved. None of us were. Not in the way children deserve to be loved. Not safely. Not freely. Not without conditions. We never were, and we never will be. Accepting that truth was devastating to the childhood "me"; I wanted her to feel love, but she never did. That truth was also freeing, though, to the adult "me." I stopped running toward something that never existed. I stopped trying to earn what was never truly offered. I stopped believing that the absence of their love was a reflection of my worth.

Today, I have my in-laws, and they are enough. They showed me what family can look like when love isn't transactional or withheld as punishment. They showed me that care can be steady, uncomplicated, and real. My future children will know that version of family. They will never know my parents, and that is a choice not rooted in anger, but in protection.

I reconnected with my paternal side of the family - the side I was kept from for most of my life. I only got three years with Papa before he passed away. Three years to know him, love him, and understand what I had been denied. Losing him made me bitter, but it also made me grateful. I mourn the decades that were stolen from me, but I hold tightly to the time we did have. I carry him with me now, not as a wound, but as proof that love existed somewhere all along.

After he passed, Mimi gave me the opportunity to speak at his celebration of life. Here's what I said:

Papa,

There are so many things I wish I could've said to you, so many questions I wish I would've asked, so many memories I wish we could've made. I wish we didn't have so many lost years, but rather than mourn what never was, I choose to be eternally grateful for what we did have. Today, as we celebrate your life, all I want to say is, "Thank you."

Thank you for loving me my entire life, even when I didn't get to experience your love firsthand.

Thank you for never giving up on me and trusting that we would create memories together one day. And we did!

Thank you for not dwelling on the past but instead welcoming me with open arms and moving forward as if all that mattered was the present.

Thank you for your service to our great nation; your service was a significant factor in my decision to serve as well. I am honored to lace up my boots and follow in your footsteps to serve a country that is dear to us both.

Thank you for walking me down the aisle at my wedding; I will cherish that memory and be forever thankful you were willing to fill a role that wasn't yours.

Thank you for loving Mimi unconditionally and showing me what not a "good" marriage, but a GREAT marriage can look like. Your devotion to her and your undying love is what fairy tales are made of, and I'm so grateful you got to meet my Prince Charming.

Thank you for showing me what a loving parent looks like. You set the bar high, and I will make it my goal to meet it when I have the honor of being a parent myself.

> *Thank you for never missing an opportunity to tell a joke - if laughter is the best medicine, then you were by far the best doctor.*
>
> *Thank you for all your words of wisdom, even though they were usually in the form of a movie line.*
>
> *Thank you for doing more for others than you ever did for yourself. You were truly selfless and never thought twice about it.*
>
> *Thank you for being the best grandfather a girl could ask for. You were the coolest guy I've ever known, a true legend.*
>
> *Thank you for being so many things to so many people - a comedian, a teacher, a supporter, a friend, a husband, a father... but to me, thank you for just being "Papa."*

I have eight siblings. I only talk to a few of them, and that is okay, although it took me a lot of therapy to get to that point of acceptance. Trauma seems to have bonded me closely to my older sister in ways that are hard to explain to people who didn't live it. What kept us siblings alive together, however, also made some relationships impossible to sustain. There are two siblings I barely speak to; we text on birthdays or anniversaries, and sometimes on holidays, but we don't have a relationship. And I don't desire to have a relationship with them. I'm content with how things are between us, which is another aspect of trauma survival that is difficult to explain to outside people. The same trauma that bonded me to my older sister somehow separated me from other siblings - that's the best explanation I can offer.

Four of my siblings are still in the cult. Still with my parents. Still under their control. My two biological brothers want nothing to do with me, and I grieve that. They have listened to what my parents have told them about me, and they are either unable or unwilling to see our childhood for what it was. They cannot or will not see our parents as abusive. Part of that could be because my older sister and I shielded them from so much, and I've blamed myself for that countless times. I mourn the siblings I lost while they're still alive. I hold hope that maybe someday we'll reconnect, but I no longer organize my life around that hope. I have learned that peace sometimes requires acceptance instead of reconciliation. I still text my brothers on their birthdays every year; they never respond, and they may even have me blocked, but at least they'll know I have the same phone number if they ever decide they want to reach out.

The youngest two adopted siblings - the Native American boy and T's younger half-sister - are back with my parents. I don't know how they're doing. I don't know if they're being abused. I don't know if they're actually doing school. What I do know for certain is that they are not being loved. My parents are incapable of loving anyone but themselves; that much I know. That cannot change. They have been parents for over thirty years, and if they haven't changed in that amount of time, they aren't going to change now.

My family is smaller now, but it is so full of love and acceptance that I never realized I was missing.. I've learned that family is not always blood, and sometimes the family you choose can be healthier than the family you are given. I have fewer people in my life, but the people I have chosen to let into my world are people who actually see me, respect me, show up for me, honor my boundaries, and love me without trying to change me. They love me without conditions.

I focus on my mental health, my husband, and our marriage. I focus on the quiet, steady love we choose every day. I focus on my job, my hobbies, the routines that anchor me. I am happy. Not in a loud, performative way. Not in a way that denies grief or pretends the past didn't happen. I am simply happy in a grounded, honest way; a way that allows space for sadness without letting it define me.

I am still learning who I am, still uncovering layers, still coming to terms with what was done to me and how it shaped me. I don't think that process will ever truly end, but that's okay. I've learned that healing isn't a destination; it isn't a straightforward journey with clear steps and milestones. It's a process; it's a relationship with yourself that deepens over time.

This book doesn't end with forgiveness; it doesn't end with reconciliation or redemption; it doesn't end neatly, all tied up with a bow. However, it does end with clarity, boundaries, and chosen family. It ends with medication bottles on my nightstand and peace in my soul. It ends with me standing firmly in the life I built for myself, no longer chasing love that was never mine to receive, no longer afraid of asking for help, no longer apologizing for choosing myself.

This is where I am now, and for the first time, that is more than enough.

Epilogue

She's four years old. Her feet don't quite touch the floor when she sits. Her legs swing back and forth, restless, like they're searching for somewhere safe to land. She is small in a way she no longer remembers how to be - small enough to disappear, small enough to be overlooked.

She doesn't know the words for what she feels yet; she just knows she's careful. She watches faces closely; she listens for shifts in tone. She tries to predict what version of the adults around her she's about to get. She's already learned that love can change without warning, that safety is conditional, that silence is sometimes the smartest choice.

She doesn't know any of that consciously; she only knows it in her body.

I step into the room quietly, the way I always had to. She sees me. She is me. She looks up, and our eyes meet. Hers are wide and unsure, waiting for instruction or correction. Waiting to be told what she's done wrong. Instead, I kneel in front of her.

I open my arms. She hesitates. So do I. Nobody ever taught either of us what gentleness looks like. When I pull her into my chest, she stiffens at first, like she's bracing for impact. Her little body is tense, prepared. It breaks something open in me.

I hold her anyway. I hold her until her shoulders soften. I hold her until she leans in. I whisper the things no one ever said to her. You're not bad. You're not difficult. You're not broken. None of this is your fault.

She doesn't cry - she's been taught not to. She just presses her face into my shoulder, breathing me in like she's memorizing the feeling. Like she's afraid it might disappear. I tell her she is strong

- not because she survived, not because she endured - but because she never stopped being herself underneath it all. I tell her she is capable. That one day, she will think for herself. That she will leave. That she will choose peace even when it costs her everything she was taught to protect.

I tell her she will grow into someone who asks hard questions. Someone who walks away from harm. Someone who builds a life that feels like home. I tell her she will be loved. Not in the way she's been taught to accept, but in the way she's always deserved.

I don't tell her everything that's coming; I don't tell her about loss or distance or the years it will take to find herself again. I only tell her what she needs to know right now. She doesn't need details; she doesn't need promises mapped out in years and milestones. She just needs to know this: She makes it.

I pull back just enough to look at her face. I memorize it - the softness, the hope she doesn't know she has yet, the strength hiding behind her eyes. I press my forehead to hers. I stay. I don't rush. For once, no one leaves her alone with what she doesn't understand.

When I stand up, she doesn't reach for me. She doesn't need to. She already knows. I leave her there - safe, held, no longer alone with questions she's too young to answer. She looks steadier. Not because the world has changed, but because she knows something now. She knows she isn't the problem. She knows she survives.

I step back once, then twice. I don't rush. I don't disappear. She watches me go, calm in a way she's never been allowed to be. I didn't give her a promise that life would be easy, but I gave her the certainty that she was never weak. That she was always worthy of protection. That she grows up.

And when she does, she builds a life that feels like peace. She grows up. She makes it out. She becomes me.

Acknowledgments

Writing this book has been one of the hardest things I have ever done.

For years, these memories existed only in fragments - pieces of conversations, journal entries, tears, and quiet moments when I wondered whether I would ever be ready to tell the story. This book became more than a memoir; it became an act of remembering, grieving, and healing.

To my husband, Mark: thank you for being my safety. You have loved me through questions, flashbacks, difficult drafts, and countless moments when I wasn't sure I could finish this story. You reminded me, over and over again, that my past did not define my future. Thank you for believing in me long before I believed in myself.

To my siblings: our stories are forever intertwined. While this book reflects my own experiences and perspective, I know we each carry different memories, different wounds, and different paths toward healing. I hope every one of you finds peace, freedom, and the life you deserve.

To my friends, beta readers, and everyone who encouraged me to keep writing: thank you for your honesty, your encouragement, and your willingness to sit with difficult chapters. Your thoughtful feedback made this book stronger, and your belief in this project carried me through moments of self-doubt.

To every survivor who has ever shared their story with me, whether through my work, social media, or in quiet conversations: thank you for your courage. You reminded me that none of us are as alone as we sometimes feel.

Finally, to every reader holding this book: thank you for trusting me with your time and your heart. Whether you picked up these pages because you saw yourself in the title, because someone you love has walked a similar road, or simply because you wanted to understand, I hope you leave knowing this:

What happened to you was real.

Your story matters.

And healing is possible.

About the Author

Stella McCormick is a U.S. Navy Reservist, sexual assault victim advocate for the U.S. Army, and writer. Through her work and writing, she is passionate about helping others understand trauma, coercive control, and the resilience of the human spirit.

Deliver Us From Mother is her debut memoir. In it, she shares her journey of growing up in a highly controlling, religiously motivated family, confronting the lasting effects of abuse, and discovering that healing is possible - even after a lifetime of believing otherwise.

When she isn't writing, Stella enjoys reading, traveling, and spending time with her husband, Mark, and their flock of chickens. She lives in North Carolina, where she is already hard at work on her next book.

Connect with Stella

I'd love to stay connected as I continue writing, sharing, and publishing future books.

Follow along for updates on future books, behind-the-scenes glimpses of the writing process, conversations about healing from trauma and high-control environments, guest appearances on podcasts, and the occasional look into my everyday life.

TikTok
@Stella_McCormick
Instagram
@StellaMc_Author

Thank you for being part of this journey!
— Stella McCormick

Thank You

Thank you for taking the time to read *Deliver Us From Mother.*

If this story resonated with you, one of the greatest gifts you can give an author is an honest review on Amazon, Goodreads, or wherever you purchased the book. Your review helps other readers discover stories like this one and means more than you know.

Books by Stella McCormick

Available Now

Deliver Us From Mother

Faith, Fear, and the Family Cult That Broke Me

Coming Soon

The *Deliver Us* collection continues with future books exploring healing, resilience, identity, and the lifelong journey of rebuilding after trauma.

www.ingramcontent.com/pod-product-compliance
Lightning Source LLC
La Vergne TN
LVHW040517210926
848480LV00007BA/1492